DESIGNING
TRAINING
PROGRAMS

DESIGNING
TRAINING
PROGRAMS
THE CRITICAL EVENTS MODEL

LEONARD NADLER
Professor, School of Education and Human Development
George Washington University

ADDISON-WESLEY PUBLISHING COMPANY
Reading, Massachusetts • Menlo Park, California
London • Amsterdam • Don Mills, Ontario • Sydney

Library of Congress Cataloging in Publication Data

Nadler, Leonard.
  Designing Training Programs: The Critical
  Events Model

  Includes index.
  1. Employees, Training of.   I. Title.
HF5549.5.T7N285   658.3'12404   81-12840
ISBN 0-201-05168-0   AACR2

Fifth Printing, September 1983

ISBN 0-201-05168-0
  BCDEFGHIJ-AL-89876543

For Zeace, as always.

Contents

10

CONDUCT TRAINING 207

11

SUPPORT SYSTEMS FOR TRAINING 227

APPENDIX 245

INDEX 247

Foreword

Designing training programs is one of the most pervasive, yet most misunderstood activities to be found in the field of Human Resource Development. As HRD is concerned with learning, particularly in work settings, the task of designing is crucial.

The actual conduct of the training is the proverbial tip of the iceberg and tends to get most of the attention. The design of training programs is not nearly so visible. Too often, the Designers are not even present or involved when their product is delivered.

"How do you design a training program?" This question was asked of me in 1965. The occasion was the first class on a university campus to whom I was teaching that subject. Prior to joining the faculty, I had been a practitioner in adult learning for some 25 years, for 15 of these years specifically in HRD. During my HRD experience, I had designed many training programs, but at no point had I ever really been challenged to teach others how to do it.

Suddenly, in 1965, I was a faculty member at a leading university and one of the courses I was expected to teach was in training program design. I reached back through my experiences to identify what it was I actually did when I designed. As I organized my thoughts, read the works of others, and discussed the activities involved in design, I began to see the process that I had been using, but had never really identified before. In fact, my first writings on this topic were under the heading of a "Process of Training."

The current title emerged during a graduate class when a student remarked that what I had done was to identify the critical events that must take place when one designs a training program. The model referred to is the one presented in this book, but what resulted from that remark was a new and clearer label: the Critical Events Model (CEM).

Over the years, the model has remained essentially the same, though there has been some minor fine tuning. "Identify the Needs of the Organization" emerged when it became apparent that the CEM is essentially based on training for jobs within a specified organization. It also reflected the tendency of too many people to rush out and start designing without first considering the purpose—to solve some kind of problem or to prevent the problem from arising.

The remainder of the CEM has stood the test of time. Some of the labels have been changed (for example, behavior to performance, and methods and materials to strategies).

Before this book, the only material written about the CEM was a series of two articles that were published in a British magazine. I made reprints available and found that others were using the CEM but apparently could not find a source for attribution. Perhaps they preferred to believe that it was their own product, or did not have the professional courtesy and ethics to acknowledge the source.

The CEM is now in print, and there should not be any question about what it is and where it came from. In writing this book, however, I have faced the usual problem one finds in trying to de-sex some of the writing. I could have opted for the numerous variations such as: he/she, s/he, he and/or she, and so on. I find these difficult to deal with grammatically and disruptive in reading. Our language poses some problems as there are times when a pronoun is appropriate. An option is to vary from "he" to "she," and I have even seen some people who count how many times each of these pronouns appears in a manuscript!

This entire manuscript was carefully reviewed by a female who has no doubt about her sex, or her role. She is certainly an equal. She has approved the use of the male pronoun in its broader and common generic use. Which brings me to acknowledgments.

Of course, acknowledgments are always in order, but frequently they are difficult to specify. The continual testing of the CEM has been done with the involvement and help of the numerous students I have had in my classes of "Designing Training programs" since 1966. I have also used it in my work with clients, both in the United States and in other countries, and those occasions have always proven to be tests of the CEM. I owe a debt of gratitude to all the people involved who helped me to see some of the implications and for providing examples of how the CEM works in a wide variety of situations.

Those who know me know that there is one other very specific acknowledgment that must be made. I could not possibly have produced this book, nor any of my other professional writings without the immeasurable contributions of my wife Zeace. She has been my professional partner from the beginning, and over the years has constantly challenged me. She does more than react to my outlines and edit what I write. She questions, probes, criticizes as needed—and supports warmly when that is needed. To dedicate this book to her is inadequate, as is this acknowledgment.

June 1981   **Leonard Nadler**

DESIGNING

TRAINING

PROGRAMS

1

Learning—The Use of

Models

This book is concerned with learning, or more specifically, with the design of learning experiences provided by organizations, usually employers. Various names are given to this activity and I prefer Human Resource Development (HRD) as I have stated elsewhere [1]. It is also called training, education, development, training and development, adult education in business and industry, and so on. Although there is no general agreement on the label, there is considerable agreement about the activity and on the fact that employers spend large sums of money for this activity.

Within the HRD field, there are many different kinds of people who are called upon to make decisions about learning programs or to actually design learning programs. Although the major focus of the book is on the actual design of learning programs, it will also be helpful to any other people who are even peripherally involved.

LEARNING

As learning is the core of this book, let us take some time to discuss what is and what is not learning, as the term will be used in this book. A more detailed discussion of learning theories will be found in a later chapter when we get into "Build Curriculum." For now, let us take a look at the general area of learning.

Learning is the acquisition of new skills, attitudes, and knowledge. (The learning psychologist refers to these as *domains*.) This definition, purposely, does not tell us anything about how the learning is acquired or whether the learner can actually use the new learning outside of the learning situation. Both of these are major areas of consideration that we will have to explore in depth as we move through the design process.

Some people would include behavior in this category. I contend that you do not learn behavior. Rather, behavior is one possible result of learning. There are many reasons why we do not use (that is, behave) all we have learned. This does not mean that learning has not taken place, but it does tell us something about the constraints placed upon behavior. It also suggests that we should avoid having people learn things that they cannot possibly use, unless the goal is just to learn with no intent to use.

Incidental and Intentional Learning

We learn through two different modes. One is *incidental,* and is happening to us all the time. We watch television for entertainment, read books for pleasure. Newspapers and magazines are read in most households. We engage in discussions, sometimes heated ones, with friends and neighbors about a wide variety of issues. As described here, these things are not done for the purpose of learning. This does not mean that we do not learn from them, but the learning is not planned, and we would not try to evaluate it.

For our purposes, we are concerned with *intentional* learning, that is, an experience wherein the individual expects to be a learner, where there are identified objectives, where time is devoted to the learning, and some kind of evaluation is planned. In organizations, this means that there must be an appropriate allocation of resources if intentional learning is to take place.

Generally, large organizations tend to allocate the physical and financial resources needed to facilitate learning. In small organizations that contend they cannot afford it, learning does take place anyway. The major difference is that the large organization provides intentional learning and reaps the benefits of this activity. The small organization forces its people to resort to incidental learning, and pays the price for employees possibly learning the wrong things.

A pervasive example is in the orientation of new employees [2]. If the organization does not have a good orientation program, one that goes beyond merely filling out appropriate forms, the new employee is forced to learn by the incidental mode. Therefore the employer has little idea of what the new employee is really learning and may be surprised by unusual behavior.

There are times when incidental and intentional learning are in conflict within an organization. The grapevine provides information (incidental learning), which rapidly becomes learned, about a new process or procedure. Employee behavior changes before any intentional learning has taken place. This forces an intentional learning program to deal with unlearning, which is frequently more difficult than learning.

Incidental learning should not be ruled out as being negative or undesirable. As it happens all the time, we should be alert to the serendipitous possibilities of integrating incidental learning into intentional learning.

This book will focus on intentional learning and therefore will drop the qualifier "intentional" and write only of learning from now on.

Teaching and Learning

Two words which we tend to use interchangeably, but which have much different meanings are:

Teaching—what we do to others.

Learning—what we do to ourselves.

Teaching is the general process of enabling the learner to acquire the learning. Teaching can range from the "stand-up classroom presenter" to fully machine-mediated instruction with no live instructor in sight. (Some refer to this as the use of high technology.) Teaching can use a facilitator who does little more than help the learner find the appropriate resources for the learning. Teaching, obviously, covers a wide range of behaviors, using both people and machines.

Even machine-mediated (for example, computer-managed) instruction uses a teacher, though the teacher and learner may never see each other and only have contact through the machine. This does not mean that a teacher is not used, but only that the teacher is not present when the learning takes place. Teaching tells us what is offered, what is presented, and what is available.

Learning cannot take place without a teacher, Designer, or some kind of facilitator. Both teacher and learner are essential to the process. It is even possible, in some carefully designed situations, to reverse their roles for the benefit of both.

The cliche "you can't learn nobody nothing" may be ungrammatical, but it communicates. Even the best teacher is useless if the learner will not, or cannot, learn. There used to be the saying that "if the learner hasn't learned, the teacher hasn't taught." The fallacy of this is that it makes the situation one-sided. Learning is a transaction which requires both parties, actively engaged, even though they are not in an interface situation.

For good teaching to take place, the teacher must have the benefit of prior preparation and the learning program must be previously designed. There are those unique individuals who can talk instantaneously, are amusing, and perhaps even instructive. In only isolated cases will this produce any real learning. Most of us must rely on the more pedestrian approach of carefully designing the learning experience to achieve the maximum return for the use of time and resources.

If we agree that teaching/learning is a partnership transaction, the learner must also be prepared. There are various ways to do this. In the model presented in this book, some of this is accomplished by involving the learner in the design process.

Learning and Performance

Learning does not necessarily produce a change in performance. We will have to deal with this dilemma in much more detail throughout the entire book. Employers, who pay the HRD bills, are not generally interested in the learning aspect. They are interested in results. In some cases the results are observable and sometimes even measurable. Results are in the application of the learning to performance in the work situation.

We should not exclude those rare and wonderful situations where employers do provide learning without seeming to be concerned with the results. Indeed we may find more of these occurring as employers become more concerned with social values, improving the quality of work life, and other activities which are not directly related to performance.

In this book, the emphasis will be on learning for performance. This is not a value judgment on my part, but an attempt to be specific about a particular kind of learning. I still believe that other kinds of learning are important, but they are beyond the scope of this book.

MODELS AND DESIGNING TRAINING PROGRAMS

Individual creativity is wonderful—it should be encouraged and rewarded. Despite this, Designers of learning programs should first explore existing models before starting to design. The unfortunate circumstance is that too many Designers start their work without realizing that models already exist and that such models can be extremely helpful.

A Designer need not take a model and apply it without some prior exploration. We will discuss some of the variables to be considered when selecting a design model, but first let us discuss models generally.

The Uses of Models

Models are not in themselves reality, but they represent the reality of those who have developed them. Developing a model is not a unique experience reserved for the privileged few. All of us are constantly "designing models" as we try to make sense out of the everyday world around us. Without those models, it is doubtful if we could solve the problems that are a constant part of daily life.

Take a simple but common experience. You want to drive from New York City to Chicago. Before you start out on your trip, you do some planning, and a significant part of that would be to consult a road map. Through the use of the map you can identify the roads to take and the major cities or other discernible points you will pass. You can even make some estimates about time and cost. You could start your journey without the road map, but you know that it will be easier if you do some planning. Your process of planning is actually using a model. The road map is the basic part of your model. You know that it shows the roads, but they are not the actual roads. You could not put your car on the road map and achieve any part of your purpose. The road map is merely a representation of what you can expect to find when you get on the real road. If you have chosen the correct map (the appropriate model), you have a much greater chance of having a successful trip than if you just started out or if you had the wrong map.

Choosing the correct road map is fairly easy. You would not look for an airline map or a railroad map. Each of these has its appropriate use, but not if you are going to drive a car.

This discussion identifies some of the questions you must consider when choosing a model for learning. What is its purpose? For which kinds of learning (that is, travel mode) is it most appropriate? Does it tell me what to look for? Does it help me anticipate what I will find? Does it provide alternatives?

There are many kinds of models, and a typology can be found in Gordon Lippitt's *Visualizing Change* [3]. Lippitt notes that "any model is valuable when it improves our understanding." In other words, the model does not do the work for us, but it enables us to understand the process or situation with which we are concerned.

A good model can help the user to understand what is essentially a complicated process. Underlying a good model is some theory, and both are interrelated. Von Bertalanffy has stated that conceptual models are basic in any attempt at theory. Conceptual models represent reality in a simplified and therefore comprehensible form [4]. This is not to say that all models must be simple, but that just because a model appears to be simple is no reason to reject it. Rather, the potential user should ascertain the theoretical base from which the model has sprung.

Models have many benefits for the user, and the 1980 *Handbook for Group Facilitators* [5] lists several, among which are:

- Explain various aspects of human behavior and interaction.

- Integrate what is known through research and observation.

- Simplify complex human processes.

- Guide observation.

More cautiously, it has been stated that "a model is something to be copied. It is intended to be close to the perfect or ideal form of something, or at least an acceptable satisfactory version" [6]. In other words, it is not necessary to look for absolute perfection in a model. It should not be confused with reality, for it is only a representation. As with any attempt to take a complex process and reduce it to a one-dimensional representation, something can be lost. The utility of the model depends upon your own understanding of the reality for which you are designing. Within this limitation, the understanding and use of models are extremely helpful.

Some people feel that using a model makes them appear dependent. They think that their organization or client might doubt their professional competence if they have to rely on a model. As in the travel example just discussed, if you rely on a map are you considered any less a good driver? Quite the contrary. Have you been a passenger in a vehicle and felt insecure because the driver hesitates when faced with unknown alternatives, such as which road to take? A map could have made the trip much more successful. The same can be said of a carefully selected model.

Open and Closed Models

There are various ways to build models, but let us focus on two kinds. The terms open and closed are used to differentiate between some model types and the philosophies expressed by each.

A *open model* is one that considers that outside factors exist which can have an impact on the design process. In creating an open model, the model builder is specifically accepting the fact that some outside forces may be beyond the scope of the model, but they should still be considered in the design process.

An open model is a working hypothesis. It provides the Designer with possible courses of action and anticipations of outcomes. The open model is descriptive, as it endeavors to describe what will happen if the model is followed. It makes no guarantees as to outcomes, therefore the design process must be carefully watched as the design process unfolds.

An open model tends to be a verbal model, as contrasted with a closed model, which is mathematical. This diminishes it in the eyes of some. Even as knowledgeable a model builder as von Bertalanffy begrudgingly acknowledges that verbal models have contributed to our understanding of human behavior and therefore should not be shunned in favor of only mathematical models.

In an open model, feedback is not automatic, and this is one of the weaknesses of many open models. The assumption is made that the user will recognize the need for feedback, but it is not built in as part of the model. There is, however, nothing to restrict an open model from having a feedback component.

A *closed model* is based on the assumption that all inputs can be identified. Closed models [7] endeavor to build all the possible variables into the model. If there is anything that can possibly have an impact on the design process, it should have been previously identified and integrated into the model.

When using a closed model, the Designer is being assured that the conclusions and outcomes are predetermined. That is, if the Designer uses the model as indicated by the model-builder, the learning program will evolve exactly as promised by the model. The Designer has fewer options, for if he strays from the closed model, it has not been used for the purpose for which it was developed. The closed model is predictive, for it is based on the model being used exactly as designed, and therefore the outcome is predictable.

As stated earlier, closed models tend to be mathematical, at least in concept. This is noted by the use of algorithms or "yes-no" choices. The movement through the model tends to be linear. The engineering/mathematical influence is quite apparent in closed models.

The contrast between open and closed models can be seen in Figure 1-1. In this, I have tried to be fair in presenting each side, but perhaps my bias has slipped through. Obviously I am generally in favor of open models, but there are times and situations when a closed model does have its advantages.

Open	Closed
Outside factors exist which cannot be identified at the outset	All factors can be identified or accounted for in the model
A working hypothesis	Outcomes predetermined
Descriptive	Predictive
Verbal	Mathematical

Fig. 1.1 Contrasting open and closed models.

Variables for Selecting a Model

In selecting a model, a Designer should consider some of the variables which are discussed in the following. The list is not complete—it probably never can be, to serve the needs of every Designer. However, it provides an indication of some of the factors to be considered when making a choice about the model to be used.

Training, education, or development?

There are various reasons for learning related to work situations. The taxonomy I have used makes a distinction among the three major types of learning programs. They are:

- Training—learning related to the present job of the individual.

- Education—learning related to a future but defined job for which the individual is being prepared.

- Development—learning for the general growth of the individual and/or the organization.

Although all three are concerned with learning, there are different models which would be most appropriate for each.

If training is the focus, the model must be related to the job as it is actually being done by the individual. Present performance on the job is an essential part of such a model.

For education, the model would have to focus on the future job which the individual is being prepared to do as a result of the learning program. It is not possible, then, to focus on present job performance, as the result of the learning is intended to result in job performance on a different job. As we will see, this strongly influences needs assessment and evaluation. Also, there is a time lag between the termination of the learning program and the use of the learning by the participant. Therefore, a model designed for education (as different from training) should contain specific activities which reinforce the learning between the end of the program and the placement of the learner on the new job.

Development models can be more general, for there is no intent for direct use on the present job or an identified future job. This should not be seen as suggesting that development is any less significant than training or education—it is different.

It is possible to modify models (for example, use a training model for education) and this is more possible with an open model than with a closed model. In either situation, the Designer should be careful to explore the implications of any changes. In an open model, changes would alter the descriptive elements of the model. For a closed model, changes could destroy the predictive elements of the model.

Skills, attitude, and knowledge.

The mix of the three different areas of learning suggests which model is most appropriate for a particular learning experience. If the emphasis is on skills and there is only one way for performance to take place, a closed model might be more appropriate. If there is a skill component but there are allowances for some individual differences in performance, an open model might just as readily be used.

For knowledge, it is somewhat the same. If there is some exact learning to take place, not based on previous experience and learning, a closed model might be more appropriate. This is one reason why some of the closed models are linked so closely with programmed instruction, computer-assisted instruction, and similar models that are useful where the knowledge to be acquired is exactly predictable. This does not mean that an open model would not be as useful, but the difference could be in how the program is designed rather than in how it is delivered.

For attitude, there are those who contend that there is little we can do about attitudes, and learning should only be concerned with behavior. Such people generally favor closed models. People who prefer open models tend to be more humanistic and consider attitudes as an area of learning. Indeed, in using an open model, the inclusion of the learner early in the process is a key element and reflects an opinion about the attitudes exhibited by the potential learner.

The learner.

Consideration should be given to the learner and his role in the learning situation. If the Designer believes that the learner should be involved, a model should be selected that provides for this in the design process. If the Designer believes that the learner need not be part of the process, (and there are those who do believe that), he should choose a model accordingly.

The previous experience of the learner, as a learner, is also important. Those who have had extensive experience in learning situations (for example, school beyond high school, out-of-school learning experiences) could have a different role in the design process than those who lack this experience. Depending upon the goals of the organization, and the Designer, an appropriate model should be selected to reflect this.

Physical distance—geography—must also be considered. Suppose you select a model that requires the learner to be involved. However, if the learner is some distance from you (the Designer) and it is too costly or logistically impossible to communicate directly, you will have to choose a different model.

Although distance can be a problem, there are alternatives. With the availability of electronic media you might choose to communicate by computer, telephone, electronic facsimile transfer, two-way television, and other ways of shrinking distance. The technology is even present so the Designer can sit miles away and observe job performance. The possibility exists, but the technology may still be too expensive or not readily available. The model selected should be carefully scrutinized for its geographical requirements.

The instructor.

The model chosen should reflect the relationship of the instructor to the design and to the instructional process. In some instances, the Designer and instructor are the same person. This is most common when the instructor is a university professor, or where the organization has the same person doing designing and instruction (either internally or externally).

In many situations, the people doing the designing are different from the people doing the instruction. Once a learning program has started, the Designer is usually out of the picture. If the instructor is to be allowed to make changes, without consulting the Designer, the model chosen should reflect this possibility. In large organizations, the physical distance and organizational placement may prevent any continuing communication between the Designer and the instructor.

The level of the learner in the organization is another factor. That is, higher level employees tend to be assigned different instructors than lower level. This can be argued, or it can be justified, but for our purposes here it should be recognized. The higher the level of the instructor (even if only in the self-image of the instructor), the more likely that he will be permitted to modify the previously designed program.

The experience of the instructor should be considered. When the instructor is relatively inexperienced (as in peer-mediated instruction), it is important that the Designer produce a program which can be conducted by a person at that level. Experienced instructors tend to want to put their own professional fingerprints on any design, and the Designer should be aware of this and select an appropriate model.

Culture of the organization.

Culture is always difficult to deal with. There are many definitions, but one can be quite sure that culture is a factor when a speaker starts a sentence with "Everybody knows . . ." It is more likely that the only people who do know are part of that cultural or micro-cultural group [8].

The culture of an organization decrees the type of model that can be selected. If there is a high degree of interaction among all levels of the organization, the model selected should reflect that aspect of organizational culture. If the culture of the organization is such that people are expected to have specific jobs, get assignments, and get the job done, the model selected should reflect that. If the culture is based on participative management or a matrix organization, that should be considered in selecting a model.

I would not want to leave the impression that identifying organizational culture is an easy task. Much work is still to be done on this important dimension of organizational behavior. The work of Fritz Steele [9] is very helpful in this area though there are those who criticize the book as being too frivolous. His analogy to the climate may oversimplified, but it is a readily usable approach to a very difficult topic.

In some organizations, certain names will trigger specific responses. I do not dare list the names and responses here but that is not for legal reasons. Rather, I would not want to trap any of my colleagues into a particular reference or defense. I have seen Organization A which would never consider a model associated with Mr. X, while Organization B thinks that Mr. X is the most outstanding person in the field of learning design. Rather, you should listen for these statements in an organization as you prepare to select a model:

■   Learning is a waste of time.

■   If you want them to learn, you tell them.

■   The only true learning takes place when the learner is involved.

■   If you can't measure it, you can't learn it.

■   Anybody can learn anything.

■   Give an intelligent person a job to do, and he will do it.

■   No learning can take place without some risk.

You could go on and add many more. Those are all reflections of various kinds of organizational culture which will influence the kind of model you choose if you design for that organization.

Your likes and dislikes.

What do you like to do as a Designer? Do you prefer to work alone, with a small group, or with the total organization? Are you comfortable and competent in doing a job analysis, or do you function more globally? How do you want to be seen by the organization? If you go around asking questions, will you be perceived as a help or a hindrance? How do you want to spend your time?

These questions, and many more like them, must be answered by you as you choose models for designing learning programs. If you are not comfortable with a model, you will probably not be successful using it. You might have to "try on" several models before you find those that are best for *you.* You might find a model that can handle most of your design needs, with some modifications. This is why I am presenting a particular model in this book. It is one with which I have had success, that my students have found useful, and that my clients have been able to relate to—so I offer it as one model. It is not the only model, but it has served me admirably since 1965, with some changes, so it is the one I like and the one I will share with you.

THE CRITICAL EVENTS MODEL (CEM)

We now turn to the main topic of this book, the presentation and discussion of a specific model: the Critical Events Model (CEM).

What is the CEM? Figure 1-2 presents the model. How can you use it? That is the remainder of this book. Before proceeding to the specifics, some general observations are in order.

An Open Model

It is apparent from the earlier discussion of models that the CEM is an open model. Recognizing that organizations and individuals are very complex, I believe it is not possible to identify and determine all the variables when a program is being designed. Indeed the actual work of designing the program will probably

THE CRITICAL EVENTS MODEL

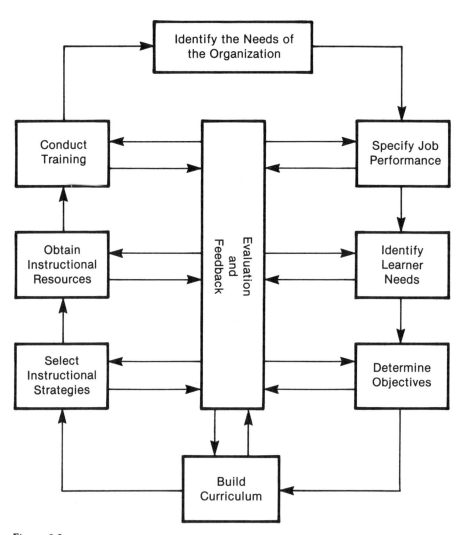

Figure 1.2

bring to light practices and policies that have either been forgotten, overlooked, or are in the organization culture category. The open model allows the design process to be halted when something other than a learning response is more appropriate.

The CEM depicts what may happen but cannot be used for predictions. After using the CEM several times, you will find that you can anticipate the responses you will get from various levels of the organization as you involve them in the design process. It still cannot predict the exact final product, but it does describe what is happening.

Designing a training program takes time. There is no exact formula that can tell us how much design time is needed for each hour of learning, though there are those people who have anxiously and eagerly searched for such a formula. As time passes, during the design process, things change. There is nothing startling in that statement except to recognize that what you start designing for may no longer be the need by the time you finish. The organization, and the problem, do not freeze just because the Designer has started the design process. Therefore the open model is more useful, particularly with organizations and industries where rapid change is the norm.

Evaluation and Feedback

There will be a whole chapter on "Evaluation and Feedback," as an event in the CEM. For now, just be alerted to the importance of this particular event.

Many models wait to do evaluation (of the design, as well as the learning) until the end. It is more helpful and extremely important to stop at each event and purposely evaluate in terms of the previous events in the CEM. I receive constant feedback from my students and clients about the CEM. The one consistent observation is that the evaluation and feedback, built into each event, has avoided wasted time and effort and contributed to a better learning program design.

The CEM and Education

The CEM is essentially useful for training—for learning programs related to the job the individual now has. This will become evident within the first few chapters.

This does not mean that it cannot also be used for education—learning for a future job. It would require, however, modification. I will comment under specific events indicating how the CEM would have to be altered to be useful for education learning programs. The major focus, however, will be on training. I might also urge you, if you are concerned with education rather than training, to search out other models which might have more direct relevance to that specific kind of learning. The difficulty is that not enough of those who write about models make the distinction among the three types of learning. They force the user to make these distinctions and therefore lessen the utility of their models.

What about development—non-job-oriented learning? The CEM is of no real use for such programs. The focus of the CEM is on the job, and if the learning is not job-related, other models would be more useful. If you are concerned about development, look for models that have come out of "adult education" which tend to be less job-related. Now, let us proceed.

REFERENCES

1.   I have discussed these distinctions in many articles and workshops. In addition, they can be found in *Developing Human Resources*, second edition, (San Diego: Learning Concepts, 1979). Also in *Corporate Human Resources Development* (New York: Van Nostrand, 1980). On tape, I have discussed these on *Leonard Nadler: An In-depth Interview with Steve Becker on Human Resource Development* (Learncom, 1980).

2.   There are too few books on orientation, despite its importance in the world of work. A recent noteworthy book in that area is *The New Employee: Developing A Productive Human Resource* by Gordon Shea (Reading, Mass.: Addison-Wesley, 1981).

3.   Gordon Lippitt has brought together different kinds of models in *Visualizing Change: Model Building and the Change Process* (San Diego: Learning Resources Corporation, 1973). Although the focus of the book is on change in general, the model building parts are directly related to the discussion in this book.

4.   A fundamental book on systems theory is Ludwig von Bertalanffy's readable book *General System Theory* (New York: George Braziller, 1968). He discusses models and systems and indicates how they can be helpful in conceptualizing and understanding even complex behavior.

5.   A longer list can be found on page 171 of the *1980 Handbook for Group Facilitators* (San Diego: University Associates, 1980).

6.   Although focusing on the health fields, the following book presents a model which would be just as helpful in other areas. Ascher J. Segall, Hannelore Vanderschmidt, Ruanne Burglass, and Thomas Frostman. *Systematic Course Design for the Health Fields* (New York: John Wiley & Sons, 1975).

7.   There are many I consider closed models. Among the more popular and well known are Leonard Silvern's *Systems Engineering Applied to Training* (Houston: Gulf Publishing, 1972), and William R. Tracy's *Designing Training and Development Systems* (New York: American Management Associations, 1971). Others will appear in references to other chapters, as well as in some of the general readings.

8.   One way of looking at culture, or micro-culture, within an organization can be found in "The Organization as a Micro-Culture" in Chip Bell and Leonard Nadler (editors), *The Client-Consultant Handbook* (Houston: Gulf Publishing, 1979).

9.   Organizational climate is deftly handled by an analogy with the weather by Fritz Steele and Stephen Jenks in *The Feel of the Workplace* (Reading, Mass.: Addison-Wesley, 1977).

ADDITIONAL PRINTED RESOURCES

The printed materials listed contain models, as well as other material, related to designing learning programs.

Banathy, Bella H. *Developing a Systems View of Education: The Systems Model Approach.* Belmont, Calif.: Fearon, 1973.

Byers, Kenneth T. (Ed.). *Employee Training and Development in the Public Service.* Chicago: Public Personnel Association, 1970.

Cooper, Susan, and Cathy Heenan. *Preparing, Designing, and Leading Workshops.* Boston: CBI Publishing, 1979.

Craig, Robert L. (Ed.). *Training and Development Handbook: A Guide to Human Resource Development.* New York: McGraw-Hill, 1976 (Second Edition).

Davies, Ivor K. *Instructional Technique.* New York: McGraw-Hill, 1981.

Davis, Larry Nolan. *Planning, Conducting, and Evaluating Workshops.* San Diego: Learning Concepts, 1975.

Donaldson, Les, and Edward F. Scannell. *Human Resources Development: The New Trainer's Guide.* Reading, Mass.: Addison-Wesley, 1978.

Fostering the Growing Need to Learn. Washington, D.C.: Government Printing Office, 1973.

Friesen, Paul A. *Designing Instruction.* Toronto: Friesen, Kaye and Associates, 1971.

Gane, Christopher. *Managing the Training Function.* Palo Alto: Davlin Publishers, 1972.

Gardner, James E. *Helping Employees Develop Job Skill.* Washington, D.C.: BNA, 1976.

Goldstein, Irwin L. *Training: Program Development and Evaluation.* Monterey, Calif.: Brooks/Cole Publishing, 1974.

Harris, Ben M. *Improving Staff Performance Through In-Service Education.* Boston: Allyn & Bacon, 1980.

Harrison, Jared F. (Ed.). *The Sales Manager as a Trainer.* Reading, Mass.: Addison-Wesley, 1977.

Harrison, Jared F. *The Management of Sales Training.* Reading, Mass.: Addison-Wesley, 1977.

Ingalls, John D. *A Trainer's Guide to Andragogy: Its Concepts, Experiences, and Applications.* Washington, D.C.: Government Printing Office, 1973.

Loughray, John W., and Barrie Hopson. *Producing Workshops, Seminars, and Short Courses: A Trainer's Handbook.* Chicago: Follett, 1979.

McLagan, Patricia A. *Helping Others Learn: Designing Programs for Adults.* Reading, Mass.: Addison-Wesley, 1978.

Michalak, Donald, and Edwin C. Yager. *Making the Training Process Work.* New York: Harper & Row, 1979.

Miller, Harry G., and John R. Verduin, Jr. *The Adult Educator: A Handbook for Staff Development.* Houston: Gulf Publishing, 1979.

Odiorne, George S. *Training by Objectives.* New York: Macmillan, 1979.

Romiszowski, A. J. *Designing Instructional Systems.* Volume 1, Theory and Design. Chicago: Nichols Publishing, 1981.

Saint, Avice. *Learning at Work: Human Resources and Organizational Development.* Chicago: Nelson-Hall, 1974.

Silvern, Leonard. *The Evolution of Systems Thinking in Education.* Los Angeles: Education and Training Consultants, 1971.

Silvern, Leonard. *Systems Engineering Applied to Training.* Houston: Gulf Publishing, 1972.

Smith, Robert G., Jr. *The Design of Instructional Systems.* Alexandria, Va.: Humro, 1966.

Tracey, William R. *Designing Training and Development Systems.* New York: American Management Associations, 1971.

Warren, Malcolm. *Training for Results.* Reading, Mass.: Addison-Wesley, 1979. (Second Edition).

2

Identify the Needs of

the Organization

Every organization has needs. These are defined as what the organization must have to attain its goals, while recognizing that there are constraints on the kinds and amount of resources available. Essentially all the organization can muster to meet its needs are the physical, financial, and human resources which it has or can obtain.

As this is a book about designing learning programs, the focus is on the human resources, but by no means can we exclude the relationship to the other resources. We will be constantly referring to these resources as we go through the events that will facilitate the design of a training program.

The objectives of this event are:

To determine the nature of the problems.

To assist in deciding whether learning is the appropriate solution to the identified problem.

THE NEEDS OF THE ORGANIZATION

We are now into the first event of the CEM. (See Figure 2-1.) An assumption in the CEM, and all models are built on assumptions, is that organizations generally will not provide training (as different from education or development) unless there is a specific need. Until that need is sufficiently clarified, it is not possible to move on to the next event. For the Designers [1], this can be frustrating. There is the drive to get on with the more traditional activities in design work that have to do with the learning. Yet this first event of the CEM is definitely part of the design process. Rushing ahead to some of the other events, without fully clarifying this one first, is courting disaster.

THE CRITICAL EVENTS MODEL

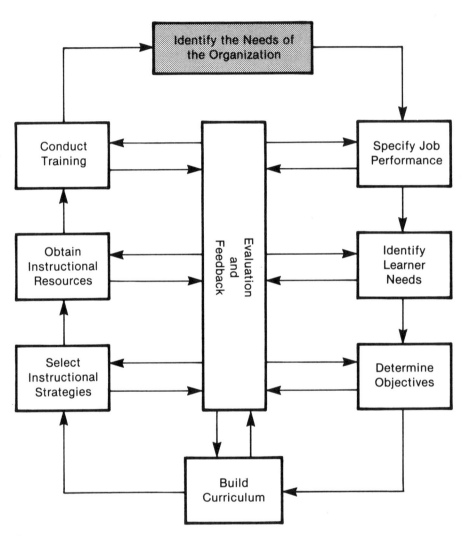

Figure 2.1

This first event has within it the components of what has been called *front-end analysis*. That is, why bother to go ahead with the design until we first have some assurance that there is an agreed upon problem, that training is the response to that problem, and that the response will not prove more costly than leaving the problem unsolved?

There is also the question of the individual and the organization. The needs of each do not have to be in conflict, though sometimes the situation is approached as if it is one or the other. The needs of both must be met if any performance change is to result that will be helpful to both. Therefore, within this first event, we have to explore some of the theoretical as well as practical issues. The Designer must seek information, talk to people, gather data, and do the myriad tasks which are the first part of designing a learning program.

Development: Individual and Organizational

Our language has many limitations, but it is what we have to work with in a book or in our interpersonal relations. For example, we constantly refer to Organization Behavior, yet we all agree that an organization is an artificial entity. It is not a real person, so how can it behave? It is the people within the organization who behave. Rather than engage in a semantic battle, let us accept the common terminology but not be trapped by it. Organizations may not learn, but people within the organizations can and do learn. If learning is effective, it is possible that people will behave differently and their organizations will function as a reflection of those changes in individual behavior.

A dichotomy has arisen which can be misleading. How would you respond to the question, "Which is more important, individual development or organization development?" This question was actually asked in a survey conducted in the late 1960s. It is still asked by some people today. It assumes that the question must be answered by opposites. It ignores the possibility that both might be appropriate—depending on the needs of the organization and the individual.

Sometimes the purpose of learning is to bring about modification in individual behavior, while at other times the reason for the learning is the improvement of collective behavior (that is, functioning as an organization). This latter purpose is one part of a related field which has been called Organization Development, or OD [2].

A long discussion about the various and varying definitions of OD would be fruitless. Between the time this is written and you read it, we can expect that more definitions will emerge. At this time, there does appear to be some general agreement that many aspects of OD do not require learning as one of the interventions.

It is possible that, when a need has been clearly diagnosed by an OD intervention, a learning experience will be required. At that point, the OD practitioner moves from the OD competencies to those competencies required of a person *designing* learning, not conducting it. Many people (too many, perhaps?) make this move without having sufficient competencies in both areas.¯

It is not proper, nor possible, to make the dichotomy that learning (HRD) is for individuals and OD is for organizations. We must return to the objective of intervention. If it is learning with an expected change in performance, training is appropriate. To do this, the relevant learning experience should be designed. This is more than just pulling an exercise out of a book or buying the latest package. Both of these resources may be chosen, after some initial design work has been done. (The make-or-buy decision will be explored in later events of the CEM.)

Another area where we have the potential of a clash between the individual and the organization is in career development. In this activity, the focus is on helping the individual move to another position, generally within the organization. This is *internal mobility*, as contrasted with *external mobility* where the employee is planning to move outside the organization.

Career development, for internal mobility, can be planned without provision for any learning experience, but this is unwise. It does happen frequently, as we can observe when an individual is first promoted and then trained.

If the identified need of the organization at this point in the CEM is to provide for career development, those individuals who are to be the learners must be involved. If this is not done, the learning situation can create new problems. If the learners perceive the experience as education (as contrasted with training), they will be looking for new jobs at the completion of the learning experience. If the new jobs are not available within their own organization, they will move to other organizations. In such a situation, the learning program will have increased turnover and created additional problems that had not existed previously.

It is important for us to identify how a need surfaces within the organization, and the expectations that relate to that need.

WHERE DO NEEDS COME FROM?

The needs of an organization are a result of the everyday experience of existing. Some needs arise very quickly and become problems. Other needs emerge over a period of time and are amenable to short-range and long-range planning.

Let us examine some of the sources that cause needs in organizations, and for the individuals within the organizations.

Production or Service

A call comes to you that production has fallen below quota and you are asked to "run a training program" to increase production. There is no doubt that there is a production problem, and therefore there is a need. Whether training is the solution or not is yet to be determined.

In production activities, the need for some kind of action becomes apparent very rapidly. As performance can be quantified in terms of output, any variation below the determined figure becomes a problem for somebody in the organization—and presents an obvious need. In the production area another need that can arise quickly is related to quality, as this is also quantifiable. Line managers recognize that it is more economical to produce the product correctly the first time rather than to have to rebuild it later.

In a service situation, we generally lack the data that can tell us that output is slipping. There are some measures for service, but most of them are not quantified—as yet. The need can still arise in very explicit terms, such as increase in customer complaints. In a supermarket operation it can be evidenced by excessively long lines at the checkout counters. This encourages shoppers to take their business to a competitor. It is certainly visible, though not immediately quantifiable.

Equipment or Regulations

A change in the equipment being used or some modifications in existing equipment can also be the source of a need for the organization. When electric typewriters were first introduced in the early 1950s, there was the contention that this would not pose any problems or needs. The keyboard was the same, so it should be easy for a typist to sit at the desk, have the electric replace the manual, and go to work on the new machine.

In practice, this is not what happened. Output decreased, and it was measurable. Morale took an appreciable slide down the scale and grumbling was audible. Researchers were called in and they determined that it was more difficult to teach a manual operator to work the new electric than to teach a person who had never worked on a manual. For either situation, a learning program was required.

We usually think of new equipment as a problem on a production line or with other types of equipment operators. How about managers and executives, faced with introduction of the computer. As computers become more pervasive, we are told that each manager will have one on the desk, and probably at home as well. What kinds of problems might arise? What training will be required?

In the early 1980s, it was identified that one problem was the change in managerial behavior required by the computer. It was now possible for managers to "talk" to each other without ever leaving their offices. As contrasted with the telephone, you could now leave a message on somebody else's computer. It was no longer possible for a manager to use the excuse, "I never got your message." It was on the computer to be readily called up whenever the manager returned to his desk, and the computer.

Complaints about government regulations can be found in almost every daily issue of a newspaper. Columnists thrive on the subject, for there is always something to write about. Politicians, particularly those out of office, find the topic convenient as a rallying cry. As Designers, we do not have the luxury of debating the pros and cons of government regulations. They exist and will continue to exist. They are constantly changing. Each new regulation or any change in an existing regulation creates some kind of new need in an organization.

Output: Products and Services

Consider the executive decision to diversify. The organization is in sound financial condition, has a good market position, so the executive level may decide that now is the time to reach out into different areas. Such decisions are not uncommon, but they produce a new set of needs.

A new company may be spun off as a subsidiary to the parent company. New relationships emerge, and old tasks are reassigned. There could be the decision to add a new product line to an existing organization and this introduces new suppliers, customers, and processes. These changes are occurring all the time. You can see this in the way companies have been changing their names in recent years. At one time, you could tell exactly what business a company was engaged in, for that was part of the company name. Today companies are changing to more generic names (industry, associates, or just the name of the founder) rather than a product name in the title. This allows for more flexibility as the product mix changes.

Manufacturing companies have a high capital investment, as compared to service companies. This difference accounts for the greater flexibility found among service companies as they move from one market to another. For all organizations, it is obvious that almost any capital expenditure will create a learning need for some group of employees.

Outside Pressures

Picture the situation of a Designer who is called in and asked to design a learning program about_____(you can fill in the blank with almost anything) because one of the company officials heard that a competitor was doing it. I can anticipate the groans from many readers who have been faced with just such a request.

This happens when a fad, gimmick, or something catches the corporate fancy. It is not too difficult to look back over the past years and produce an impressive list that would include: sensitivity training, transactional analysis, transcendental meditation, programmed instruction, video-tape recording, behavior modeling—and the list goes on. In themselves, each of these does have something to offer when it is built in as part of the design process—as we will see under later events in the CEM. At this point, they are being discussed because sometimes the need only arises when a company official wants the organization to be able to report that they are in the forefront of learning, whatever it happens to be at the time.

As an organization recognizes the importance of the human resource, so does the marketplace. The proliferation of vendors in this field is one of the major growth areas in recent years, and it is destined to grow even more. Some people dislike being called vendors, preferring the more glamorous title of consultant. (The glamour was tarnished a bit by the discussion in Congress in 1980 when consultants were castigated for some of their practices.) As a group, in relation to learning design, vendors include those who: provide external consulting; provide training, education, and/or development programs; sell hardware; sell software; provide facilities and sites; and so on. The list can go on and on. If you have any doubts about the length and variety of such a listing, just look at those publications in the HRD field that have monthly or periodic buyers' guides. These sections are increasing in thickness and complexity. In addition, the daily mail brings attractive brochures, and the ringing telephone heralds the approach of a vendor's salesperson. There is certainly nothing wrong with this situation, since increased competition is helpful, both in quality and in price. It also means that many members of your organization are at the receiving end of those sales efforts, and they then turn to the HRD people and ask, "Why don't we have that kind of program?" The implication appears to be, "How come you are not smart enough to know that such a program exists, and that we 'need' it?" The tendency is to give in and obtain the program, film, package, or individual, so you can show the company that you know what is current.

It takes a great deal of strength to resist this kind of pressure from outside the HRD unit, particularly if the budget is in the hands of others. If you don't respond, it is not difficult for them to use their budgets to purchase the program externally and by-pass you. In very few cases will "they" (whoever has the budget) admit that perhaps the external program they purchased did not really make any difference in their operations.

You

People in your organization may be coming to you because you have an admirable track record. In the past, you helped solve problems through the kinds of learning programs you designed and provided. The new request may be completely different, but you are still looked upon as having the solution rather than being part of the problem-solving process.

It takes a strong will and satisfactory self-image to respond by slowing down the process. "Identify the Needs of the Organization" is the first event in the CEM and indicates that you are willing to respond, but some up-front questions must be asked.

If you are doing a good job of helping managers solve their people problems, of course you will get repeat calls. This provides one measure of feedback on your performance. Once you have been accepted as part of the problem-solving resources in the organization, you will have little difficulty in encouraging a process rather than a quick response based on little data.

When you are new in an organization, and particularly when the HRD activity is just starting, it may be necessary to respond fairly rapidly with learning programs just to gain validity and recognition. You should, however, recognize that you are doing it for those reasons, and you may not be coming close enough to the reality of the situation to really solve problems. You should be able to differentiate between those programs you are doing to gain acceptance and those that are directed towards meeting the identified needs of the organization.

ORGANIZATION DIAGNOSIS

Diagnosis is a continuing process. All managers in an organization are continually engaged in diagnosis as they solve problems, even if they do not use that label for their activities. This first event in the CEM is directly related to diagnostic activity in the organization.

Managers may not be using standardized instruments or even some of the available organizational diagnosis models [3]. They are asking themselves some questions, and if you can be part of that questioning process, you are closer to helping provide some appropriate solutions.

How Are We Doing?

Within the organization somebody is asking that question. It sometimes comes out in terms of the "bottom line"—are we making a profit or a loss? This type of question is asked throughout the entire organization, but in different ways. Sometimes this is done by an organized data-gathering process. At other times, it is through staff meetings.

A different but related approach is the use of *quality circles* or groups. Although the technique started in United States, the practice gained wide acceptance and publicity in its use in Japan, so that some people think of it as a typical Japanese management technique. Essentially it is what was generally called participative management long before the term quality circle became common. The practice is based on the premise that those who are doing the work are more likely to know their own problems and will be able to suggest solutions.

If your organization has such an activity, no matter what it is called, you should be attending those meetings. One purpose is to listen carefully and to identify organization needs for which training could be a response. If you are accepted by the group, you can also be helpful in having them avoid the "training is the answer" response before exploring the need further.

How Can We Do It Better?

The pressures of the marketplace dictate that the organization that does not change is doomed to either die or to spend much of its resources in an attempt to survive. A need of the organization is to constantly seek ways of doing things better in order to retain or improve its position.

When this search arises, it is phrased in terms of money. In many situations it is possible to do better, but the cost could price the organization out of the market. There are alternatives, and training may be one, but careful exploration is required. We must avoid the possibility that the cure would turn out to be worse than the illness.

Some organizations function in a different kind of marketplace. There is the government organization which does not have any competition. Some say that this is what keeps the government from operating as efficiently as it could, but that observation is based on limited insight into the forces that control the behavior of government employees. They are always under the microscope of citizen groups, the media, and special interest groups. In our form of government, with its checks and balances, the legislative group is always looking at the executive and vice-versa. It would be in the best interests of all concerned if government employees could find ways of doing things better. The numerous awards for suggestions are one indication that this is part of the organizational norm, though perhaps not as prevalent as some would like.

Nonprofit organizations (such as the American Red Cross) are also constantly seeking to do things better. They work with limited financial resources and are under continuous pressure to improve the job performance of all their employees.

What Problems Do We Have?

An organization always has problems. The job of a manager is to constantly solve problems. It is not the problems that are of concern, but the solutions. If, after identifying, selecting, and applying a solution the problem still remains, the organization could be on the way to crisis.

To be effective, all the people in an organization should constantly be solving problems. There are many dimensions to this, as the range of problems varies from the very simple to the extremely complex. Some of the problems involve only one kind of resource (for example, physical), while most of the problems involve all three resources. Some of the problems are concerned with only a single individual, while many of the problems involve several people and sometimes the whole organization.

Solving these problems is a basic need of the organization. The difficulty arises as people in the organization try to determine just whose problem it is, and how important. For one person, solving a particular problem could seem like the most important task of the day. For another person in the same organization, that particular problem could have very low priority.

A good question to ask, and we will be asking it several times in this and future chapters, is: What difference does it make? What if we do not solve this problem? Asking this question does not mean that there is no problem or that it isn't important. For organizations with limited resources, the reality is that not every problem can be solved. What would the impact be on the organization if a problem were put aside or if an agreement were reached not to solve a particular problem?

Asking it another way, what is to be gained or lost? If the problem is not solved, what is the relative cost—and cost is always relative. There was a factory, in the mid-1960s, where water was an important component of the manufacturing process. At times, workers would not shut off the water completely but let it flow even when it wasn't being used. There were adequate trenching and sewers so the water could run off with no negative effect on the plant or the workers, but water costs money, and this presented a problem that was put on the agenda of the plant manager's meeting. After some discussion, it was agreed that to police the situation and perhaps arouse the negative feelings of some of the workers would be more costly than the water bill. An alternative was suggested: to place appropriate notices at each valve with eye-catching cartoons using the workers to turn off the spigots. Very soon, the workers were adding very interesting additions to the cartoons, but little change in the way of performance.

Some years later, in the same factory, the identical situation became a significant problem. The cost of water had risen dramatically, there were workers in the plant who were concerned with conserving resources, and the city that provided the water gave notice that it might have to resort to rationing. At that point, the waste of water became a significant problem, involving many both inside and outside of the plant, and firm action had to be taken to limit the waste of water. The need of the organization had changed greatly as the internal conditions (water rates and work force) and the external forces (the city) altered the nature of the problem.

The Future

Organizations must constantly be looking towards the future [4]. There is no longer the luxury of slowly sliding towards the future, for that point is now being reached at a much faster pace than ever before. A need of the organization is to anticipate that future and to take appropriate action immediately so the company will be prepared for changed conditions. Despite this need, some organizations ignore the sign-posts. Perhaps there is the tendency to think that some problems can best be solved by ignoring them or by reacting only to those problems that are on the verge of becoming crises.

A major example is in relation to the work force. We know that this will change, though we do have some managers who are waiting for the return of the "good old days." As of now, it does not appear that we will ever return to the past we have known. Even a new depression will not be like the old ones, for we now have unemployment insurance and similar buffers. On the other hand, we are now much more dependent upon international trade than we have been previously.

What is being done in your organization to prepare for the future? Some companies have recognized the impact of the changing work force which will produce different conditions than we have known. In one organization, a fast-food chain in the Midwest, they did a comprehensive market study to determine how the changing population would impact upon what they were selling and how they were marketing their products and services. The results were astounding, and the company became involved in developing significant changes to accommodate the data provided by this comprehensive market study. At the same time, as I met with the officials on the human resource development side, nothing was being done regarding their work force. The same data on population trends for the areas they served could be applied to their own work force, but they had not taken the available data and used it to do work force planning or considered its implication for HRD.

PERFORMANCE ANALYSIS

No matter what the problem, our concern in this book is performance—or designing training programs to improve performance. In conjunction with organization diagnosis, we must also ask: What is the performance component? How does the need of the organization relate to some kind of performance problem?

How Did the Need Arise

A place to start is to identify how a need arises. More specifically, who says it is a need? As we will see, the source of needs can be either external or internal to the organization. From whatever source, there must be some person within the organization who has responsibility related to that need, or it may be a stimulus to which the organization cannot respond.

There may be complaints from customers about the quality of merchandise, late shipments, damaged materials, or incorrect shipments. If service is involved, customer complaints can arise rapidly and require immediate actions to meet the need.

The source of the need should have been processed through some of the organization diagnosis steps indicated earlier in this chapter. At this point, agreement must be reached that, no matter what the source, it is a human performance problem for which learning could be a solution.

The need can also arise from an internal source. Reports can show that a supervisor is having difficulty keeping up with production, either quality or quantity. Or, there may be damage to equipment which goes beyond normal usage.

A manager may be planning for a new process or product and does not know if the workers will be able to perform as needed for this change. In these instances, it is relatively easy to identify the internal person who has responsibility related to that need.

There is a specific reason for seeking the person, or people, who have the responsibility related to the need. They are the ones who must agree that there is a human performance problem, and they are the people who will be looking for results at the end of the learning program. These people should be involved early in the design process, and at various stages they will have to make decisions about that design process.

Too often it is a case of the Designer being given the assignment with the admonition, "Now go away and do your work and don't bother me. It's now *your* problem." It is never the Designer's problem. The purpose of the design process is to meet the need of some individual or group within the organization, and the Designer is helping them and must avoid making it his problem. The solution to the problem will occur when the learning is applied back on the job, and the Designer is not part of the job. When the Designer does become part of a job performance, there is a question as to whether that person is a Designer or a supervisor.

The Designer must, however, be able to *follow* the design process to its ultimate conclusion, which is not the learning, but job performance. Therefore those who initiated the request to meet a need must be prepared to allow the Designer to follow the process on to the job.

I would not want to leave the impression that Designers want to do this and that the line people object. Too frequently, I have observed just the opposite. The line people want the Designer to see how the work gets done, after a learning program, but they do not want the Designer to get in the way of the supervisory relationship. This becomes an acute problem when the Designer is also the instructor. Then, a relationship can build between the Designer/instructor and the learner, with the supervisor being the odd man out.

Which Human Resource Area?

In other writings I have identified three current areas of human resource endeavors, and that typology is very appropriate as we try to clarify performance problems.

The area of Human Resource *Utilization* (HRU) is commonly called personnel. It is concerned with recruitment, selection, placement, compensation, and appraisal. Some refer to this area as Human Resource Management.

In looking at who is doing the job, we may find that the wrong people are in some jobs. (What we can do about this will be discussed under alternatives.) This may be due to a breakdown in recruitment criteria as related to other organizational needs, or the selection process may not be screening for the kinds of people the organization needs at this time. Placement is too often done without consulting the line people.

A long time ago, we discovered that people tend to do those things they are rewarded for and to avoid doing those things for which they get punished. Perhaps the reward system (compensation) is not related to performance. Indeed, we have seen instances where good performance resulted in a negative reward. This was prevalent in earlier days (note my optimism about today) when piece work rates were used. That is, workers got paid by the piece produced. A rate was set, and if a worker had a higher level of performance than the standard rate, this would result in extra pay. This was frequently followed by the practice, in some companies, of then reducing the rate—paying less per piece produced and therefore requiring the worker to produce more units for the standard rate. The term "speed-up" was the label applied to this practice. The result was increased productivity, but it also challenged the worker to use creative thinking to find ways to beat the system. Industrial relations have come a long way since those days, but we still have isolated pockets of such practices, and perhaps more than is commonly recognized.

An area that has developed more recently is Human Resource *Engineering/Environment.* I am forced to use both terms, engineering and environment, for that is the common usage at this time. Essentially they both relate to the same activity and the differences tend to be semantic rather than conceptual.

Within this area a specific question can be raised. Has the employee been provided with the appropriate equipment to perform the tasks assigned? This may seem like an obvious question, but it is easily overlooked. Those who are looking at performance from a distance, from higher levels of the organization, often make assumptions about the equipment available to the person performing the job. If the equipment is not correct, is outdated, poorly maintained, or in some other way deficient, that could be the cause of poor job performance.

In most organizations, people do not work alone. They work in relation to others in the organization, including others at the same level. This produces an important aspect of human behavior which is called *peer pressure.* The worker may know the appropriate performance, but does not perform because of reactions from others in the same unit or group. The literature has many instances of this, and when a worker does violate the peer norm the term "rate-buster" is applied.

Peer pressure can also be positive. In some of the newer and innovative approaches to improving the quality of work life, we are finding that facilitating peer relationships and cooperative behavior can produce pressure to improve performance.

When performance is not up to standard, it can be because the worker does not want to meet that standard. This comes as a shock to some, but some people report to work with different standards and expectations than their employer. For such workers, you could provide the best equipment, environment, financial reward, and they still would not perform. This may be a result of a deficiency in the HRU aspect of selection and placement. There would be other needs in that area, but we could be faced with the wrong people on the job, and a need to be met.

We now return to Human Resource *Development* which, as previously defined, is based in learning. Before rushing off to design and conduct another learning program, we should ascertain if there had been a previous one. If so, why did performance not change? If there had been a previous learning program, why does it need to be repeated?

The answer to these questions should have been built into the design process for the earlier HRD program. If such was the case, as in the model described in this book, the answers to these questions will be readily available. If not, the Designer is required to find out something about the previous programs and their relation to learning and performance.

ALTERNATIVES TO TRAINING

Given the previous discussion, it is obvious that some alternatives may be more related to meeting the need of the organization, than designing a training program. It is not that training should be considered as a last resort, but once one starts the design process, a commitment of time and resources is required. We owe it to our organizations to at least explore other alternatives. This is a part of the design process and is the first event of the CEM.

The Designer who does not explore alternatives is bordering on disaster. Though the range of alternatives keeps expanding, this does not diminish the need for training programs. It does help us focus on what training can and should do, and when other alternatives are a more appropriate way of meeting the identified needs of an organization. Hackman and Oldham [5] suggest four in wide use, which are:

1. Change the people who are doing the work.
2. Change the people who are related to those doing the work.
3. Change the work place.
4. Change the contingencies, benefits, and rewards.

Let us look at some of these and other changes as alternatives to be explored as part of the first event in the CEM. Although we may decide not to continue the design process, the information gathered in exploring alternatives can be helpful to the Designer in other situations.

Fire and Hire

It may seem cruel and lacking in humanity, but sometimes the best alternative is to fire some people and hire others.

Some years ago, I was asked by a major bank to design a sales training program. This was at the time when banks were becoming competitive in New York City, and marketing was being introduced into banking as a new and necessary activity. The bank could provide more than 35 services, but its customers were using very few of them. The bank hired a vice-president for marketing (an almost unheard of position at that time) and asked me to design a training program for selected personnel. The trainees would be the Platform people. These were the persons who, in early banking days, did actually sit on a platform, or behind the swinging gates. In more recent times, these are the people at the desks away from the tellers' windows. The Platform position was a step up in the banking world and a position to which many people aspired. It meant being in control, making bank assets available, and was considered prestigious. Essentially this individual sat at a desk and customers came to him.

The change the bank officials wanted to bring about was for the Platform person to get out from behind the desk and visit customers to sell more of the bank's services. The goal was fine, but the approach caused some difficulties. As part of this first event, I interviewed some of the Platform people and determined that they had no intention of getting out from behind their desks. They had worked for years to reach the point where the desk was a reward and symbolized success on the job.

My suggestion to the bank officials was to either fire or reassign the Platform people and recruit new employees who would not see sitting behind a desk as a reward for good prior performance. The organization was asking for too great a change to be brought about through a learning program. The Platform people, at least those interviewed, just would not do the job as redesigned.

My advice was ignored, and a contract was given to somebody else to design the training program. Within six months the vice-president for marketing was fired, and a different person was hired. Jointly, with this action, new people were recruited and selected for the new job category. Some of the Platform people were retained for those activities which still needed to be done behind the desks. The new people hired knew that their main job performance was outside the bank, visiting customers, and selling bank services at the customers' place of business.

There are times and situations when a training program cannot bring about the massive change in job performance that somebody expects. We need to have the courage to say this at the beginning of the design process and not to wait until the final evaluation provides these data.

Internal Mobility

Jobs are constantly changing. The proliferation of technological advances, new demands from the marketplace, and other factors that require organizational changes also bring about changes in individuals and jobs.

It is not uncommon to find that, after several years, an employee wants to change jobs because, "They now expect me to do something I wasn't hired for." We could suggest a training program for such an employee, but what might be the result? The problem is not one of getting the employee to perform better on the present job. The job and employee are no longer compatible.

We now have increased research into life-cycles and the ways in which people change over the years. Their needs change, and they may be looking for either more or less responsibility.

In these changing situations, training should not be considered the first response. Many organizations have a variety of jobs. Moving the employee to another job (that is, internal mobility) may be a more satisfactory response than a training program.

With internal mobility, we may find the need for an education program to prepare the employee for the new job. In fact, an education program often can be helpful in assisting the employee to discover what the new job requires. In that way, a thoughtful decision can be made as to the relevance of the new job to the identified needs of the individual and those of the organization. When an employee is transferred prior to any learning experience, training will probably be required.

Reengineer the Job

Towards the end of the 1970s, we had a nuclear accident which highlighted the need for constant concern with the way jobs are engineered. The Three Mile Island accident had multiple causes. One, as determined by the investigating group, was the lack of sufficient education programs and adequate standards of performance. It was also found that no amount of training or education could have helped, as the workplace had been engineered in such a way that no single employee could possibly perform all the functions that were required. The work situation had to be reengineered to take account of people.

Engineering in the workplace can also be used to bring about improved performance. One provocative approach is that suggested by Gilbert [6] who contends that we can measure most of performance and engineer the situation to increase the potential of improving performance. Others have taken different approaches which have launched a quality of work life movement [7], though this group tends to prefer the term environment rather than engineering.

Performance is a result of many factors. In some cases, by redesigning the workplace we may be able to improve performance far beyond what can be accomplished by training.

Change Equipment

If equipment is not consistent with the expected outcomes of the job, it is unlikely that learning will have any effect. This appears to be so obvious that one wonders why we must constantly restate it.

U.S. steel mills have been criticized as having some of the lowest productivity in the steel-producing world. In many plants this is absolutely true, and no amount of training will make any significant change. The reason is that the equipment is old and has severe limitations. No matter how trained or skilled, the workers can only produce what the equipment will allow. The criticism is usually accompanied by comparisons with Germany and Japan. What is omitted from the picture is that both of those countries had their steel-making capacity obliterated by World War II, so that in the postwar period they were able to build a new capability, including oxygen furnaces which require less scrap metal and are geared to a much higher level of productivity than the earlier older furnaces.

Until an organization (such as some of those in the steel industry) is prepared to face the reality of needed capital expenditures, training may be sought as the solution to obsolete equipment. Training may suffice as a temporary measure, but it is no substitute for equipment replacement.

Organization Change

The term organization development is used very broadly, so perhaps we can be more specific when we talk of organization change. That is, performance can sometimes be improved vastly by making an organizational change, rather than by training.

Various kinds of organizational changes are possible. To make a unit more effective, it might be desirable to have the unit report to a different level or group than before. This can improve performance of the individuals and the unit.

Traditional organizational patterns are slowly giving way to more innovative relationships in order to improve organizational effectiveness. The matrix organization is one example. Though it retains some elements of the traditional, it uses project groups or task forces. People function in a variety of temporary relationships to get the job done [8]. For people who thrive on the ambiguity of such work relationships, the organizational change can be very effective in improving performance.

THE DECISION TO TRAIN

As the first event in the CEM, we have explored the sources of the need and possible alternatives. To proceed further, let us assume that you are now convinced that training is the appropriate response. Still one further question must be asked. What would the *cost* be if the training did not take place? This is an extremely difficult question to answer at this time because there is a lack of cost data at this stage of the design process.

This is where the previous experience and professional background of the Designer becomes an important factor. Costing out the design and implementation are exercises in guesswork, but they must be done. Estimates have to be developed covering the total training program.

By contrast, another set of cost data is required. Suppose no performance change, attributable to learning, were to take place. What is the current "cost"?

An organization can keep records of production that will show how much was lost because manufactured items did not meet quality standards. There is an identifiable cost for rebuilding, scrapping, or whatever the practice is in the organization. The question that must be asked is: What is the comparison between the cost of the present quality deficiency and the cost of conducting a training program to improve quality? Based on these comparative cost data, a decision can be made as to whether or not to proceed with the design and implementation of the training program.

Costs are not always possible to state in financial terms. How can an organization quantify the cost of the loss of its reputation when quality fails? Reduced sales may be only one manifestation of poor quality. The decision to train, in such a situation, may be based on the need to produce a quality product for market image, rather than to reduce the actual cost of production.

Organizations that provide services rely less on cost data for individual items or jobs. For many jobs, from supervisor on up in the organization, cost data are difficult to obtain. Where sales is a function, an organization will try to quantify using sales quotas. Yet, even sales organizations recognize that direct cost data are difficult to obtain in this area.

If the organization does have cost data, the Designer must have access to that data. This further suggests that the Designer should know how to interpret this data and how to use it for comparison with the cost estimates for designing the training program.

DECISIONS

Before going further, the Designer must ascertain if there is agreement on the problem and the need for a training program. This can be done by obtaining responses to the following questions:

1. Is there agreement on the problem?

At some point, the problem should be clearly stated, preferably in writing. Those concerned should review this and reach agreement on the statement of the problem. This is crucial if the training program is to have the sharp focus required.

2. Is it agreed that training is the solution to the stated problem?

The response to this question may have to be hedged. The Designer should avoid making promises for training that may not be possible. All the Designer can promise is that the learning will take place which can produce the possible performance change. The intent of this question is to commit all who are concerned to support the efforts of the Designer as he seeks to design a training program that is directed towards solving the previously stated problem.

If appropriate, it can be an education program instead. The Designer should avoid putting both training and education in the same program. As will become apparent in later events of the CEM, if the distinction becomes obscured, the resulting design will be less effective.

3.   Is there a specific decision to start designing a training program?

From all the exploration and discussion there must now be a specific decision. This should come from those who have the problem or feel the need to have the problem solved. If they have concurred on the previous two questions, it may seem superfluous to ask this one. The intent is to be sure that all agree on starting the process, before there is further use of any resources. Indeed, some of those involved in making this decision may be asked to provide some of the resources needed during the design process.

When affirmative responses have been received to all the questions, the Designer can proceed.

MOVING FORWARD

Having completed this first event in the CEM, the Designer would then move on to the next event. In practice, this is what takes place. For purposes of this book, we will take a slight detour into evaluation and feedback.

REFERENCES

1.   Throughout this book, the word "Designer," with a capital D is meant to designate that person who has the responsibility for designing the training program. Where a team is used for this process, and this is frequently the case, the term is meant to designate the entire team. The word itself is sexless, but I hope the readers will pardon the occasional use of "him" or a similar male designation. My wife, who is certainly not a "him," has helped me in writing this book. We have agreed that the use of alternatives can be confusing so there will not be the use of some of the terms such as: he/she, s/he, she/he, and so on. Whenever a male pronoun is used, please accept the fact that it is used in a nonsexist mode.

2.   The distinction I make between these two terms, and the fields, can be found in my article "Defining the Field—Is It HRD or OD, or . . .?" in the December 1980 issue of the *Training and Development Journal.*

3.   A variety of approaches are presented in Edward E. Lawler, III, David A. Nadler, and Cortlandt Cammann, *Organizational Assessment: Perspectives on the Measurement of Organizational Behavior and the Quality of Work Life* (New York: John Wiley & Sons, 1980.)

4.   I wrote an article for the *Management Review* entitled, "If You're Planning for Tomorrow, Remember . . . It's Not What It Used to Be." (May, 1978) The ideas are still valid, but some of the data would have to be updated. You can also keep up to date with publications like *The Futurist* from the World Future Society, Bethesda, Maryland.

5.   *Work Redesign* by J. Richard Hackman and Greg R. Oldham (Reading, Mass.: Addison-Wesley, 1980) has in-depth discussions of the various factors which influence job behavior, outside of training.

6.   In his book *Human Competence: Engineering Worthy Performance* (New York: McGraw-Hill, 1978) Thomas Gilbert presents a model for improving performance which has little to do with training. The material is helpful in this front-end analysis event for the variety of alternatives to training that are presented.

7.   A good review of the literature can be found in *Productivity and the Quality of Work Life* (Forestdale, N.Y.: Work in America Institute, 1978). The same organization publishes a periodic newsletter which contains specific examples related to these vital areas.

8.   Some years ago the book *The Temporary Society* by Warren G. Bennis and Philip E. Slater (New York: Harper & Row, 1968) discussed what is happening in business relationships under the impact of accelerating change. Their discussion of the social consequences of temporary relationships was perceptive and almost prophetic. It should be reread from time to time.

ADDITIONAL PRINTED RESOURCES

Bass, Bernard M., and James A. Vaughan. *Training in Industry; The Management of Learning.* Belmont, Calif.: Wadsworth Publishing, 1966.

Cohen, Allan R., and Herman Gadon. *Alternative Work Schedules: Integrating Individual and Organizational Needs.* Reading, Mass.: Addison-Wesley, 1978.

Harrison, Jared F. (Ed.). *The Sales Manager as a Trainer.* Reading, Mass.: Addison-Wesley, 1977.

Levinson, Daniel et al. *The Seasons of a Man's Life.* New York: Alfred A. Knopf, 1978.

Mager, Robert F., and Peter Pipe. *Analyzing Performance Problems or You Really Oughta Wanna.* Belmont, Calif.: Fearon Publishers, 1970.

Mayer, Nancy. *The Male Mid-Life Crisis: Fresh Start After Forty.* New York: Doubleday, 1978.

3
Evaluation and Feedback

There is one event in the CEM that is involved in every other event from here until the end of the program. Therefore we will stop the process for a moment and discuss that event in depth.

Evaluation and feedback (E&FB) is built into the first event of "Identify Needs of the Organization." In this event, it is part of the process, rather than a specified happening that must occur at the end. In that respect, "Identify Needs of the Organization" is different from the other events in the CEM. Upon completion of that event, the Designer will move on to "Specify Job Performance." We are digressing here so that the flow of the rest of the CEM can proceed uninterrupted.

From "Specify Job Performance" and for all subsequent events, the Designer must engage in identifiable E&FB activities. The actual behaviors will vary with each event, so in this chapter there will only be a brief discussion of the purpose of E&FB, planning for it, and some indication of how it will work.

WHAT IS E&FB

In general, evaluation includes feedback, so why make a special point of it? If everybody agreed, the event might just be called "Evaluation." Unfortunately there are too many instances when evaluations are conducted and then carefully filed away to be used at some later date. In the design process, this cannot happen. If, at the end of each event, the evaluation is not immediately built into the bridge to the next event, the entire design process can fail.

Evaluation is often thought of in terms of learning, job performance, or performance appraisal. Those are not the only kinds of evaluation. In this instance, we will evaluate the results of the activities within a particular event of the CEM. The relationship is shown through the arrows in Figure 3-1.

THE CRITICAL EVENTS MODEL

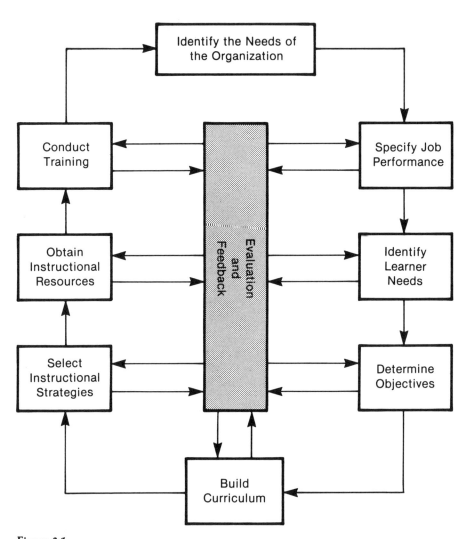

Figure 3.1

During the design process, the Designer is working for others in the organization. The provision for E&FB is to assure that what is happening is directly related to the needs of those in the organization who are involved as learners or decision makers. It is not the performance of the Designer that is being evaluated, but the outcomes of the activities for which the Designer has responsibility.

As we are discussing evaluation, it is important to make a distinction between evaluation and research. They are different, and a fuller discussion can be found in Appendix A. In the CEM, we are only concerned with evaluation. This does not mean that research is not important. If the organization, in addition to the evaluation, wants to conduct research, it is certainly possible. It is very important to recognize that every Designer must be able to include evaluation in the CEM, but not every Designer has the competencies required for research. Those same competencies are not required for designing learning experiences.

Evaluation, as used in the E&FB, is concerned with how the Designer is meeting the objectives of a particular event. For example, for the E&FB the objectives might be as follows. By the end of this event, the Designer will be able:

To determine if the design, up to this point, meets the needs and criteria established by earlier events.

To identify those individuals who should have been involved, and receive specific feedback from them.

To modify the design, as appropriate, based on the feedback from selected individuals.

To obtain necessary approval from those concerned to proceed with the next event of the CEM.

E&FB is an automatic stop device built into the CEM. It is much like the "hold" which is built into our space flights. It does not signify that anything is wrong, but alerts everybody to the necessity for some decision making before proceeding further. As a result, the Designer cannot proceed to the next event until there has been agreement on what has been accomplished by the end of a particular event.

The E&FB underscores a concept of the CEM, that the Designer cannot do the job working alone. Others must be involved, and the roster of these people will change from one event to another. Some people will be involved in almost every event, while others may only be related to one particular event. Using the E&FB reinforces the idea that the Designer is not a loner, and that he requires interaction with others, particularly within the organization, if the design process is to be successful.

EVALUATION AS A PROCESS

Evaluation is not a single activity, but a process. As with designing, there are many models to choose from. Figure 3-2 depicts the process model which is represented by E&FB. Recognize that at this point in the design process we are not evaluating the learning. That is necessary and will be covered in a later event, and with reference to other models. In the E&FB we are concerned with evaluating the progress of the design process.

The process is shown in Figure 3-2, but planning to use that process is accomplished in almost reverse order. Let us show this by a series of questions:

1.   Who will be asked to make the decisions? *(Decisions)*

2.   Who must receive the feedback so they can make the decisions? *(Feedback)*

3.   Who must receive the analysis so they can provide feedback? *(Analysis)*

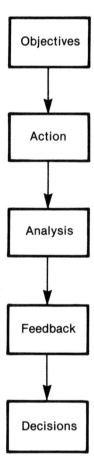

Figure 3.2

The objectives and action steps are conducted independently of those three questions, but produce the data that become the basis for responding to those three questions.

The answer to these three questions will be different for each event of the CEM. (As noted earlier, some people will be involved in almost every event, but others will be involved in only one event.) The Designer must plan carefully so that all the necessary people are included, without involving people who cannot contribute by responding to those three questions. It can also be anticipated that the same group of people will not have to be involved in all three questions, even in a given event.

Some people will get the feedback only for information. They need to be kept informed of the process, though they are not expected to do anything with the evaluation. For others, the feedback is crucial. It can be important, for example, that the supervisors reach agreement before the event can be considered satisfactorily completed.

The intended audience influences how the feedback is prepared and disseminated. For some people, it may be necessary to have a face-to-face meeting, while for others, a brief check-off sheet might suffice. The form, and the audience for the feedback will indicate the appropriate kind of analysis. For some of the events, and for some people, written reports will be required. For other events, and other people, an oral report or a meeting will be the mechanism. The analysis should be prepared considering the audience, and the form most appropriate for that audience.

In essence, then, as the Designer reaches the end of each event, the appropriateness of the design will be tested out. This will be done before proceeding to the next event. Sometimes this can prove frustrating, particularly if it takes time to gather the necessary people for the E&FB. Similarly, written comments can be sought on the feedback element of the evaluation process, and then there is a delay while waiting for the responses. Even this can be important. If people do not want to meet, or give written feedback, perhaps the original need no longer exists. The E&FB is another way of assuring continuing relevancy of the design process.

E&FB AND THE DESIGNER

There are many values to the Designer, and the organization, in carefully planning for the E&FB event. It assures that the Designer does not become isolated from the rest of the organization. Most Designers do not seek this isolation, but end up in that state because they have not built in an identifiable activity that involves others in the organization. As others will be involved, coordination becomes essential. The Designer cannot expect to control the situation, though the Designer is expected to assert the initiatives necessary to implement the E&FB.

For the Designer, and the organization, the E&FB provides an ongoing check that the program being designed is still relevant to the identified need of the organization and to the people who are concerned about meeting this need. In isolation, the Designer can go through the design process and not be aware of changes that have occurred which impact upon the original need.

For the Designer, the E&FB is a cumulative function. It is not possible to overlook the E&FB for the first few events and then introduce it at a later stage. The E&FB must be prominent and observable at each event of the CEM. As the design emerges, through the events, the Designer can expect that the E&FB will take more time than in the earlier events. There is more to be processed, and more options may open up. The Designer must plan for this time and control it so that the time used for E&FB does not become disproportionate. There is no formula for a balance between time spent on other events and time spent on the E&FB. There are other factors, beyond the control of the Designer, which must be considered.

Key to this is prior experience in the organization. In previous design experiences, has the E&FB or something similar to it been used? Generally, in the organization, is project work or participative behavior encouraged? The answers to these questions will influence how to plan and use the E&FB event.

Not Previously Existing

First let us look at an organization that does not have such prior experience, and therefore does not have the norm of crossing unit lines or other forms of participative management. As the E&FB is based on bringing together individuals from various parts of the organization, the Designer has to be aware of the need to change some norms.

The insular organization is exemplified by the statement, "Don't bother me with details, I am only interested in results." When this is said to the Designer, it becomes difficult to try to involve such people in the design work. Yet, if they are not involved, it is doubtful that they will know what to look for in results.

The Designer must help these people see why they should be involved. What is in it for them? It is not that the Designer needs help. Quite the contrary, the Designer is doing the work to help others. Therefore those others should be involved if they have the need. (If they don't have the need, why is the program being designed?) When the managers, supervisors, or others can see how a well-designed program is of benefit to them, they are more likely to want to be involved. They must see it as their program, not the program of the Designer or the HRD manager.

It may be that working together is accepted in some units of the organization, but this has not been the practice in the HRD operation. Then look for those places where cooperation exists and build on that model. For example, do your production people involve the sales people in their meetings (or vice versa)? Then use this as an example of what you are doing with the E&FB. You are involving those people who can see their own self-interest served best by being part of your process.

Participating in the E&FB takes time. At the outset, you cannot tell how much time it will take, but there is no doubt that some time will be required. For some in the organization, time is a scarce commodity. The amount of time available for a group may determine the way you handle the E&FB.

When people have not been involved in this kind of process previously, a distinction must be made between influence and control. The purpose of E&FB is to allow for influence from various parts of the organization. The Designer must still retain control, as the Designer has the ultimate responsibility for the design. Many people are prepared to influence without seeking control. Some, however, do not want to be involved if they cannot control. If possible, such people should not be part of the E&FB. If it is expedient to include the control-types, it may be necessary, at each meeting, to clarify the mutual responsibilities. If there is no agreement, it may indicate the need for a training program for them.

Previous Cooperative Behavior

If the Designer has used a similar approach previously, the task is much easier. In those earlier situations, the Designer may not have had an identifiable E&FB event but had involved others in some aspects of the design process. If so, build on this. (The assumption is that the previous experiences were successful.)

Identify the practices related to designing where others have been involved. Before starting the new design, have a short workshop to explore how the people involved can be even more effective. This would be a good time to stop and look at some of the task and maintenence behaviors exhibited in the past [1]. The E&FB event then becomes a learning and growth experience, rather than just an administrative chore.

Prior experience with some of the individuals will suggest to the Designer the best ways to involve them. Some people are good conceptual thinkers, while others can only deal with hard reality. Each has a contribution to make to the process, even though the contributions may be very different.

Once the designer is comfortable that involving others is not a big problem, some work must still be done so that using the E&FB becomes as productive as possible. The most important step to take is to make sure that every person who will be involved knows the CEM. They do not need to know each detail, but they should have a brief overview of the model. Then, for each meeting of an E&FB group, the following should be planned by the Designer.

Preparation

Generally some premeeting reading will be sent to those who will attend. At the beginning it could be a report from the Designer. As the design process proceeds, the materials will be more closely related to that event of the CEM as added to previous events. For example, it might be a list of job performance requirements with several levels of detail. It is unlikely that the entire group would be interested in how the list was derived, as many of them would have been involved in that process and therefore are already familiar with this. If it is possible that there will be questions, the Designer should prepare additional materials necessary for clarification.

Sometimes the preparation might be face-to-face premeeting conferences with the Designer. These should not be attempts to manipulate people or to plan the outcome of the meeting, but considering the variety of people who will be participating, some might want more information than others or perhaps the opportunity for a personal briefing. Such premeeting conferences should be carefully arranged so that there is not even the slightest implication that the Designer is going behind the backs of other members of the group. It is difficult, however, for the Designer to reject an invitation for a premeeting conference with a particular member.

As with any meeting, a notice should be sent to all those concerned. This should state the time and place, and both are significant for the E&FB meetings. The design of a training program, no matter how important to job performance, may still not be the prime area of interest to all those who should attend. They may have other priorities. The time should be carefully selected to meet the needs of as many people as possible. Reality dictates that not everybody will attend every meeting to which they have been invited.

The place is also important. Space communicates, and where the meeting is held will send a message to those who are invited. Although the meeting is concerned with HRD, the venue might best be someplace else. It could be close to where the job is being performed, in the manager's office, or some other relevant place. This can be expected to change, depending upon the particular event of the CEM.

The Meeting(s)

As the heading indicates, there could be more than one meeting to accomplish the objectives of the E&FB. If a second meeting is required, specific objectives should be agreed upon, and a commitment obtained from those attending to be present at another meeting, if needed.

Some issues might be referred to a smaller group, with the understanding that the larger group will abide by whatever they decide. Such a tactic can be a sound use of the human resources, or a signal that most of the people just do not care. In the latter, the Designer should re-examine those who have been involved in the E&FB. Are they the right people? If so, why are they ready to pass the issue on to another group? There might be a problem with either the selection of the participants or the designation of the issues.

Roles at the meeting should be clarified. It is best for the Designer not to be the chairperson but rather to function as the convener. I have observed situations where the Designer agreed to be the secretary of the group and then became completely passive. This is certainly not the appropriate role for the Designer. Of all the people at the meeting, the Designer probably has more information and the best grasp of the total design picture. The Designer should be a resource to the meeting, not just a record keeper.

The norms for the conduct of the meeting will reflect those already existing in the organization, as modified by the Designer. Probably this will not be the first meeting within the organization for most of the participants. A certain protocol will have to be respected. This can be reflected in a range of behaviors including seating, asking questions, summarizing, and whether agreement is reached by consensus or voting.

Follow-Up

Each meeting should have a designated follow-up activity. If all has gone well, it may require only a brief note of the decision of the group to proceed to the next event of the CEM.

More specifically, there should be something in writing that states where the group ended on that particular event. This information will be needed in building the design and is more than just the minutes of the meeting. It could be the list of specific job behaviors, the identified needs of the learners, the stated objectives, and so on. For each event, it will be different.

If some invitees did not get to the meeting, the Designer should see that they receive the relevant information which was the outgrowth of the meeting. This is particularly important if those people are to be included in a future E&FB meeting. If they have missed a part of the picture, they will feel inadequate, and perhaps excluded. A brief memo may be all that is needed to effect inclusion.

THE E&FB IN THIS BOOK

As noted earlier, the E&FB does not end with this chapter, for in every subsequent chapter a discussion of the E&FB will be one of the final activities discussed. It must be, for without having the E&FB built in as a part of each event, the value is lost.

The E&FB can only be discussed generally because of variations in each situation. There will be a sharing of some experiences where I and others have used it. For your particular organization, the E&FB can be played out in a wide variety of scenarios. As different people are directly involved in this event, we can anticipate wide variations in acceptance and behavior.

On the practical side, some aspects of E&FB can take place even before the event is completed. While working on any event, the Designer may find the need for an E&FB meeting because a contradiction has emerged or new data have suddenly come to light. Nothing in this open CEM model prevents the Designer from moving right into the E&FB for what is referred to as a *formative evaluation*. That is, doing some evaluating while the action is in progress without waiting for the final result.

In this book the use of E&FB will be limited to *summative evaluation*, when the event is nearing completion. It will be the decision point for proceeding with the next event or taking some other kind of indicated action.

CONCLUSION

Do not be misled by the brevity of this chapter. It does not signify that the E&FB is not significant. Rather, by intervening in the description of the CEM at this point, I am highlighting its importance.

We can now return to the regular flow of the CEM. In an earlier chapter we explored "Identify the Needs of the Organization" and found that there was an identified training need. As we are dealing with training, we now move to the job and "Specify Job Performance."

REFERENCES

1.   An exercise which can be used to explore this is found in *A Handbook for Structured Experiences for Human Relations Training*, Volume II, J. William Pfeiffer and John E. Jones, (San Diego: University Associates, 1970), page 76. Of course, there are many others, and if you have any favorites, you should use them. The important aspect is to recognize that the Designer needs competencies in group behavior to be successful in the feedback aspect of the E&FB.

ADDITIONAL PRINTED RESOURCES

So little has been written about this area, that it is difficult to find relevant books. Articles will be found in some of the publications and journals where the E&FB is described, but not using that label.

Evaluation of learning will be discussed in several of the events of CEM, and appropriate note will be made in those chapters of references and additional readings.

4

Specify Job Performance

We are now ready to look at the specific job. As discussed earlier, it is a job that has been identified as relating to a need of the organization. In some way, the job is not being performed the way somebody (or some group) in the organization thinks it should be performed.

This event of the CEM is crucial. In some models for designing training, the first activity is given as identifying needs. The CEM is based on the premise that needs can only be assessed against some kind of standard, which is based on agreement about the job to be performed. (See Figure 4-1.)

Within the organization, agreement about the job to be performed is essential. Experience has shown that until agreement is reached on what the job contributes to the organization, it is meaningless to attempt to find out how to improve the job. Perhaps, and we will see this later, there is no need for that job.

By the end of this event, the Designer will be able:

To specify the performance expected of a person who is doing a designated job.

There is some slight controversy in the field regarding the words *"behavior"* and *"performance."* Earlier versions of the CEM used the word "behavior" but at this time I perceive the tendency for more people to use "performance" to describe what we are concerned with in this element.

WHAT IS JOB PERFORMANCE?

To take a close look at a job, we must separate it from the person who does the job. Of course, the separation is only temporary, and we will have to consider the person at some point as part of this, and much more specifically under the next element of "Identify Learning Needs."

THE CRITICAL EVENTS MODEL

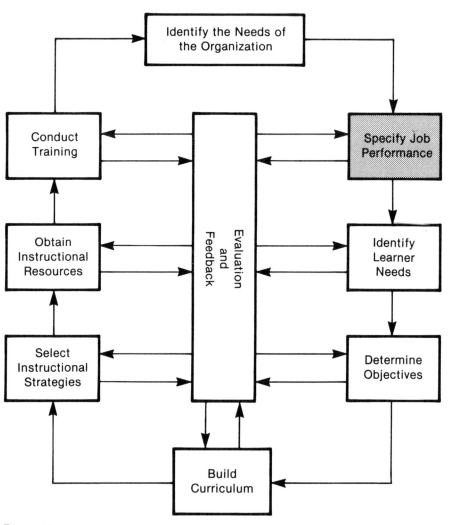

Figure 4.1

When we discuss job performance, the first area of concern is the *concept* of what people do, which is labeled as a job. The term *job* is used to represent the work done by anybody in the organization from the lowest to the highest levels. Those at the executive level may not see themselves as doing a job, and if they wish to use a different label, that is acceptable. The label can change, but what must be done to reach the objectives of this event will remain the same.

Perceptions of the Job

In this design process, we are dealing with a job that already exists. If the purpose were to design for a new job, this event could still be used, but it would require some minor modifications, as will become apparent. As the job already exists, we must deal with *perception*, or what various people think the job is, or what they think somebody is doing on that job. A major part of the work under this event will be gathering and clarifying perceptions.

The Designer should not be dismayed if the result of this event is the discovery that there is not a training need, once perceptions have been clarified. This could happen during the event, but it will certainly be one of the factors to be checked out during E&FB.

The perceptions of the job will be based on expectations. What is it that the organization, as reflected in different individuals and groups, expects takes place when the job is accomplished?

A key element is, what does the *supervisor* expect? In this discussion, the term supervisor is used very broadly. The most obvious use, (and the one that probably encompasses the largest number of individuals) is the first-line supervisor. This is the first level at which an employee gets the work done through the efforts of others. There are, however, supervisors at various levels of the organization. To move to the highest level, the Chief Executive Officer (CEO) has a private secretary, and the CEO supervises the work of that secretary. All through the organization, there are people supervising others and the term supervisor is used here to identify that person who is responsible for the person doing the job. In this event we are looking at the perception of the supervisor as to what that job contributes to helping him (the supervisor) meet his goals in the organization.

There is also a perception of that job, as held by various other people in the *organization*. In the next section of this chapter I will discuss the interrelatedness of jobs. At this point the focus is on the fact that there are many people in the organization, in addition to the supervisor, who have some perceptions of what is being done on the job we are looking at. Some of the perceptions have been evolving over a long period of time, while others may be fairly recent. There are perceptions by people who have actually seen the job done, as contrasted with perceptions by people who have only heard about what somebody does on that job.

This latter perception frequently gives rise to a good deal of erroneous information. It even contributes to the "grass is greener" feeling. You have heard it—"If only *I* had that job, I could do it much better." This is sometimes voiced by people who do not know the job. They might be able to do "it" better, but they are not always sure what the "it" is.

In a large or complex organization, perceptions may be contradictory or in conflict. When viewed from one perspective, the job appears one way; when viewed from another, it appears much different. It is evocative of the blind men and the elephant [1]. The Designer should gather these perceptions, as one way to "Specify Job Performance," but not be surprised at the variance in the data gathered.

In situations where we are dealing with organizations, it becomes obvious that people do not work alone. Except in very rare situations (for example, the CEO), there are *peers*. These are people at the same level in the organization, work-related to the person doing the job, but not necessarily even in the same work unit. Those in the work unit who are doing related jobs certainly have something to contribute to help the Designer understand the job under discussion. Those working in similar jobs must definitely be involved in developing and clarifying the perceptions of the job.

The Designer can expect that peers have much different perceptions from the supervisor, and different from others in the organization who are not close to the job.

Naturally we should determine the perceptions of the *person doing the job.* There is little doubt that the person on the job has much to offer. We have tried various ways to unlock this treasure house through participative management, suggestion systems with monetary awards, and one of the new approaches called Quality Circles (where the workers continually discuss their jobs in planned group sessions) [2].

Some designers hesitate to go directly to the employee on the job, anticipating that the employee will behave defensively and will not share relevant data. If this is expected, it may indicate immediately that there are some other problems. This once again poses the question as to whether training is the appropriate response. If there is a low level of trust, that may be a factor influencing job performance.

The Designer should not be surprised if the employee counters with, "I would like to do the job better, but 'they' won't let me." Finding the elusive "they" can be the most important activity of the Designer. If the first event, "Identify Needs of the Organization," has been done well, this situation should have been uncovered during that event. If not, it may surface here, and the Designer should recognize it and anticipate it. As the Designer works further with the employee, it may appear that there is no "they" but rather some misperceptions.

A large multisite organization asked me to do a program on motivation for its managers. A group of 30 were brought together from various parts of the United

States, and we spent several days together exploring concepts and practices related to this crucial aspect of managerial behavior. At one point, in reporting on a case I had presented, one group said that they recommended a bonus for employees who had handled a difficult problem and actually brought about unexpected economic benefits to the company. Some of the managers immediately protested that the case solution presented by the group was unfair, as the company did not permit bonuses due to union trouble in the past. Some of the managers questioned the source of this information, as they had been giving bonuses to employees regularly, for several years, for just such savings for the organization.5

It took quite an effort to quiet the group down. Obviously one factor was that each manager had evolved a different perception, had been managing based on that perception of the latitude a manager had, and was now defending his previous behavior. We finally determined that the awarding of bonuses was done at the discretion of the plant superintendent, but prior to this, none of the managers had been aware of this basis for permitting bonuses or denying them.

When there is no incumbent or employee on the job, the Designer is being asked to design an education program rather than a training program. This event can still be used, but it is obvious that data cannot be gathered from the person actually doing the job. Others doing the same job can provide some basis for data. There will need to be clarification, though, that those presently on the job are not among the potential learners. A lack of such clarification can raise anxiety levels and interfere with effective data gathering.

Interdependency

People working together in an organization depend upon each other, so job performance must be viewed as being interdependent. The very nature of an organization is that the tasks that must be accomplished to reach goals require more than one person. Each person makes some contribution to the general effort that is required if the goals are to be reached.

The essence of interdependency is depicted in Figure 4-2. It can be stated as: one employee's output is another employee's input. Where people work in groups, one group's output is another group's input. Although this appears to be an oversimplification, it is a core concept related to work, one too infrequently stated or recognized.

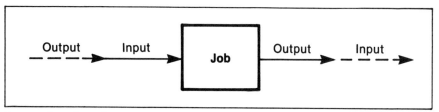

Fig. 4.2 Interdependency of Jobs.

As part of understanding job behavior, the Designer must look at the input side. Where does the input come from? The two major sources are from within the organization and from outside the organization.

When the input is from *within the organization,* the Designer must trace the source. In the process, the Designer may discover that part of the problem is that there is a default on the input side and no amount of training for the job under observation will improve the situation.

This arose in an assembly operation in a manufacturing plant. The problem had been identified, at the first event, as being that the assemblers were not working up to the standard that had been set. Repeated runs of the material showed that it was possible for the tasks to be performed in the time designated, but production was still suffering. In this plant, the work came to the assemblers from several points, brought by fork-lift trucks.

As part of this event of the CEM, the Designer looked at the input side. The fork-lift trucks scurried around as if they were choreographed. There were near misses, but an examination of the accident rate showed that there was no real problem in that area. There was never a time that the supply area was bare, yet the assembly production was below what could be expected. On closer observation, the Designer (working with the supervisor) determined that there was a fault in the input. Sometimes there was a surplus of Part A, but not enough of Part B to enable the assemblers to complete the job. The supervisor acknowledged that this happened, but thought it had been built into the assembly quota. It had not been.

Further examination by the Designer disclosed the reason for the problem. The fork-lift operators had their quotas, which had not been fully coordinated with the flow on the assembly line. With the input in this uncoordinated state, the assemblers could not possibly meet the assigned quota and no amount of training of the assemblers could have changed the situation. The Designer had found the problem in the input side.

When the input comes from within the organization, adjustments are possible. It may be scheduling, the state in which the input arrives, or the storing of the input until it is ready for use. If these are at the core of the situation the Designer has discovered the problem, and the solution can follow. It may not be a training solution for the job being looked at, but it indicates a possible training need for another job in the organization. That is the essence of interdependency.

Inputs also come from *outside the organization.* The sources can be suppliers, subcontractors, the government, or customers. In a retail establishment, some of the input is from the customers. If there are no customers, the salespeople have little to do. Providing training for the salespeople will not increase sales if the customers are not coming in.

Input from external sources may be more difficult to examine, but the process must take place. In the assembly plant incident described earlier, another problem arose in a different part of the plant. The problem was quality control, and rejection of some of the finished assembly. Once again, probably because of faith in the HRD department, the department manager requested a training program.

The Designer, using the interdependency approach, began looking at the input side of the situation. (On the output, it was clear that there was a problem, by the level of rejects.) Some of the parts were manufactured in-house while others came from external suppliers. Presumably all were carefully examined before being sent on to the assembly department. It was determined that internal production was carefully examined and tested.

The external parts were receiving only a superficial examination, for what appeared to be a good reason. As parts were delivered, the loading docks had to be cleared. The trucks and spur line railroad cars had to be emptied as rapidly as possible to minimize demurrage charges. With the docks loaded, the parts had to be moved off very rapidly to make room for the next flow of railroad cars. The receiving dock manager could only provide for examination and/or testing of a few items out of each shipment. The result: faulty materials were being moved into the plant and not identified until they had been assembled.

The solution to this problem proved complicated. It required that additional space be provided for incoming shipments, additional personnel be assigned to inspection of incoming parts, and a training program provided so that these inspectors could work rapidly to make the whole effort cost-effective. Once this was put in place and records of rejects were maintained, the suppliers were forced to improve the quality of their shipments.

This incident is not meant to indicate that input is always somebody else's problem. However, the Designer must be very sure that the fault does not lie in input before going further with the design process. If input is a problem, it must also be determined whether there is somebody on the input side who needs training in order to provide the appropriate output.

Satisfactory input and unsatisfactory output indicate that the problem is within the job. The employee may be working satisfactorily, but the output being produced is not what is required for somebody else's input.

Do not be misled into thinking that this is only a production situation. It happens just as frequently in office or managerial situations. A manager looks to subordinates to provide reports so the manager can make decisions. These reports are the manager's input. If the reports are not satisfactory, perhaps there is the need for some training down the line so that the output of the subordinates (supervisors and other managers) can provide the necessary input.

Standards of the Job

The output of the job must be stated in some kind of standards. The two most common are quality and quantity. These appear to be easy labels to work with, but actually they are very difficult to determine. Until agreement is reached on these two components, it is not possible to "Specify Job Performance" which can produce the desired quality and quantity.

In each organization, these terms have different meanings. The Designer must determine very specifically what is meant by those terms within the organization, and by the people who are involved with the job.

Quality can be either very observable or extremely elusive. Where the output of a job is compared to a specific standard, quality can be determined. The most obvious case is: either it works or it doesn't. When Chrysler went through its critical financial crisis in 1980, the company stated that from that time on, cars would be produced at such a quality level that they could be driven off the line. To the nonmotorist this may not be clear, but the message to the workers was strong and to the point. At the completion of assembly if a car meets at least basic quality standards it should be possible to drive it off the production line. If it has to be pushed off the line, the work had not been up to the quality that had been engineered into the car.

By contrast, and with a different product line, GM had commercials on television concerning the locomotives that they manufactured. They emphasized that careful quality control and high standards of work performance meant that the completed locomotive could immediately be driven off. (Have *you* bought a locomotive lately? Obviously the message to the average consumer was quality of work, not the product.)

It is possible to hedge on quality by using alternative approaches. When I lived in Japan in the early 1960s, I bought a Japanese combination radio–record player. At that time, quality control focused on service to the consumer, rather than on the manufacturing side. The set I received did not work. The manufacturer sent a team to my home and the men spent several hours making the necessary repairs to the errors of production. Within a week, the set once again needed repairs. Another group of men showed up and likewise spent several hours making repairs. (Ultimately I returned the set and bought components.)

Later, during my work with industry, I asked questions about this practice of making repairs at the site of the consumer. I found that this was the general practice at the time and extended far beyond just consumer goods. It was partly a cultural factor. Providing service in the home of the consumer or the plant of the customer indicated an interest on the part of the manufacturer for the people being served. Culturally it was appropriate, but economically it was a disaster! As markets expanded, the Japanese discovered that quality must be built in during production and not handled as part of service. They trained their production workers and their inspectors so that quality became a reality.

Quantity is easier to deal with. For a job, either things are counted or they are not. If there is no quantification, the Designer should consider that possibility. With increased emphasis on productivity (which implies measurement of quantity), we are gaining further insights into ways of counting and measuring.

Perhaps this would be the time to introduce quantity into a job that did not previously have that dimension.

It is not possible to consider quantity alone. It must be related to the amount of time used to perform the tasks and the relation to the input/output consideration. We can never forget the interdependency of jobs and particularly when measurement is required.

When a job is quantified, it can raise other issues. During the late 1960s, when we were concerned with disadvantaged people entering the work force, an incident occurred in a Westinghouse plant. A "new hire" (the euphemism for the disadvantaged) entered the work force at the rank of sweeper, which was the general entry level for all new employees in that plant [3]. He rapidly showed his capability and in a very short time was promoted to machine operator. He received materials, processed them on his machine, and then put them in a basket to be taken by a sweeper to the next operation.

At first, there were accolades of various kinds to the HRD people who had done such a good job with this new employee and thereby facilitated his rapid rise with a merited promotion. Very soon thereafter, disaster struck. The floor supervisor visited the HRD unit and complained bitterly that what they had done in their training and education program was a waste! No sooner did the new employee get his promotion than he began "goofing off." His shift was to end at 2:30, yet after 12:00 noon he was nowhere to be found. "A lot of good the training did," said the supervisor.

The HRD manager talked with the supervisor and then suggested they talk to the new employee. The core of the conversation took place when the new employee said, in his argot,

New Employee: "What did ya hire me for? You keep telling me I got 'ta do the work and do it right. What's the beef? Did you have to throw out any of my work?"

Supervisor: "You left your machine!"

New Employee: "It was shut down."

Supervisor: "Of course, because you weren't working. You were supposed to be at your machine until 2:30."

New Employee: "I done the work."

Supervisor: "Not if you left early."

New Employee: "You told me to do all the pieces in the three bins the sweeper got me. I finished the three bins and took off."

Supervisor: "But you are supposed to stay until 2:30."

New Employee: "Do you pay me for the time or for how much work I do?"

And therein is the rub! We talk of production and productivity, but tend to pay people for elapsed time. If an employee works more than a certain number of hours we pay time and a half, but we do not pay for production and a half. The message being sent is one of time, not production. Yet, will organizations allow a training program to advocate working more slowly to fill up the amount of time the worker is expected to remain on the job? It is a conflict that can be surfaced by the Designer but must be reconciled by management.

There must be clear agreement about the standards for the job. That is important in this event of the CEM and will become even more important when we encounter evaluation of the learning. If the Designer is to show the benefits that resulted from the training, there must be base line data on standards. This is the event where agreement must be reached on quality and quantity.

Group or Individual

For the most part, we have been looking at a job as if a single individual is doing it. The tendency is increasing for people to work in groups. This complicates the situation, particularly when the employees are free to rotate jobs, within limits. It does not mean that we cannot "Specify Job Performance," but such a specification must relate to the reality of how the work is actually done.

Much of the work so far in designing training programs has approached the situation as if one person were working alone or alongside others. Working *with* others has not fully been explored in terms of job performance.

Of course, we do have those situations where people must work together, and this has produced training programs in team building and similar activities to improve group performance. Usually such programs deal with interpersonal relations but not with job skills. There are few published examples of situations where people had to be trained to be substitutes for each other on a regular but unplanned basis. Yet this is the direction in which the work place is moving at this time.

Though we lack sufficient specifics, we can recognize the phenomenon and build it into the specification of job performance. It means that there are two sets of specifics: one for what an *individual* does on that job, and the other for what the individual does when exchanging or substituting for another member of the same *work group*.

GATHERING DATA

To "Specify Job Performance" it is necessary to collect data. There are many ways to do this and no one way is best. Each method has its exponents and its critics.

The Designer must identify and select the method that seems most appropriate to him, the job, and the organization.

The Designer

Each Designer has certain competencies. It is expected that you, as a Designer, tend to use those methods in which you feel competent and with which you have had success. It is a good idea to continue to do those things that have proven successful.

But success can be a trap. You can continue to use the same methods even after you discover they are not relevant for a particular task. Therefore Designers must develop a wide range of competencies, in a variety of methods, for gathering data about job performance.

There are some tested and commonly used approaches to gathering data on job performance. The designer should be familiar with these and know when to use them. In a sense, they are "safe" as they have the backing of having been published. Somehow this lends credence even to a seldom used methodology.

The professional journals have a constant flow of "how I did it" type of articles. Some of these can be very helpful to the Designer, in opening up new vistas about other ways of gathering the required data. A shortcoming in many of these articles is that they do not tell all of the story, given the limitation of space, and the need to appeal to a wide readership. If you are interested in a data-gathering experience shared in a magazine article, by all means write to the author for the additional information you may need to make it more helpful to you.

A designer with experience will also recognize that methodology can change and these changes can be the result of many factors. There are constant changes in the work force, and there is now more openness in providing data than existed in the past. A higher level of schooling, which is a trend in the American work force, produces people who are more articulate and can provide more data.

The use of data-gathering instruments requires a higher rate of literacy than the interview. Yet employees can be instrumented to death and completely overwhelmed by the constant flow of forms which must be completed to gather data.

The Designer must continually ask, "Why am I using this particular method for gathering the needed data? Is there another way? Is there a better way? When I used this (whichever it is) method previously, what did I learn about how I can do it better?"

One way of helping yourself is to keep a file on the methods you use and your suggestions to yourself as to how you would improve your use the next time. Then, be sure to read that file before your next activity in data gathering on job performance.

The particular job influences the source and methods for gathering data on job performance. Some jobs are readily observable, and gathering the data does not pose any particular problems. Those are the easy ones. They are jobs in which the output is immediately and easily discernible. It can be a production job or a service job.

In production, the output is always observable and almost always measurable. The way the job is being done tends to be standardized. The job is generally composed of smaller units, tasks, which are required to be done exactly the same way by anybody who is doing that job. Of course, individual variations do exist and some of these can be important in helping to understand how job performance can be improved.

In the service area, there are also jobs that are easy to observe. The clerk servicing a customer, the waiter in the restaurant, and similar service jobs have an observable component. It is also possible to establish quality measures in such jobs.

When we move into the supervisory area and above, the work of the Designer becomes more complicated. The output is the result of many factors, of which the performance of the employee is only one minor element. The quality of the job is only generally measurable. At the higher levels, there tends to be less agreement on how the job should be done. At those levels in the organization, employees are not as eager to have data gathered about their performance or any significant inquiry made into how they do the job. The emphasis is on the results of the performance, not the performance itself. This makes data gathering extremely difficult and, in some organizations, almost impossible.

The complexity of the job is a factor that contributes to the methodology to be selected by the Designer. The more complex the job, the more difficulty can be anticipated in collecting the data. In some complex jobs, collecting the data must be done in a way that will avoid interfering with the job. Continuous or complicated operations require the complete attention of the employee, and the data-gathering process cannot be allowed to interfere with the performance of the job.

When the Designer is not adequately familiar with the job or the operation, there is no negative implication if another resource is used for data collection. The Designer should discuss this with the supervisor and the subordinate to be sure that the alternative resource is acceptable. This resource could be somebody else within the organization who knows the operation and can observe without interrupting with questions and will have no need for explanations. It is also possible to use an external resource, but this should be carefully checked out. It could be looked upon with disfavor by those involved in that particular job. There is a positive side, in that the external resource may bring to this activity some information on similar jobs in other organizations.

As with any job under scrutiny, we have to be aware of the Hawthorne Effect [4]. As soon as the Designer starts the process of looking at a job, to gather data, the job can change.

In the 1960s, as one consequence of the British Industrial Training Act, there was a need for more people with competencies in designing training programs. In 1966 I was invited to England to conduct a workshop, and used the CEM (then called the Process of Training) as the core of my workshop. It was agreed that the participants would actually design a program, as part of the workshop, and we sought a common job which everybody could see and would find familiar. At the first tea break, the answer to our need became obvious. All of us could have firsthand observation of the woman serving the tea and therefore could use her job as the basis for designing a training program. Can you picture what happened during the tea break following the session on "Specify Job Performance?" Each participant, as he passed the table where the young woman was pouring, was taking quick mental notes on how the job was being performed. By the time the young woman had experienced the piercing scrutiny of the first five participants, performance had deteriorated. After serving the next five participants, she fled, crying, to the rest room! The remaining participants never did get to see the job performance.

Of course, you would not usually have that many people observing a single employee in such a short period of time, but the depth and intensity of the observation could be just as disruptive to performance over a longer period. Recognition must be taken of the premise that a worker under scrutiny may no longer perform the job in the usual manner. This is applicable to all levels of the organization.

There was an earlier reference made to the difference between a job being done by an individual and one in which there is group performance. In gathering data, this is extremely relevant. Different methodologies are required as some are more useful for individuals than groups. Also some group methods are irrelevant when individual job performance is the factor.

The organization is the third variable that must be considered. The Designer is always trapped, at the beginning, by organizational history. It is possible to get out of the trap, but the Designer must start by determining if it does exist.

A usual way this is expressed is, "But Designers never asked for this information before; they sat in their offices and did the design without bothering us." You may be getting a signal to do the same. Perhaps the data can be gathered without observing the actual job site. If so, do not go against history just to be different. If, however, on-site presence is necessary for understanding the job, the environment, and so on, do not hesitate to develop the strategies that will induce the people on that site to extend an invitation to you. If they view you as being helpful, it will not be difficult to receive such an invitation.

Every organization has a climate, even if we cannot always be sure of what it is [5]. As climates change, so must the methodology change for the Designer activities under this element of the CEM. What worked last time might not work this time, if there has been a change of climate. It is not possible to provide a list which says, "If this is the climate, then . . ." The variations in organizational climate have not been categorized to the extent that this is possible.

It becomes incumbent on the Designer to continually sense the subtle changes in climate that occur in every organization. The wind is constantly shifting. There are times to go against the wind and times for the "bamboo approach" of bending with the wind. The Designer must be related closely enough to the entire organization to be able to sense the changes and to know the appropriate design behavior that will be congruent with the current climate of the organization.

In general, when gathering data for this event, the Designer should consider sources and methods. In some models, these two elements are considered as one activity. That approach deprives the Designer of some of the alternatives that are possible within this activity. Therefore we will discuss each of these separately: sources and methods.

SOURCES

The Designer must identify the sources of the information necessary to "Specify Job Performance." Before actually gathering the data, the Designer must do some intensive planning. In some situations, it is not possible to go back to the same source a second time. Therefore, before proceeding to gather the data, the Designer will have carefully planned for the sources to be tapped.

Some sources will be inside the organization, and these may be more readily available than some of the outside sources. Where alternatives do exist, cost may be a factor in determining which source is to be explored.

Sources, generally, can be people, or records and reports. These are not mutually exclusive. Records and reports are produced by people, though sometimes the records and reports seem to have a life of their own. If you will not be repulsed by the analogy, it is easier to put an end to people than to terminate records and reports!

Even going to people may require that, to provide the data you seek, they in turn must go to the records and reports. Though there is a mixture, let us start by looking at people as a prime source.

People

When dealing with people, we deal with perception—as discussed earlier. This should not dissuade us from going to people, but we should recognize the subtle perceptions or unsubtle biases that we will get from using people as a source of data.

A major area to be wary of is the mixture of *what is* as contrasted with *what should be*. People may confuse what they want the job to be, while presumably telling you what is actually being done on the job. Both of these areas are helpful in understanding job performance, but must be separated within the data.

A prime source is the *person actually doing the job*. Here too, the caution is that the person may describe how he would like to do the job, rather than how the job is actually done. The employee can consider this an excellent opportunity to influence job changes. The Designer should gather this data, but separate what is being done from what the person on the job would like to do. The person on the job is a very good source for ideas on job improvement, but these ideas should not be co-mingled with the reality of the job performance.

The interdependency of jobs requires that before any changes are made, based on a single source, the possibilities should be explored with those on both the input and output sides.

At this juncture, it is important to separate the job from the individual. The focus here is on the job, no matter who is doing it. The interdependency aspect requires that a job be done within the organization. How the individual is doing the job will be explored in the next event of the CEM.

There are several groups that can be called *peers*. Others in the organization, usually at the same level, can be included in this category. As used here, peers does not mean only those at the same salary or grade level. The concept of level should be broadened, but kept small enough so as not to include those who are either in a supervisory or subordinate position. They would not be peers.

You can anticipate that the peers would have different data to provide regarding the job you are looking at. If they anticipate that your data could bring about changes in their jobs, you will get different responses than if the job under design has no direct impact.

By stretching the peer concept, you could also identify people outside the organization who do the some kind of work. Looking at salespeople, there could be significant data from salespeople outside your organization, but in the same general product line. Of course, the performance of your competitors in such a situation is extremely important, but very difficult to determine.

The *supervisor* is another good source. Indeed, it will most probably be the supervisor who called you in to start the design process. If so, the supervisor must certainly be included as a source. If the supervisor's supervisor (i.e., a manager) asked you to design the program for subordinates of the supervisor, there is a different situation. The supervisor is still a good source, but may be overly cautious. You can be perceived as an instrument of the manager, appointed without even consulting the supervisor, and hence there is some question about your true role. You need to gain the confidence and trust of the supervisor, if he is to be a valuable and reliable source.

Consumers can be external or internal, but the term is usually applied to those outside the orgnization, and more generally describes the ultimate purchaser. The data from the consumers are usually gathered by other components of the organization, in which case you would be relying on the records and reports gathered by others.

When the consumer is internal (for example, in another part of the organization), there will be records and reports, but the consumer is more readily available to you. The consumer is the individual or unit that is directly in the path and receives the output. The consumer can also be somebody or some unit in the organization that is influenced or affected by the output, but does not directly receive it.

Another source of people outside the organization is through *conferences and meetings.* There are various trade associations, professional groups, and other temporary meetings (also called institutes, workshops, and so on) where job performance is discussed. The content of these conferences and meetings can be related to a specific job or to what is happening in the general field, which can be expected to impact the job under design.

Internal meetings, though not called specifically for job design, can be another source of data. Of course, timing is important. It is of benefit when the people at a particular meeting are discussing the job under design, although the meeting is called by somebody other than the Designer. Under this heading, however, reference is to those meetings called by others in the organization, but to which the Designer has been invited. Such meetings may be very general, not job-specific, but helpful to the Designer in understanding the broader context and the trends.

Outside the organization there are *professionals* who constitute a valuable source. This includes university faculty who are teaching and researching the same kind of job for which you are designing. Engineering and management faculties represent a significant source. There are also vendors of services (sometimes erroneously called "consultants") and product vendors who have broad knowledge of the field and can be a valuable source.

Records and Reports

Written documents seem to have a life of their own. Though there is some indication of change, we are still people who put a great deal of value in the printed word. Some people seem to think that if they reduce something to writing and distribute it broadly, the inherent value has been increased. In recent years, two technological advances have increased the storage and dissemination of written material and can be expected to have an even greater impact for the future.

One innovation has been the computer. With the proliferation of microcomputers, we are told that desk terminals for many employees will be a common sight. The computer, in relation to the CEM, contains a vast amount of information and therefore becomes a vital source for designing training programs. It also suggests that Designers must either develop computer capabilities, or find someone with such a capability who can serve as an adjunct to, or on the staff of, the Designer.

Another innovation is word processing. This technology allows for the production of much more written material than in the past. Whether for better or worse, it puts more written information into various channels and into filing cabinets. (I know that much can be stored in the word processor, but there is still a great deal of printing and filing.)

Despite these technological innovations, some of the sources we will be discussing will still be found in standard filing cabinets, on bookshelves, piled on desks and tables, and stored in other exotic fashions.

A major source of data are *production* records. Within this category are included those records that tell us about sales, customer complaints, back orders, and all the other data that are related to production. For a nonmanufacturing organization, the term production may have to be modified, but what you would seek are those records that indicate how the organization is meeting its goals or accomplishing its mission. There is the global approach of looking at the production records that are related to the total organization and then at the records that tell us of performance in selected units or departments. In some situations, there may also be records of individual performance.

When we look at an individual or a related group of individuals, a related record is the *performance appraisal.* Not all organizations have a formal procedure or form for appraising performance, but the tendency to keep written records of individual performance is increasing. Recognize that performance appraisal is not intended for the purpose of Specifying Job Performance, but without some agreement on job performance it is difficult to see how there can be appraisals. The Designer should seek out the criteria for performance appraisal to identify expected job performance. (We will return to performance appraisal when we move to the next event of the CEM.)

Designers are concerned with learning, but in most organizations they must also be concerned with *financial statements* [6]. By themselves, these statements do not tell of performance, but rather of the results of performance. For higher levels of the organization, or for certain specific individuals or groups, what is reported on the financial statement indicates the job performance that is expected.

One of the most used sources is the *job description.* Indeed, some Designers go to the job description as the primary source, and then get trapped in the past. For the most part, a job description does not tell you what is expected of job performance at present, but rather what was expected when the job description was written. An analogy can be found in the dictionary. People go to the dictionary to find the meaning of words. Yet, dictionaries do not tell us what words *mean* but what they *meant* at the time the dictionary was published. If you want to test this, write down your own meanings for words like: mediocre, and sanction. Then, look at the dictionary and see how these meanings differ from common usage, which has changed over the years.

The job description is important, for it is the agreed upon document which is relied on to indicate something about job performance. It should not be ignored, but it should not be accepted at face value. The designer should not put the personnel office in the position of defending the document, for that is not the purpose of obtaining it for the CEM. As a result of looking at the job description and at actual job performance, the description might be changed. In some organizations, the job descriptions are written in very broad and general terms because the personnel office recognizes that actual job performance cannot be fully stated in such a document.

It is a rare organization that does not have meetings and produce *minutes of internal meetings*. Some of these minutes have very limited distribution, and it may be inappropriate for the Designer to be on the route slip. Some meetings produce minutes which are then made available to selected people within the organization. If the Designer can be put on the route slip, as a routine step, this provides another source of data concerning job performance. It requires a great deal of reading about other factors that are not related to job performance. If possible, the Designer should evolve a screening mechanism to avoid his reading the unrelated material. A common practice is to have a staff member (if you have more than a one person operation) read all the minutes and highlight those parts that relate to job performance. With either the computer or word processing, some of this can readily be "filed" for instant recall, as needed.

Despite the movement towards the paperless office, it will still be years before this is a general practice. Therefore we can expect the flow of *memos and reports* to continue. These also are a source of data about job performance. As with the previous source, the Designer must take steps to be on the distribution lists and set up a screening and filing process so the relevant data on job performance can be retrieved.

A common practice in many organizations is the *reading file*. This may contain minutes of meetings, memos, reports, correspondence, and so on. In fact, it becomes a significant vehicle for keeping all informed of what others are doing. If such a reading file exists, the Designer should be on the route slip. If it does not exist, the Designer will have to devise alternative methods for gaining access to the various printed pieces of data that circulate within an organization.

As the use of computers expands, much of this written material will be put into the computer, and the Designer may find more ready access. It can be anticipated that not all of the various kinds of written reports, memos, and so on will appear in the computer for general consumption, as a limited distribution may be essential for some. Whatever the mode, the Designer must stay alert to the various ways in which these source materials are circulated and stored.

In the earlier section under "People" it was indicated that conferences and meetings are a source. Very often this source is reduced to a report referred to as *conference proceedings*. In the technical fields, these conference proceedings can be extremely valuable as representing the state of the art. Many items will be reported on during the conference and will appear in the conference proceedings. There may not be sufficient material for a book and, therefore, it is not published, but the material can contribute to the general understanding of expectations of job performance. This source can also be helpful in indicating trends and future directions. It enables the Designer to raise questions about how the job is changing or can be expected to change. This can help the Designer avoid the trap of designing for a job that is becoming obsolete or is on the verge of heavy impact by new technology or processes.

The Designer is not expected to be an expert in the various technical fields. This limits the kinds of proceedings that the Designer can read, understand, and use. This limitation must be explored by each Designer. Do not try to become an expert in a field that takes years of study. The role of the Designer is not as an expert in the subject matter, and the Designer must avoid the temptation to become an instant expert.

There is another source of written materials which we can generally refer to as *literature*. The two major categories are magazines and books. Many occupational fields have specialized magazines which can be a source of data about job performance. They range from a simple one-page flyer or newsletter, to a several-hundred-page quarterly. Once again, the caution is that the Designer should not try to become a subject matter specialist, but should be familiar enough with the terminology and trends to be able to understand what constitutes job performance possibilities in that field. If it is a completely strange field, the Designer must find other people as the appropriate resource, as discussed earlier in this chapter.

Books in the field are a similar source. The same advantages and limitations exist as for magazines. Given the wide coverage of a topic presented in a book, the Designer might seek help from others in the organization as to which parts of the book are relevant to understand performance on the job under scrutiny.

There is a tendency to scoff at *government documents*, but they can be a very valuable source. Frequently large sums of taxpayers' money (yours) have gone into the research and related work to produce some of the government documents related to occupational fields. The Government Printing Office is probably the largest publishing organization in the country, and their output is available to all at relatively low prices. To ignore this source is to refuse to accept the results of some of your organization's tax dollars.

METHODS

There are different ways to tap into the sources we have been discussing. Some of these are fairly easy to use, while others require significant levels of skill in order to be effective.

It would be relatively simple to make a laundry list out of this section of the chapter. Instead, I believe it would be more useful to discuss the various methods by grouping them. For example, the heading "Questionnaire" includes checklists, various types of data gathering instruments, closed questionnaires, and so on. Each of these is different and will be discussed, but all under the same generic heading.

Questionnaire

The general group of methods under this heading are all concerned with some kind of written data-gathering device. The questionnaire could be developed by the Designer, or the Designer can use some of the standardized instruments that are available. The data can be hand-processed or machine-processed, depending upon quantity and complexity. We cannot possibly cover all the variations here, but we will explore some of the most significant concerns of the Designer when using a questionnaire.

Of prime importance is the impact of the questionnaire. If the respondent (that person who is responding to the questions) has a low level of literacy, the questionnaire can be a frustrating experience. (An alternative is the scheduled interview, which will be discussed later.) At the other end of the scale, a highly literate respondent may react negatively to a forced choice questionnaire and prefer an open-end type of questionnaire. Therefore let us look at some of the possibilities.

Before using a questionnaire, the Designer should be sure that the data are obtainable. That is, that it is possible for the respondent to supply the answers required. What could you expect if the respondent (a machine operator) is asked, "Indicate the ways in which the redesign of your machine could contribute to increased productivity of your unit." The operator may have some ideas, but the question is asking for something that is probably beyond the ken of the operator. The question also assumes that productivity (as differentiated from production) is a concept the operator can deal with. Many managers cannot yet cope with the concept of productivity.

If the data are obtainable—so what? In other words, if you do get the responses that will be helpful to you, what could you do about them? Some are predictable. "Get me a different supervisor and I would work better." Or, "If they let me design this car we could save a lot of money—it has too many unnecessary gadgets on it." If the questionnaire is well designed, it should produce usable data which the Designer can then use to "Specify Job Performance." The questions should all be tested in terms of the possible responses and their use by the Designer.

When developing a questionnaire, avoid the common trap of a "fishing expedition." Do not throw a broad net hoping that at least some of the questions and responses will prove useful. You have probably had your own experience of being asked to respond to questionnaires that were either so broad or lengthy that part way through you gave up. If you had the option, you just threw the darn thing into the nearest wastebasket. If you were required to complete the instrument, you did not spend too much time on valid responses, but just made sure that every question was answered—somehow.

To be effective, the questionnaire should be long enough to gather the necessary data, but short enough to be accomplished in a reasonable period of time. Reasonable will vary from one situation to another, but for each situation there is a limited period of time that we can expect the respondent to devote to the questionnaire.

It is important to pilot test the questionnaire, that is, to administer it to a selected small group (could even be two people) and ask their feedback on the clarity and form of the questions. For job performance, testing the questionnaire on the supervisor is essential. If the supervisor will not participate in this phase, the problem may not be with the job performance of the subordinate.

In some situations, it is helpful to share the data with the respondents. This builds a level of trust for similar activities in the future, as well as providing for another check on the quality of the data gathered.

Questionnaires can take many forms. A common one is the *checklist*. The respondent is presented with a series of statements and essentially asked to check off those that are done as part of the job. Or, the various tasks of the job are listed and the respondent is asked to prioritize them in order of importance. Given the problem that triggered the request for the training program, the respondent might be asked to number the tasks in the order in which they are performed.

A variation of the checklist is the *Likert Scale*. This is named for the eminent behavioral scientist, Rensis Likert, who introduced this type of instrument. Statements are presented to the respondent, with an option of marking them on a linear scale which might go from 1 to 6. The respondent is provided with a definition of the scale (1 is low and 6 is high, or some similar distinction). The statement should be one that is linear and where the respondent can select some appropriate point on the scale without having to qualify the response. Note the use of a scale, 1–6, which does not have a midpoint. If the scale were 1–5, there could be a tendency to select 3 which is a noncommittal way of responding. The scale could be 1–4 or 1–10 depending upon the nature of the statements, the respondents, and the way in which the data will be used.

Another type of scale is the *semantic differential*. It is much like the previous scale, but the difference is that the respondent is usually presented with words that are diametrically opposed, with a line between them. The line will have graduations, which can be numbered or unnumbered. The respondent is asked to circle the point on the line that represents the desired response. It is important that the words selected be direct opposites.

There are many other ways of constructing questions, such as forced choice, multiple choice, and even the old standby true and false. In each case, the Designer should keep in mind the factors discussed earlier, of respondent, nature of the data, and use of the data.

Another type of questionnaire is the *open-end*. You might be familiar with it as the *essay* type examination question you experienced during your school experiences. Though it appears simple, the questions for this instrument are difficult to construct. The questions must seek the data, without indicating any bias on the part of the questioner. The questions must be clear enough so that the respondent does not have to seek assistance just to understand the question. Provision must be made for the response. Should it be on the same page as the question (within a limited space) or can the question be answered on other pages?

Another type of open-end questionnaire is the *completion* format. You could present the respondent with "If I could change any part of this job, I would_____." The same factors about length of response apply as indicated about the open-end question. Although similar to the essay, some designers report better results with the completion as it tends to stimulate the respondents' thinking more than the essay type question.

It is possible to have a questionnaire which *combines the checklist* and the *open-end*. The respondent could be asked to complete the checklist, but under each item there is space for the respondent to write something. This is usually labeled "comments" but better data can be obtained if the checklist item is followed by either a completion option or a question that focuses the attention of the respondent.

The type of questionnaire will be influenced by the number of respondents. If there is a large number (whatever that is within your organization) of respondents, it might be easier to use a checklist or closed type of questionnaire. This makes for uncomplicated processing and comparison of the data obtained. Where large numbers are involved, the data usually have to be presented in some quantified form, and the checklist questionnaire fits right into this.

It is difficult, if not impossible, to quantify the responses to open-end questionnaires. Each must be read, and the data assigned to preconstructed categories. This is acceptable and even desirable for research, but can be time consuming and counter productive to "Specify Job Performance." If the numbers are small enough or the job sufficiently controversial (as in management), the open-end questionnaire will gather more substantial data and will be worth the additional effort and resources required to process the data.

If you anticipate using questionnaires, it is helpful to develop a file of questions related to particular jobs. The next time you are in this event of the CEM, for the same job, you can readily construct a questionnaire. Before using it, review the questions in terms of their usefulness in prior situations, any changes that have occurred in the organization or unit since that time, and what additional competencies you have acquired in developing questionnaires since the last time.

For some jobs, it is also possible to use external sources. There are companies that produce standardized questionnaires for some common jobs, such as those in supervision and management. Other vendors have questionnaires that relate to specifics, such as morale, interpersonal relationships, and communications. The availability of these materials varies from year to year, so it is not possible to provide a list of these companies that would be helpful for any long period of time. The companies that provide such products are usually listed in buyers' guides published by the American Society for Training and Development and in other magazines in the HRD field.

Interview

The interview is a face-to-face situation between an interviewer and one or more people. The interviewer in this situation is the Designer or represents the Designer. The interviewee (or respondent) is the person from whom some kind of data, information, or opinions are being sought.

Interviews can be either *group or individual*. It is a very active process in that the respondent will be doing most of the talking, with the interviewer listening and possibly using some data retrieval device such as note-taking or a tape recorder. There will be a further discussion on interviewer competencies, but at this point I will just indicate that one of the factors determining whether group or individual interviews are appropriate is the skill of the interviewer in working with individuals or groups.

Where job performance is the result of group behavior, a group interview might be more appropriate. Conducting individual interviews, in such a situation, could communicate that somebody is trying to split up the group. The interview may gather the data, but at the cost of reducing the morale and perhaps the effectiveness of the group.

A limitation is that if the entire work group, perhaps five people, is to be interviewed as a group—work stops. Provision must be made if the interviews are to take place "on the clock," particularly if interdependency of jobs indicates that if this group does not perform for a period of time, the work of others is affected. To do the interviews "off the clock" raises several issues. It could communicate that management does not think the process sufficiently important to provide for company time, and such a perception can seriously limit the validity of the data gathered. If the interview is held after work hours, will the respondents be paid for their time or given compensatory time? These issues should be clarified before planning to use an interview.

The individual interview must be handled very openly but cautiously. When an employee is taken off the work situation for an interview, rumors can be expected. When the employee returns to the work site, he will be greeted by, "They had you on the hot seat, didn't they?" or, "Do you still have your job?" Unless the situation is clear to all, negative implications can be expected. To turn this around everybody who is concerned should recognize that those being interviewed are valued resources and that the work of the Designer could not be accomplished without significant help through the interview process.

To get the most from an interview, careful attention must be paid to *climate setting*. The interviewee and those associated with the interview must receive prior notice. This should include the time, place, purpose of the interview, and a clear indication that this has the support of the supervisor of the person (or group) being interviewed.

The place of the interview is extremely important as it relates to the concept of the territorial imperative. Obviously the place for the interview should be carefully selected, as it communicates nonverbally the importance placed on the interview by all concerned. The two places that should be avoided are the work site itself (unless it is necessary to provide some specifics about job performance) and the office or desk of the supervisor. It is best to find some neutral space. This is not always easy to find and some compromises will have to be anticipated. If there are no other alternatives, the office of the supervisor could be used with the explicit agreement that the supervisor is not present—and that he will not stroll in and out of the office with muttered excuses. If the interview process calls for the supervisor to be present and this is an acceptable approach, it is still not desirable to use the supervisor's office unless there is absolutely no alternative site.

The interviewee should be put at ease. This is cultural behavior and may be difficult to determine absolutely. For example, in the United States, offering coffee is accepted practice. When both parties are sipping coffee it tends to produce a friendly and sharing atmosphere. How is coffee drinking viewed in your organization? In some organizations, drinking coffee at or near the work site is absolutely forbidden. In others, there may be no restrictions, while still other organizations actually provide the coffee pot and a continuous flow. ("Coffee" includes other drinks, such as tea and soda, depending upon the norm in the organization.) Do not make too big a production of this, such as providing a big tray of donuts, pastries, or other confections that might accompany the liquid. Overabundance of these amenities can impede the interview process and even produce a negative effect.

In setting the climate, the interviewer should have some opening questions which establish the norm—the interviewer will ask and the respondent is expected to answer. The first questions should be those that can readily be answered, so the interviewee experiences success in the initial stages of the process. As the interview proceeds, it can be anticipated that more specifics will be required, with the possibility of arousing some internal conflicts in the interviewee.

There are different *types of interviews.* One is closely allied to the questionnaire and actually uses questionnaires which have been discussed earlier. The difference is that the interviewee is not expected to write the answers. As the questions are asked and the interviewee responds, the interviewer records the responses on the questionnaire form. This is appropriate for almost all of the questionnaires that have been discussed. The interviewee can be presented with the questionnaire so he can follow the questions as they are being asked. If the interviewer does not want the interviewee to see the questions until they are asked, the questions can be put on individual cards and handed to the interviewee as the questions are asked.

When specific questions are being asked and the order is predetermined and not to be changed, the questions are referred to as an *interview schedule.* This is particularly important where similar data are being sought from different people, and where more than one interviewer is involved.

It is also possible to have some key questions, the open-ended type, which serve to stimulate the interviewee to talk about specific aspects of the job. Such an interview can probe in-depth issues, but can also provide a good deal of extraneous data. In one interview situation with which I am familiar, the following took place. The interviewer was an upper-middle-class white woman and the respondents were generally blue-collar workers on the lower fringe of the employment ladder, both black and white. They were employed at the Sparrows Point Plant of Bethlehem Steel and had been in a company-union-government program on literacy. The purpose of the individual interviews was to gather data on their perceptions of how the program had influenced their job performance.

At first, I expressed hesitation about the comparative socio-economic gap between the interviewer and the interviewees, but was urged to allow the interviewer to at least try. After the first few interviews, the interviewer met with me and we discussed the process and the data. In my own mind, I was prepared to offer the interviewer the opportunity to disengage from the project.

Quite the contrary. The interviewer had done a good job on climate setting and her only problem was that the interviews were taking much longer than anticipated. Her reading of the situation was that these respondents did not lack oral, verbal skills, but on the job there were few opportunities for conversation and they had acquired the reputation of being verbally inadequate as well as illiterate in the written word. This was not the actual situation. The interviewees wanted to tell her how the program had improved their family life as well as their job performance. For many, it was one of the first times that anybody with the aura of management had ever asked their opinion.

A general limitation of the interview process is the difficulty in organizing and analyzing the data. When a closed-end questionnaire is used, this should not present any problem. More commonly, an interview is used to allow the interviewee flexibility of response and this provides data with a wide scatter. It would definitely not be quantifiable, though some interviewers then take the raw data, put them into categories, and statistically compare within and among categories. Such quantification of interview data is highly questionable, and may not even be necessary for the purpose of specifying job performance.

We now come to *interviewer competencies*. What is required is more than the mere ability to ask questions. The interviewer must be able to establish the climate and maintain it, so the respondent feels free and comfortable in providing responses. The interviewer must also be able to terminate responses that are too lengthy or not particularly helpful, without communicating a negative feeling to the respondent.

There is a great deal of nonverbal communication that takes place during an interview. My wife and I work together, and we have used the interview technique. At first, we adopted the practice of my asking questions and she would take notes. This would allow me to maintain eye contact with the respondent and give him my undivided attention. Although she might also ask questions, her major role was to take notes which we could review at a later time. We soon discovered that this division of labor encouraged interesting behavior on the part of the interviewee, who would look at me as I asked a question, but then quickly turn to her when responding.

After a few experiences of this kind, my wife and I reviewed our process and respective roles. What we found was that her taking notes was a controlling factor in the interview. The interviewees responded to the note-taker as being more important. After all, I only asked questions and they were my questions. She was recording what the interviewee was saying and that was much more important.

Our mutual observations also indicated that she could control the interview by how she took notes. When she stopped taking notes, the interviewee stopped talking. When she closed her book, it signaled that the interview was terminated and no coaxing by me could encourage the interviewee to continue. We had to each develop competencies in questioning and note-taking so the roles could be switched as appropriate for each interview situation.

There is also evidence from other sources that the behavior of interviewers can influence the flow of conversation. It is a cultural factor, but particularly in the Americas (North and South) the interviewer must provide a steady feedback flow. This can be done by repeating, "Uh-hum," "I see," "Yes," and similar noncommittal, but overt signals that the interviewer is interested. It resembles a conversation by two Japanese over the telephone. If one speaker does not hear an audible response from the other, the first speaker will interject "Moshi, Moshi" which defies translation, but, essentially, is just a means of checking if communication is still going on.

In a face-to-face interview this is also communicated by nodding the head or other body language that communicates that the interviewer is involved in what the interviewee is saying. It has been noted that when the body language stops, the verbal behavior of the interviewee is influenced, and slowly the flow of oral language will ebb.

In addition to these competencies, the interviewer may also need skill in collecting the data. Where mutually agreed upon, a tape recorder might be used, though at one time this was a laborious process requiring heavy and elaborate equipment. Today, with micro-tape recorders, it is even possible to record an interview on a small concealed device, but this obviously raises ethical considerations.

Some interviewers start the tape recorder when the respondent enters the room, and then ask, "You don't mind this, do you? If you do, I will gladly turn off the tape recorder." This does not provide the respondent with an alternative. It puts the respondent in the position of having to request a change, with the implications that perhaps there is something to hide. If for any reason the respondent wants to discuss the use of the tape recorder, that discussion is already being recorded.

In using a tape recorder or similar device, the respondent should be informed prior to the interview that this is a possibility and be provided with the opportunity to merely say yes or no without having to defend a position. The respondent will understand that the interviewer is respecting the privacy of the interview. Of course, if privacy is not a concern, there is no problem.

Technology is constantly changing, and so is the methodology for gathering interview data. It is also possible to use the video-cassette recorder. There are units that are portable, easily set up, and operated with just a flip of the switch. The VCR enables the interviewer to capture not only the verbal responses but also the nonverbal behavior. For some interviewees, such equipment can be percieved as even more threatening than the audio-tape recorder, and the same protection of the interviewee should be provided as discussed earlier.

The most commonly used method of collecting data from an interview is still pencil and paper. When this is to be used, the interviewer must develop the competency for taking notes without disrupting the process. Some experienced interviewers develop skill in shorthand or some other system of speed writing, while others develop their own system, which has the added value that nobody else can read it. Whichever approach is used, all interviewers should recognize that taking notes during an interview requires special skills. It is not easy to ask, listen, and write—all three operations taking place almost simultaneously.

If the Designer does not have such competencies, or does not wish to acquire them, it is always possible to contract for outside professional interviewers. When outsiders are introduced into their situation, however, other issues may arise so the Designer will have to choose from among several alternatives. If the Designer is part of a sufficiently large HRD unit, there might be people within that unit who do have those interviewer competencies. If there is a great deal of interviewing to be done, contracts with external sources might prove to be a better alternative.

Meetings

Here the reference is to meetings called by the Designer. There was an earlier discussion of using meeting reports as a source. When used as a method, the reference is to meetings that the Designer has called, for the specific purpose of gathering data in order to "Specify Job Performance."

It is probably not necessary at this time to go into all the fine points of meetings [9], but some aspects must be highlighted. It is critical that the Designer have a sharply focused meeting, with identifiable results. The purpose of the meeting should be clearly stated, and that should be only to gather data about job performance. The Designer must avoid having the meeting focus on how a particular individual is performing. That is part of the next event in the CEM. When all those who are invited are notified of the specific purpose, they can more readily prepare for their participation. They are notified of and have a clearer picture of the expectations of the meeting.

As with most meetings, an important element is the selection of those who are to attend. The Designer should consider the interdependency of the job. If possible, all those who are related to the job should attend. In most situations, this is not possible, as it would be too costly, disruptive, and so on. Therefore a careful selection must be made. The Designer should discuss the list of proposed participants with at least the supervisor of the job. If the supervisor disagrees with those listed by the Designer, it is important that this be discussed. It can clear up misperceptions about the job or the extent of interdependency.

During the meeting the Designer should consider using a chalkboard, flip-chart, overhead projector, or other devices that can put the data in front of all who attend. This allows for constant revision of the data during the course of the meeting and that the end result is evident to all. There need not be any other written report or minutes, for what is important is not the process, but the end result. Participants should feel free to put forth ideas that they can change later. An early freeze will bury important data.

If the Designer is using meetings to collect data, it indicates another competency need for the Designer. We know a great deal about small group behavior in meetings, and most Designers have probably had some prior learning in this area. If not, developing skill in conducting meetings is essential. For example, this kind of meeting cannot use Robert's *Rules of Order* or any other parliamentary approach. The Designer must seek consensus rather than agreement by voting. It is not expected that at the end of the meeting there is complete agreement on all the specifics of job performance. The meeting may have focused on the need for some supervisory or managerial decisions about the particular job.

For most meetings, the results are shared with all who attended, but for this kind of meeting it may not be appropriate. The results of this meeting must be added to other data. Probably just a meeting will not be able to provide all the specifics. It is just one method of gathering the data.

Literature Search

As the earlier discussion of sources indicated, many of them are written, and we will use the generic term of literature to encompass them all.

As you probably realize, the improvement in printing technology and the increase in literacy levels have contributed to a situation which has been described as "print pollution." Unfortunately this is too derogatory. Not all of what has been printed is valueless, but the proliferation of printed material does make retrieval increasingly difficult.

If your organization has a library, that is helpful. If you have a librarian, you are extremely fortunate. Some of the retrieval of literature requires the services of a skilled librarian, and preferably several, who have the competencies to conduct the kind of *computer search* which facilitates retrieval. They know which computer services or banks are likely to have the required data. Even more crucial, they know the descriptors that are the pathways into the computer.

It is also possible to obtain such a service through external sources. There is presently an increasing trend towards computer services companies that have a wide variety of sources included within their machines. For set fees, they will do the search and provide hard copy.

The proliferation of conferences has implications as a source for information that is very valuable to "Specify Job Performance." Some work-oriented conferences produce voluminous proceedings, which are too often filed and forgotten. Some of these proceedings are a storehouse of vital information regarding expectations for job performance. Those words may not be used, but the information is there. Some of the proceedings are in the traditional printed form and appear as books, in both hard and soft cover. A growing tendency has been to provide audio-cassette recordings of particular sessions, some of which contain information related to expected job performance. It is not unlikely that future conferences will provide video-cassettes which would be helpful to "Specify Job Performance."

Observation

Actually observing the job being performed would appear to be one of the best methods that could be used but it has its limitations. When an employee is aware that performance is being scrutinized, performance will probably be altered. Very few of us, while being observed, will produce our usual behavior. When observation is used, the employee(s) should be fully aware of the process. This requires a high level of trust, and previous experience in which the results of the observation have not been used punitively.

The purpose of the observation should be made clear to all concerned and the process of observation discussed with the supervisor and the subordinate. If the purpose is shared, the results of the observation should also be shared with all concerned before becoming part of the data on job performance.

Observing job performance is more than merely watching what is happening. The observer should have some competency, and know what to observe and how to do it. Checklists might be used as well as narrative statements describing some particular actions. The observer must be unobtrusive yet close enough to the action to make the observations valid. There should be periodic checkpoints when it can be determined that the information being gathered through observation is valid and meaningful. In some situations, repeated return trips for further observation can be wasteful and disruptive [10].

Critical Incident

The critical incident approach can be used by the person performing the job, with a minimal amount of training in the technique. A variation is to help the performer keep a log. The Designer should provide the guidelines as to the kinds of material that should be recorded in the log and the form this should take. Of course, the performer should have a sufficient literacy level, though a tape recorder could be used to compensate for this shortcoming.

The critical incident is a value judgment. What the person performing the job chooses to include may not be the crucial elements of the job performance. Criteria for inclusion should be as specific as possible, with frequent checks to assure that the material being recorded is what is wanted and is helpful.

For managers, using the critical incident can be useful, but it can also be disastrous. It forces the manager to look at his specific performance and to determine which are the critical elements that enable him to perform or hinder his doing the job effectively. Too often, managers function under the pressure of tasks to be accomplished and consider it a luxury to stop and take a look at their own performance. The critical incident method forces the manager to take verbal snapshots of performance, rather than look only at results. If the job of the manager is under scrutiny, the Designer may have to proceed much more cautiously than where the position is on the production line or in the office.

Trade-off Situations

I have been discussing various methods, and trying to give the pros and cons of each. It is obvious, then, that selecting the appropriate method involves trade-offs between the desirable and the possible.

A method may be entirely appropriate, but too costly for the benefits that can be derived from collecting that information. The Designer is always working against some kind of budget and some limitation of resources. Frequently it is not possible to get the ideal job performance data. The decision must be made on how much can be gathered as measured against the cost in either direct expenditures or staff time.

In this particular element of the CEM, the Designer may find that management will become more involved than previously anticipated. New insights can evolve about what kinds of job performance are actually occurring as contrasted with what management thought was happening, at several levels removed from them. If the Designer can involve management and the possible benefits are identified, additional financial and human resources can suddenly become available.

At the other end of the spectrum, limitations may force the Designer to use a method that involves little of what has been previously discussed. One limitation could be the lack of the resources discussed earlier. The Designer might have insufficient budget for some of the methods that require direct financial outlays. Or the Designer may not have sufficient or qualified staff who can use the methods.

There is an alternative. It is not highly desirable or recommended, but in some situations it may be the only alternative possible.

The Designer, using job descriptions and similar information, can try to "Specify Job Performance." This requires making assumptions about the job and how it is performed that may be far from the reality, and that is why this alternative is not recommended. It is included because some situations may make it the only course open to the Designer. When the assumption route is chosen, the Designer should still try to verify the assumptions by as much direct contact with the job as the situation will allow. This could be a memo to the supervisor or to those who use the output of the job. The closer the assumptions can be brought to the reality of the job, the greater the possibility that the ultimate list of job behaviors will be accurate.

EVALUATION AND FEEDBACK

As noted in the previous chapter, each event culminates in evaluation and feedback (E&FB). Following the model presented in that chapter, we first look at the objective of this event:

> To specify the performance expected of a person who is doing a designated job.

The *action* step is what the Designer has done during this event.

During this event, a wide variation in the expectations of job performance may have been discovered. That may be the problem, and it can lead to the solution. It is possible that a training program is not required, or at least, not yet. First, those involved must agree on the job performance. The Designer may have to become a consultant rather than a Designer in order to help the members of the organization reach agreements on the job and the expected performance.

Analysis

The data must now be synthesized and organized in a form that communicates to all who are involved. There are many ways to do this, depending upon the nature of the job and the group that will be involved in feedback.

A common method is to list the individual steps that must be accomplished as part of job performance. The listing will be sequential, in the order that is required for the work to be performed. This is fairly straighforward where the job is in the area of production or where the steps must be performed in a given and fixed sequence. The level of detail should be sufficient so that it is clear to all, though it may not be necessary to describe each hand motion that is required as part of the tasks.

Where the job is not sequential (for example, management, supervision, or customer relations), the data may be organized around areas, or similarity of functions. These might be writing, speaking, responding, questioning, or decision making. For some positions, the time of day may provide the framework for organizing the data for review. The job performance may require that the worker be doing certain tasks at specified times, and this can become the format.

Jobs in the sales area could involve both sequential and nonsequential activities. There are some given steps to a sales approach that make it almost sequential. (For example, do not start by writing out the order.) However, selling involves a personal relationship which means that variations should be anticipated. The data might be organized to indicate those activities that are sequential and those that are random.

Feedback

Who should be involved in feedback, and why? If it appears that training is the response, usually the feedback would involve the person who will be trained, or a representative if the group is large. This is not always possible, and perhaps not even desirable. If the potential trainee(s) is geographically far from where the feedback session will take place, it may be too costly to expect involvement. Also, taking the potential trainee from the work site is a cost to someone in terms of lost production. A manager may be willing to be trained, but not be interested in being part of this feedback session. This is unfortunate, but close to reality. Too few managers want to be involved in deciding on their own training, and this problem must be addressed as part of the total HRD function.

The supervisor of the potential trainee is a must. If the supervisor, at whatever level of the organization, is not prepared to be involved in the feedback, it raises the question as to whether the learning will be used on the job. Where the proposed training is fairly obvious (a secretary moving from direct dictation to word processing), perhaps the supervisor need not be involved. But, if we are concerned with job performance, the supervisor must have some degree of involvement to be able to reinforce the newly learned behaviors.

Generally supervisors want to be involved. If contacted appropriately, supervisors can see that the feedback sessions are of benefit to them. It is the rare supervisor who will pass up the opportunity. This means that the session must be carefully planned and scheduled so that it does not conflict with other responsibilities of the supervisor. As this type of feedback session will occur at each step of the CEM and will be repeated with each design task, the climate should be a positive one. This will encourage the supervisor to take part in future feedback sessions. The Designer should be sure that the session is well planned, specific, and within a limited and agreed upon period of time. After several successes, most supervisors will welcome this opportunity.

Given the interdependency of jobs, discussed earlier, others might be involved in the feedback session. The group should not be so large as to become an unwieldy meeting, but sufficiently large to encompass those who are directly related to the job under scrutiny. Once again, when various people in the organization find these meetings of benefit, the Designer will not experience too much difficulty in encouraging the related people to attend.

An alternative to a meeting is to have the data and analysis shared by written memo or report. This is not desirable, but may sometimes be necessary. If those involved are at different geographical locations, the written memo may be requested. If there is the possibility of significant disagreements, the Designer may arrange for a telephone conference call to enable direct communication about the disagreements.

Decisions

The E&FB final session should address some specific questions that require decisions. This means that the decision-making people should be present, or at least involved, in the final E&FB session.

Some of the decisions that need to be made are:

1.   Is there still agreement on the problem?

The problem is the one agreed upon on the conclusion of the previous event. Unless there still is substantial agreement, it is fruitless for the Designer to go ahead. There could be a situation, of course, where there are many facets to a problem, and then only one item may be singled out for the training response. It is also conceivable that it is agreed that there is a problem, but there is a lack of agreement on the specific dimensions. There could be agreement that the Designer is to proceed, at least to the next event, to explore the problem further. If all agree on this, there is no difficulty with the Designer proceeding.

It may sound simplistic, but the problem should be written down as clearly as possible. Every concerned person should have the problem statement, as there will be constant reference to it during the next events.

2.   Is there agreement on job performance?

The response to this question could cover the entire spectrum from yes to no with even a strong maybe. The desirable response, of course, is that there has been agreement.

If there is a lack of agreement, this too should be clearly stated. If it is possible to indicate the specific areas where there is a lack of agreement, this should be made clear to all. The Designer should not feel compelled to reconcile the disagreements, but should point out that a training program cannot be designed in the absence of agreement on job performance.

3.   Should consideration be given to alternatives?

In this and the previous chapter, we have discussed some alternatives to training. Once again, this is the time to raise the issue of whether there are other alternatives to training, such as job redesign, reassignment of personnel, or change in procedures. After one of the alternatives has been selected, it may still be necessary to have a training program, and the Designer can pick up from that point.

    4.   Will time be allocated for training?

Although the actual "Conduct the Training" is still in the future, this is the time for some initial commitment on making the potential learners available. This is the time for the supervisors to recognize that it is their people who will be trained, and they must be made available in the future when the training is to be conducted.

Depending upon what is determined during later events in the CEM, the training may be several hours a day or several days a week. If there are time constraints, this would be a good time for the Designer to learn of them.

If the training is to be off-the-job (at some distant site), the supervisor should agree to release the employee for the necessary time. If there is a limit as to the number of employees who can be assigned to training at one time from any one unit, this would be the time for this information to be shared with the Designer.

Where training is the objective, the learner leaves the job and returns to the same job. The decision to assign the learner to training rests in the hands of the supervisors.

If the program is for education rather than training, who makes the decision to assign the learner to the program? Where education is the purpose, the learner may not return to the same job. If the learner does return, presumably it is for a short period of time before going to the new job for which the education is provided. It is also possible that the learner might go directly from the education program into the new job. In either case, the responsible supervisor(s) should be identified and be part of the decision-making process.

CONCLUSION

When the Designer is confident that the appropriate decisions have been made, it is possible to proceed to the next event, to "Identify Learning Needs."

REFERENCES

1.   There are many versions of the Blind Men and the Elephant story. Essentially, several blind men touched an elephant, each touching different parts, and then were asked to describe the animal. The blind man who touched the trunk said it was like a snake. The blind man who touched the legs said it was like a tree. As each blind man touched a different part of the animal, he gave his perception which, of course, was different from that of his other blind colleagues.

2.   Quality Circles is a movement which started in the United States (as one aspect of participative management) but has been much more widespread in Japan. The essence is that groups of workers, in similar or related functions, have regular meetings where they discuss the work (usually production), how the quality can be improved, the work done more ef

fectively, and so on. It is part of the trend to involve every employee in constantly re-examining how their part of the organization is functioning and how it can be improved.

3.   The study was reported as "Helping the Hard-Core Adjust to the World of Work," *Harvard Business Review,* March-April 1970.

4.   The "Hawthorne Effect" comes from the famous study conducted at the Hawthorne Plant of Western Electric during the 1920s. Out of this came the whole field of industrial psyhology and many aspects of human relations. One finding was that workers being studied tended to behave differently than those who were not being studied. Today this does not seem unusual, but it is too often ignored when studying a job. At one time, it was proposed that workers being studied would perform slower, particularly when the data were to be used for setting pay rates; Experience has shown that it is just as likely, in protected situations, for workers to perform better than their average.

5.   Using the weather as an analogy, Fritz Steele and Stephen Jenks wrote *The Feel of the Workplace* (Reading, Mass.: Addison-Wesley, 1977). The climate of the workplace is seen as having storms, rain, sunshine, and so on. Perhaps this is overdramatic, but it does highlight the climate of the workplace as being important. More on the cultural side is "The Organization as a Micro-Culture" in Chip Bell and Leonard Nadler, *The Client-Consultant Handbook* (Houston: Gulf Publishing, 1979).

6.   One way of looking at some financial statements can be found in my article, "What is Your Financial I.Q.?" *Training and Development Journal,* October 1980.

7.   *The Territorial Imperative* by Robert Ardrey (Atheneum, 1966) makes fascinating reading, but is based essentially on animal behavior and space. Edward T. Hall discussed some of the same material, but with more emphasis on human use of space in *The Hidden Dimension* (New York: Doubleday, 1966).

8.   See Linda Gordon, "Perceptions of the Cooperative Steel Project as seen by Planners and Participants," unpublished doctoral dissertation (School of Education and Human Development, The George Washington University, 1971).

9.   Organizing and conducting a small meeting requires more than sending out an announcement and arranging for a room. Leslie This has given us *The Small Meeting Planner* (Houston: Gulf Publishing, 2d Ed., 1979), which provides much in the way of written help for anybody responsible for small meetings.

10.   The basic article, by John C. Flanagan, is "The Critical Incident Technique," *Psychological Bulletin,* July 1954, pp. 327–358. Although much has been written since then, the reader will find that the basic article provides the essence. If it is not available, more recent material will be found as parts of chapters in other books.

ADDITIONAL PRINTED RESOURCES

Gilbert, Thomas. *Human Competence: Engineering Worthy Performance.* New York: McGraw-Hill, 1978.

Mager, Robert F., and Peter Pipe. *Analysing Performance Problems or ('You Really Oughta Wanna').* Belmont, Calif.: Fearon Publishers, 1970.

Vough, Clair F. *Tapping the Human Resource: A Strategy for Productivity.* New York: American Management Associations, 1975.

5

Identify Learning Needs

In this element of the CEM we are focusing on the specific learning needs of those who are to receive the training or education. As noted in the previous chapter, it is not possible to identify the learning needs until there is agreement on the job and how it is to be performed. In this event, the focus is on the individual and the group—on the person or people who are doing or will do the job. (See Figure 5-1.)

In Chapter 1 there was a discussion of the difference between training and education. It is possible that the significance was not obvious, at that time. If the Designer has not been accustomed to making this distinction, it is very easy to overlook the difference. This oversight can result in disaster, or at the very least an inappropriate learning experience.

The objective of this event is:

To identify the learning needs of those who are doing the designated job.

(Obviously this would be modified for education.) The focus on the previous event was on the job—the focus of this event is on the person in the job.

THE INDIVIDUAL

People are different. One of the purposes of a good learning program is to bridge the differences between the person and the job so the individual can perform in a way that meets the organizational goals. At the same time, the goals of the individual cannot be overlooked. When individual goals are in conflict with organization goals, the training or education can be a waste of valuable resources.

Values

In the last event, we developed specific data on how the job should be performed. Our first determination must be: does the individual want to do the job as

THE CRITICAL EVENTS MODEL

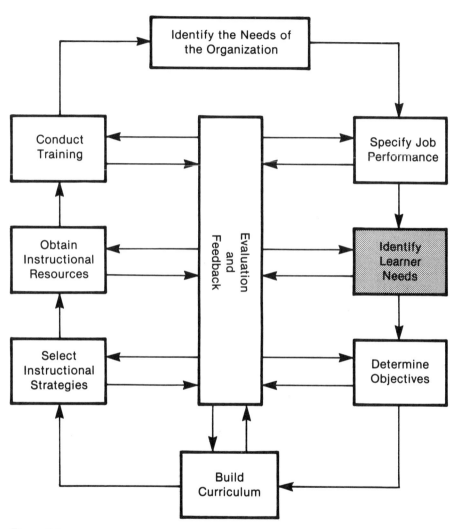

Figure 5.1

specified? There may be reasons why a particular individual does not want to do a particular job.

An all too frequent example is in sales. Certain sales techniques may conflict with the values of the individual who is selling. Let us take a case where an analysis of the job followed by an analysis of the performance of the individual, shows a shortfall. The individual is not "selling up" or engaging in other sales activities that are perfectly legitimate, though perhaps more "pushy" than the individual wants to be. The training program would have to deal with values, rather than techniques.

When we have specifics about expected performance, we may find that the individual is not suited to the job. Reassignment may be a more appropriate response than a training program.

When there is an education program, it is even more important to consider the individual. By definition, education is learning for a job that the individual is not now doing, but will be doing in the near future. The most obvious example is when an individual is to receive education to become a supervisor for the first time. The movement from being a subordinate to becoming a supervisor is the greatest change that most people make in their entire work career. As a subordinate, it appears that the supervisor has a tremendous amount of power, many perks, and real control. When education is provided in presupervisory programs, the glamor and rumor will be replaced by reality and fact. It is not unusual to find an individual, during or after a supervisor education program, opting to remain as a subordinate. The common remark is, "The pay isn't worth the hassle!"

When there is direct interface with other people, rather than machines, the question of values is highly pertinent. What does the job require in the way of performance which may be counter to the values of the individual? If the individual enjoys talking to other people, serving them, and generally being helpful, a job involving customer contact would seem in order. Accordingly, an individual might take a job as a bank teller because of the constant contact with customers and the opportunity to serve them. The teller finds that because of good service, customers keep coming back to the same window, there is chit-chat about family, the weather, the political situation, and generally a personal relationship builds up.

In the midst of this relationship, management decides that more efficient service can be rendered by the teller through the use of the "bull pen" or ropes and stanchions strung out so that people must line up. Service is provided by the next available teller, and choice by the customer becomes extremely limited. Many of us, as customers in the bank, may prefer this arrangement, for we always seem to get in the slowest line. For other customers and tellers, the bull pen is just another obstacle to be overcome. The customers pass up available tellers while they wait for "their teller" to become available. Tellers view themselves as depersonalized and as mere extensions of the computers that swallow their output.

Additional training for tellers, on how to work more efficiently with the bull pen method may be counter-productive. If the teller took the job for the opportunity of interacting with and serving people, the new, more efficient method runs counter to this value. All that training can do is to reemphasize the need for speed, accuracy, and avoiding long conversations with customers.

Needs

The term *needs* is used frequently, and often incorrectly. To begin with, what is a need? As usually defined, it is the difference between a goal (or what is expected) and what actually exists. In essence, then, there is no need unless somebody feels a lack of some kind. That is one reason why the CEM has two events before we can begin to "Identify Learning Needs." There must first be the identification of the "Needs of the Organization" as measured against its goals, then we can "Specify Job Performance," and finally we can come to the element of "Identify Learning Needs," for the individual(s).

At this time we are only going to discuss those needs related to job performance. This is not to deprecate other needs that individuals have, but that is not the purpose of the CEM. If other needs are surfaced, there must be exploration of other appropriate ways to meet them.

We must also take into account *wants*. These are the things individuals ask for, but not because they are related to job performance. Wants are legitimate, and when we are dealing with education, the wants are important. An organization may provide learning opportunities for employees, even though not related to a specified job change in the near future. Such learning opportunities are better classified as *development* (see the discussion in Chapter 1) and represent a legitimate want for an employee. Of course, the employee may see this as a need, for the employee has goals and aspirations which are not always congruent with the goals of the organization. Although we should not ignore the wants of individuals, the CEM focuses on needs.

One way of looking at needs is to recognize that there are three major types. The first are *stated needs*. These arise directly out of the previous event, "Specify Job Performance." From the specifics, it is possible to identify exactly what a person should do and therefore to give a specific indication of the need of somebody who is doing that job.

There is the *implied need*, which is not specifically stated but likewise arises from the situation. If somebody is being considered for a promotion or transfer, there is at least an implied need for some learning so that the individual will perform effectively when placed on the new job. For a person on the existing job, the implied need can arise from a change in process, technology, or materials.

The implied need can also arise when a new worker enters an existing unit. Tasks may be reassigned, requiring those already doing the job to perform differently. In a sense, some of the implied needs are really stated needs that have not been spelled out by the organization or by those introducing change into the work situation.

The strongest need is the *felt need*. There is almost universal agreement that learning takes place much more effectively when the learner feels the need to learn. The stated and implied needs flow from the individual. When a person wants to perform better and the gap between performance and expectation is clear, there is a felt need.

One problem in going to the employee to determine needs, without first having completed the event "Specify Job Performance," is that the Designer is more likely to get wants than needs. Wants are legitimate, but will not meet the target indicated earlier of improving job performance. Needs are directly related to job performance, now or in the identifiable future.

An experience I had may help to clarify the distinction among the three types of needs. I was appointed to the Training Advisory Board of a large police department. The internal HRD group had conducted a survey to identify the needs of the police officers. For this, they had gone to a selected sample of the police officers and had generated a rather lengthy list of "needs." One need, fairly high on the list, was that the officers wanted more "target shooting practice." The Training Advisory Board discussed this need.

After protracted discussion, a consensus emerged that what the officers really wanted was a program in "Shoot, No Shoot." The focus of such a program is to clarify when a police officer might discharge a firearm, and then, how to do it most effectively, given the variety of situations that could arise. We had, however, made a quantum leap from "target shooting practice" to "Shoot, No Shoot." These are not the same. Put into the framework of different kinds of needs we had the following:

- Stated—There is a specific department policy on discharge of firearms by police officers. It specifically lists those situations where it is permissible and those in which it is not. If performance review indicates that the policy is being violated, training might be necessary. Also, the board suggested, perhaps it was time to review the policy (expected job performance).

- Implied—Whenever a police officer discharges a firearm, even accidentally at home, the case has to go to a review board. There are also court decisions on police use of firearms. A general implication is that more training in the discharge of firearms is needed. (The board did ask the internal HRD people to provide more specifics on just who would need such training, based on job performance records.) The implication from the review board and court experiences was that training was needed.

- Felt—The police officers felt a need for more "target shooting practice." From this statement, it was not possible to identify the exact nature of the need. Obviously the police officers feel a need of some kind related to firearms, since they indicated this in their responses. The board was told that it could not be a proficiency factor as each police officer (including the chief) had to qualify twice a year on the range. When an officer did not qualify, his weapon was withheld until such time as the officer qualified. Therefore, what was the felt need of the police officers?

The Designer will continue to use the word "need", generally but will be more specific when it is important that the distinction be made.

GATHERING DATA

The material that follows will, in some areas, read very much like the previous chapter. This is understandable, as many of the sources and methods are the same. The difference is in the actual data being gathered, and this is extremely important. Because there is a great deal of similarity, some Designers attempt to do both events "Specify Job Performance" and "Identify Learning Needs" at the same time. "After all," it is suggested, "this would mean one less trip to the job site, one less interview, and so on." The difficulty with this is that the Designer is collecting data on needs before the performance has been agreed upon.

Another problem that is encountered when these two events are not separated is that the Designer, and others, may have difficulty determining the extent to which the individual influences the job. Of course, the individual is important. To look at both at the same time, however, is to "Specify Job Performance" as done by the incumbent. Realistically the job must be done in certain ways to meet the needs of the organization and the interdependency factor. Employees put their own fingerprints on a job, and for some jobs this is not only permissible but desirable. If this is so, it should be reflected in the latitude determined in the previous event.

Sampling

The earlier discussion of training and education must be reemphasized here. When training is the purpose, there are incumbents on the job, and the Designer should "Identify Learning Needs" as evidenced by those performing in that job slot. This is not always possible. The employees may be scattered at widespread geographical locations or are so numerous that the cost of direct contact outweighs the benefits.

A possible approach is the use of electronic data gathering by teleconferencing, computer conferencing, and other devices which are becoming widely used in many organizations. Alternatives include some of the methods described earlier. There are questionnaires and other data-gathering instruments, and they will be dealt with later in the chapter.

Still another alternative is to use a sampling technique. You are probably familiar with this as used in our national elections. The polls conducted before the election do not reach all the electorate, but focus on carefully selected individuals or areas. By polling this sample, pollsters are able to make predictions, many of them highly accurate. It is possible to use a similar approach in this event, but it should be done cautiously.

There are criteria for drawing samples, but the Designer is not dealing with the kinds of data that require a high level of sophistication. It is possible, for example, to use this sampling approach with supervisor training programs. The number of supervisors in an organization may be quite large, but the common aspects of their job performance will have been gathered in the previous event. The Designer can develop a data-gathering instrument to identify some of the common needs that supervisors feel they have when compared with what was agreed upon under "Specify Job Performance." The Designer must determine the size of the sample and how it will be drawn. This determination will reflect the diversity of supervisors in the organization.

A simple method is to list all supervisors alphabetically, and then draw a sample by taking each fifth name, depending upon the total population and the size of the sample desired. If geography is a factor, the list can be organized to reflect that variable and the sample drawn from a proportional number from each location. Where a particular unit of the organization is significant, the lists for selecting the sample can be drawn up to reflect that factor.

For an education program, the problem is more difficult. It is important to first identify the population. If they are internal to the organization, it is probable that the total number is not too large and sampling would not be necessary. If the prospective learners are from outside the organization, it may be difficult to identify them early enough before the start of the program to take a sample. If it is a recurring program for new employees entering the company, the sample can be expected to vary over time and not be adequate.

Sources and Methods

It rapidly becomes obvious that this event requires many of the same sources and methods discussed in the previous chapter. This is both a positive and negative factor.

On the positive side, it means that the Designer can use some of the same competencies that were required earlier. Also, some of the relationships built in the previous event will also be useful in this event. The groundwork to identify the sources and methods will already have been done.

The negative is that the similarity may cause the Designer to make some significant mistakes. The purposes of the two events are much different, and unless this difference is constantly kept before all those involved, the data can easily become mingled and garbled.

The focus of the previous event was on the job, no matter who was performing it. The emphasis, as you will recall, was on the interdependency aspects and how that job related to others in the organization. Even the question of whether that job was necessary was raised. All of this had to be done without significant consideration for the person or persons doing the job.

In this event there is a dramatic shift in focus. Here we are primarily concerned with people. For training, we are concerned with those who are actually on the job at this time. The theoretical of "what should be," must be replaced by the reality of "what is!" For education, we must develop a profile of the kinds of people we can anticipate will be filling that job in the future. Admittedly this is very difficult, and there is no question but that education is more difficult to design than training. The difference is that when designing training we are confronted with real people on the job. They cannot, and should not, be ignored. For education, we must frequently rely on guesswork, unless the potential learners have been previously identified.

Let us look, then, at sources and methods. I will endeavor not to repeat what you have read in the previous chapter, such as specifics on different types of questionnaires. Rather, reference will be made to using a questionnaire.

SOURCES

The sources of data should be as specific as possible. For training, it must be the people actually doing the job—the potential learners. The sources should be those reflecting performance on the job.

Production/Output Records

When the program being designed is for a production job, specific production records should be available. These take many forms, and the Designer must determine what is usable and what is not. The records may report unit or group output, rather than individual output, and such a record is not very helpful when identifying individual needs. Group performance is the result of all the employees in the group, but the needs should be individualized.

Where a product is produced, there are probably records of quantity and quality. If such records are not kept, the Designer should not try to reconstruct them from other sources. Rather, accept the fact that these data are not available and question the reason for the absence of such data. It could indicate that the employee has not been told the criteria for effective job performance and that there has been no feedback on quantity and quality given to the employer. Training may not be the need, at least, not training for the producing employees. It may mean that the need is for supervisor training, to help the supervisors learn how to give instructions about expected job performance.

Where there is no measurable production, look for other output records. These could be a log of calls completed, letters processed, or some other observable and quantifiable output. As noted earlier, when we move up the hierarchical ladder, such data become more elusive. We must search for other sources of data on actual job performance in order to identify the needs.

Relative time must also be watched very closely as the data can age very rapidly. Some Designers prefer to obtain what is termed *longitudinal data*—data that is gathered over a period of time. For some purposes, this technique may have value, but where the situation is changing, that approach can be meaningless. What value is there in seeking data on prior performance, when there has been a change in process, technology, or supervision? The most recent data on performance are all that can be effectively used.

This time factor can prove to be a problem at a later point in the design process. If the designing takes a long time (and long is relative), the Designer may find that the data gathered under this event is no longer relevant. As the needs are individual, the data are meaningless if those individuals are no longer on the same jobs. Also, the relevance is questionable if there have been other changes in the workplace related to performance. Although the Designer must gather individual data at this time, care should be exercised if the sources are altered by the time the actual learning event is ready to be delivered.

Performance Appraisal

Performance appraisal is a very important source, but the process of performance appraisal reminds one of the waves and the tides. Interest in performance appraisal has its peaks and valleys, and therefore the actual use of this technique tends to vary. Like the tides, some of it is highly predictable.

In some organizations, it is an annual ritual which most detest but which must be performed. It is approached with fear and trepidation, which frequently includes hostility. The actual appraisal may be more a reflection of the supervisor than of the subordinate. If, for example, the climate in the organization is not supportive of the supervisor, the appraisal is a source, but a questionable one, for it may be more useful as an outlet for supervisor frustration.

At one time, when working as a employee in an organization, I had a secretary who was woefully inadequate. She violated many of the actual rules and regulations which, in that organization, were extremely significant. She was unreliable, in that she would openly discuss the letters, memos, and phone calls to which she was privy. This sometimes caused embarrassment, as I had to document why some people were not being accepted for learning programs. The potential learners were always informed, but sometimes they learned this because the secretary was discussing it with others, rather than directly through me or their supervisor. I could go on to document, but let me not vent my anger at this late date.

When it came time for performance appraisal, I made out the requisite forms and called her in for the mandatory (and usually helpful) discussion. As you might expect, she felt that she was entirely correct in what she was doing and that everything we did in our office should be shared with everybody. After several discussions, it became apparent that we would never reach agreement and I forwarded the negative appraisal, as was the organization practice.

Shortly thereafter, she was transferred to a different supervisor. In her mind, and she said this out loud, it vindicated her performance. She had not been fired, reprimanded, nor lost any increment in pay. Therefore she felt she was performing satisfactorily despite her supervisor's appraisal. In a case such as described, what would happen if the Designer relied on the appraisal? Obviously it would be irrelevant, as the secretary was no longer in the same position, though she was still working for the organization as a secretary. If a need were indicated for her to learn how to respect the privacy of the material that passed over her desk, she would certainly not have a felt need. After all, the result of the appraisal was a transfer but with no implication that it was the result of any lack of performance on her part. The performance appraisal, in that instance, could not be used as a valid source.

It is even more frustrating when there are performance appraisals, but they are kept secret. At times this is necessary, but some organizations tend to be overcautious. In one situation, where I was the external Designer, the organization had elaborate appraisal forms. I met with the CEO of that organization, and he was very proud of their appraisal system. I listened to a lengthy and detailed description of how the system worked, how it had been validated, and so on. Then we came to the point when I asked to see the appraisals for the managers I was asked to design for. The response was, "I cannot let you see them, they are confidential." We explored how I could get that important and vital data. The final accommodation was that the CEO would digest the information, being sure that no single manager could be identified, and then share it with me. The result, of course, was a long list of generalities with no way of connecting them to individual learning needs.

Most performance appraisals are not designed to indicate individual training and education needs. It is possible, frequently, to tease that out of the form, but that involves a good deal of judgment on the part of people other than the potential learners. It is not being suggested that the performance appraisal be seriously altered to include identification of learning needs. However, when performance is not up to the standard required, it does suggest the possible need for some learning. If your organization has this built into your performance appraisal system (not only the forms), this can be a valid source.

Supervisor

The supervisor is a basic data source. The supervisor is the one who most often will have requested the training program. Therefore the supervisor will generally have some data or information that supports the need for the individual training. By going to the supervisor, the Designer is involving the supervisor in the identification and specification of the learning needs. As the Designer is able to function in a variety of units at one time, the Designer can determine if various supervisors have identified similar needs for their subordinates.

To "Identify Learning Needs" it is necessary to be as specific as possible. The Designer should seek out examples of behavior, preferably the observable which would indicate the need. The supervisor should have this information available. If the Designer is seeking the quantifiable, the supervisor should also be a source for such information.

Employee

Here we are directing our attention to the employee/subordinate for whom the training is being designed. If it is a need of a single employee, with no significance for other employees, training may not be the appropriate response. It is not that the individual does not have needs, but to "Identify Learning Needs" can be costly in terms of the possible return. One possibility is to do nothing, with the concurrence of the supervisor and the subordinate.

When going to the employee as the source, the Designer will automatically be verifying if the employee knows what is expected in job performance. As has been said many times, the lack of performance may be due solely to not having helped the employee understand what is expected performance. When using the employee as a source, the Designer must take the job performance expectations that were produced in the previous event of "Specify Job Performance." If the employee had been involved, this statement of the job performance will not be new. The Designer may now be faced with the employee indicating why the expected performance is not possible. If the previous E&FB were accurate and successful, this should not happen—but it is always a possibility.

Going to the employee is necessary, but it presents a critical problem. The implication, if not the stated fact, is that the employee is not working up to the level of expected performance. (This would not be the case if the training is the result of a new process or product.) The Designer is in the position of confronting the employee with this gap in performance. The employee may become hostile and negative. Few of us enjoy confronting our inadequacies. Going to the employee in this element requires skill in interpersonal relationships, asking questions, and dealing with hostility.

METHODS

The caution bears repeating, that the methods discussed here appear to be similar to those explored in the previous chapter. The major difference is that the focus should be on those who are actually working at the job for which training is being designed.

Meetings

Meetings are always costly and not always cost effective. Some levels of employees are not familiar with meetings and may need some training to enable them to function effectively.

The most desirable practice is to include in the meetings all those to be trained, as well as their supervisors. This could produce a total shut-down of the operation. Therefore some selectivity is required. The Designer should provide some criteria to the supervisor(s) as to who should be involved in the meeting. The participants should be those who are doing the job. Expectations of how the job should be done will have surfaced in the previous element of "Specify Job Performance." Now, the focus must be exclusively on actual performance. The ideal would be to involve only those who have identified learning needs. A result may be to create a group of employees who appear to be the low performers, and the meeting then becomes a pejorative event which blocks future learning possibilities.

There is a question as to whether employees, at all levels, are capable of seeing their own performance. Experience has shown that this is not only possible, but can be used effectively. For years there have been managers in the United States who have used the concept of *participative management* which included involving employees at all levels in a variety of small meetings. This idea was picked up and used extensively by the Japanese in a process called "Quality Circles" [1].

It is important that the agenda for these employee meetings be short and concise. The Designer should avoid discussions of elaborate concepts or generalities. The focus should be specifically on comparing the expected job performance with the actual, and identifying the learning needs of the employee participants.

A complication arises when we are dealing with education, as contrasted with training. In the training situation, we can reach those who are actually doing the job and get very specific data on performance. In education, this is not possible.

There are two groups to consider in education. The first consists of those who are currently employees, but not on the job under investigation. (If they were on the job, we would be talking training.) When we are involved in providing learning to prepare them for the job, we are into education. In such a situation, it is not possible to have a meeting of the employees and obtain data on how they are performing. They are not performing on that job—yet.

A meeting might still be useful in terms of asking them to compare their previous learning and experiences with the performance required of them when they get to the new job. For the most part, this will produce very subjective data and some that will be unreliable. This is not because the employees are hiding anything, but because they are being asked to guess how they will perform on a job they have not yet done. A meeting can still be helpful, but the Designer should not expect too much specific data.

The second group presents a more difficult problem. They are not employees, and in some instances have not yet been recruited. These are people who will be recruited and selected from outside the organization. It is generally not possible to meet with them beforehand to identify their learning needs.

An alternative is to provide a learning program as part of the selection process. During the mid-1970s, I found a practice which I called "prior to hire." (As you can see from the reference, the editors of the magazine that published the article gave it a different title. [2]) The organizational need arose from an economic decline which made more people available for jobs. In some cases, they were people who were looking for a job, any job, but would not remain on the job for a satisfactory period of time. (The reasons for it are discussed in the article.) In some of the organizations I studied, there was a real problem of turnover of new employees. There were many approaches to the turnover problem, but generally the organization provided some kind of education experience before the final selection was made. Upon completion of the learning, the prospective employee and a selected member of the organization met to discuss the results of the education experience. The organization was represented by someone from the personnel office, the possible supervisor, or a staff member from the HRD unit. These meetings focused on the performance of the prospective employee during the education and the possible job placements. In these meetings, they discussed additional learning needs which had been identified for specific learners as a result of the education experience.

Interview

When interviewing the potential learner, the Designer should endeavor to ascertain the relationship of the felt needs with those that are stated or implied. The interview should be as specific as possible.

The preferred approach is to interview all of the employees who are the potential trainees. This may not be possible because of the size of the group or their geographical location. In such instances, the Designer may have to rely on sampling, with its limitations as discussed earlier.

The Designer should avoid interviewing only those who are readily available, as they may not be representative of the group. The cautions to be observed, which were discussed in the previous chapter about where to interview, climate setting, and so on, are equally applicable here.

Observation

There can be observation of the employees actually doing the job when there is the possibility that they will be the learners. The supervisor is the one to identify those who will probably need the training. After the observation, the Designer may indicate those who do not need the training or those who could not benefit from the training. This latter decision is a difficult one to make, but it is sometimes necessary. There are many reasons why a particular individual may not be able to improve performance even with the best training. If the Designer can identify this and discuss it with the supervisor, it reduces false expectations and wasteful training costs.

Observing the work actually being done presents some problems to the Designer. It may become evident that some coaching of individual employees is all that is needed to bring performance up to the agreed upon standards. Of course, coaching is a valid learning strategy. The question is: who should do the coaching? It will be very tempting to the Designer to do the coaching while observing. This could almost appear to be cost effective, but what of the supervisor? Would the supervisor feel that such coaching by the Designer has usurped the regular supervisory function? If a supervisor does feel that way, this could block any further observations by the Designer. The Designer must remember that the role is one of designing, not that of supervising.

Questionnaire

The questionnaire is particularly useful when the job cannot be observed and where measurement is not a factor. If measurement is to be considered, there are better methods for obtaining this information, though the Designer may still choose to use a questionnaire to obtain related information for verification. If the measurement information is available from a basic source (for example, production records), the Designer may wish to verify this by having the employee respond to a question on output. The Designer could discover that the standard production records and the employee record of output are not congruent! There could be a discrepancy in how output is tallied and that the training need is in recordkeeping.

The questionnaire should be kept simple and relate directly to the job that the employee is performing. Too often, those who design questionnaires go on a "fishing expedition." That is, as long as time is being spent on the questionnaire, what other information can be obtained? This weakens the focus of the questionnaire, takes additional time, and raises doubts in the mind of the employee as to the purpose of the questionnaire.

A serious limitation of the questionnaire, when used to "Identify Learning Needs," is that it is best used for obtaining data about knowledge. A carefully constructed questionnaire might elicit valid data about attitudes, but a questionnaire cannot assess skill behavior. Where skill is a factor in the possible training program, a questionnaire should not be used.

When education is the purpose of the program, the questionnaire can be helpful generally. It allows the Designer to reach those who are not yet on the job. When the potential learners are outside the organization, the questionnaire can surface those learning needs that are essential before the individual is placed on the job, and perhaps those that can be left for training after the new employee has been placed on the job.

Tests

For a training program, tests are generally not helpful. The data are best obtained by interview, observation, and records. The actual job performance will yield much better and more realistic data than a test which is an artificial situation.

When the purpose is education, a test is helpful to "Identify Learning Needs," as there is no previous job performance to help the Designer. Therefore the Designer must create artificial situations which the individual will find on the job. The tests will vary, depending upon the nature of the job, the availability of the potential learner, and the resources available.

One testing method is a variation of the assessment center. The basic purpose of the assessment center is *not* to identify learner needs but rather to assess the potential of an individual to do a particular job. With modifications, the assessment center has been used to "Identify Learning Needs"—and this is not new. Before the term *assessment center* entered the literature, Designers were using an approach termed *simulation*. That is, to design a situation much like the actual work situation, but without the penalties for failure. Individuals could take part in the simulation, try out new behaviors, and not confront the limitation that failure would be costly. Used in this manner, assessment center/simulation is a form of testing.

For management level work, the case study [3] method has proven very valuable in helping an individual identify how they might possibly behave when given a particular problem. For people who have never been managers, the case study can readily be adapted into a test situation.

LISTING OF NEEDS

We can now make a specific list of the learning needs that have been identified. One approach is the "subtraction" method. This is illustrated in Figure 5-2. The need is the *difference* between expected job performance and actual job performance. This appears very simple, but unless the work under the previous event ("Specify Job Performance") and this event has been done well, the differences may not be apparent enough to serve as the basis of a training program.

Sometimes a Designer may have to compromise. For example, it may not be possible to obtain the specifics for each individual who is assigned to be a trainee. Therefore it is possible that some learners in the learning situation can already perform as expected. Despite this, supervisors send those individuals to learning sessions. There is little that can be done about this in the design phase, and we will discuss the situation further when we are in the event "Conduct Training" and are exploring the problem of selection and assignment to the learning situation.

Listing and Organization

The results of the differences (expected performance minus actual performance equals differences) should be indicated as specifically as possible. Various forms are possible, but it is important to find the form or reporting mechanism that makes the Designer comfortable and communicates to all concerned. A Designer might make a note of some of the various forms in the literature, or those distributed at workshops, and retain them in a file to be referred to as appropriate. Caution must be exercised not to accept somebody else's form without first testing it out for its appropriateness for the Designer and the situation.

Some common pitfalls can be avoided if the Designer gives adequate attention to this phase of the event. *Be specific,* as specificity lessens the possibility of designing and training for the wrong performance. There are limits, of course, to specificity, and that is what makes designing as much an art as a skill. Those who have been directly involved in the job performance may have difficulty seeing the specifics, and even block on them. By forcing them to see the specifics, the Designer might engender hostility and a blocking of the whole process. There is a very fine line between specificity and overkill.

The *meaning of words* becomes crucial. The needs should be stated in a manner that is not pejorative or critical of the performer or the supervisor. Very few of us enjoy being told that we are not performing as the job demands or as well as we can. The Designer must find the words that communicate effectively and have the same meaning for all concerned. As the listing is shared with a variety of people in the organization (and later outside of the organization), it is important that meanings be as generally accepted as possible.

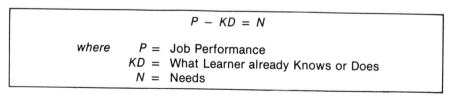

$$P - KD = N$$

where P = Job Performance
   KD = What Learner already Knows or Does
   N = Needs

Fig. 5.2 Formula for needs.

An aspect of meanings is *local usage*. In American English, we have absorbed words into our language which we assume are known to all. Actually they are known only to those who share the same cultural experiences, and a breakdown can occur even within cultural groups. Take the following words and ask for meanings: Kleenex, Ping-Pong, Frigidaire, and Vu-graph. All of these words are product names but are common usage for products manufactured by a wide variety of manufacturers. The products are: tissues, table-tennis, refrigerator, and overhead projector.

An experience many of us have had is to ask a new employee to "burn a copy." Do not be surprised if the result is ashes! The phrase "burn a copy" was common during the 1960s when copying machines using intense heat first came on the scene. Today, it could be equally disastrous to ask for a "Xerox" of a document, and have the employee go outside the company, since the copying machine within the company is made by another manufacturer! These may seem like extreme examples, yet I have seen these occur within organizations and lead to personnel problems for the supervisors who thought the subordinate was just being contrary.

One more example can be taken from my experience. For many years I have been counseling prospective students who wanted to take a graduate program in Human Resource Development. The materials describing the program are in clear written form, or so I thought. The confrontation came when I was asked by a prospective student, "What is a semester hour, and how does it differ from a credit hour?" My first reaction was that this was obvious, and then I discovered it wasn't. Actually both mean the same in our situation, but much of our written material used both terms! To those of us who use the material, the similarity was obvious. To an "outsider" it was confusion.

Most work situations have their own language, or jargon, and it is important that these be clarified on the listings of needs. All those who are involved should have clear agreement on all the terms or the design process will break down at a later element of the CEM.

EVALUATION AND FEEDBACK

Having identified the needs of the learners, the Designer is now ready to implement the E&FB event before proceeding further. As noted at the outset, the objective of this event is:

To identify the learning needs of those who are doing the designated job.

We have had to make the distinction between training and education, but in either case we should now have a list of those needs, as identified through the actions taken during this event.

Analysis

With the data in hand, the Designer must organize it for presentation to those who will be involved in feedback. As a start, the Designer should compare what has been gathered in this event with the listing gathered under "Specify Job Performance" to ascertain how the identified needs are related to job performance. If there is a discrepancy between these two listings, it may be necessary to return to "Specify Job Performance." If the current event has been done effectively, there should not be any needs that do not relate to job performance. This is the point at which that check is made.

The Designer will have, at this time, a list of needs. Now the list should be categorized and items that are related grouped together. For example, all the items related to "communications" might be put under one heading. However, care should be exercised that the subitems are not lost as then the word "communications" becomes too general and useless for design work. Under the heading of "communications," the specific items that have been identified earlier should be retained.

If there are variations due to individuals, this is also noted at this time. That is, not everybody will have all the needs listed. Therefore the analysis should show which individuals have specific needs. The Designer should not make any judgments at this time as to which needs are to be met or which are most important. That will evolve in the next element.

Feedback

Almost the same people should be involved in feedback for this event as for the previous one. Here, however, it is crucial that the supervisor be directly involved. It is helpful if the subordinate can be involved, but this will depend upon how comfortable the Designer is with the data that has been gathered during this entire event. The method of bringing the subordinates together will be a reflection of the leadership style of the supervisor. This is another point at which the Designer must realize that the work is being done for the supervisor and the organization and that the design process should not interfere with the work situation.

If the needs have been clearly listed, it is possible to have the list circulated among all those concerned and have them return it with comments. This is particularly appropriate when the group to be involved is either spread geographically or has different work schedules. This can be expected to be more prevalent as we explore more forms of alternative work scheduling.

A factor of privacy enters here. It may not be desirable to have everybody know the needs of all the others. One way this can be accommodated is by giving each subordinate the list of only their needs. Obviously the supervisor will have to react to the list of all the needs of all the subordinates.

Where training is involved, it is relatively easy to provide each of the possible learners with the appropriate list. For education, we must once again separate those who are currently employees in the organization from those who will be employed in the future. For those who are currently employees, the list of their learning needs should be reviewed by their potential supervisors. For those who are not currently employed by the organization, there is a role for the personnel office. The needs for somebody who will do the job should be directly related to the recruitment and selection efforts of the personnel office. As the people in this office have had experience, their feedback could indicate factors that must be considered in proceeding with the design process.

Decisions

Before proceeding, the Designer must obtain specific answers to the following questions, and the decisions implied in each:

1.   If the needs are met, will job performance become acceptable?

Assuming that the identified needs are met, what will happen to job performance? It is possible to satisfy needs, and yet have little or no effect on job performance. If this were to happen, the training program would have been meaningless.

In responding to this question, it may become apparent that the problem lies in what was indicated under "Specify Job Performance." That data may have looked good at the conclusion of the previous event but, on reevaluation it is obvious that something on the job has to be changed.

2.   If the needs are met, will the problem be solved?

This skips over the previous event and ties the identified needs into the previously identified problem. If the needs are met through learning, will the problem stated at the end of "Identify the Needs for the Organization" be solved? Of course, much more must happen before the final answer to this question is evident, but at this time speculation is in order. If meeting the needs will not solve the problem, why go further?

3.   How important are the needs?

There are times when a process develops a momentum of its own. This can easily happen during the design process. It is possible to "Specify Learning Needs," but the listing may not be significant enough to warrant further action. One important aspect is, of course, the financial one. Would the benefits be worth the cost? There is no easy response. Even if the benefits to be gained are below the cost to be incurred, it may still be desirable to provide the learning. Cost should not be the only factor, though it may be the main one. The decision on this should rest with the supervisor and management, not with the Designer.

4.   Should the job be redesigned?

The needs may be valid, but performance might be improved through job redesign. This was raised in the previous event and becomes more significant here. Under "Specify Job Performance," the Designer was looking at the job, no matter who performed it. Now we have data on those who are performing. Perhaps some minor redesign of the job would be more appropriate than providing training for people.

5.   Should tasks be reallocated?

The Designer may have uncovered strengths among the subordinates that were not previously known. There could be employees who have compentencies in exactly the areas needed, but who are not doing that part of the job. Rather than train, some reassignment of the tasks within the unit might improve overall job performance of that unit.

6.   Should subordinates be transferred rather than trained?

This is an extension of the earlier question. Perhaps the competencies that have surfaced during this event indicate that some subordinates can make a more effective contribution to the organization and get more job satisfaction, if they were in other units. The answer to this must start with the subordinate and the supervisor. Then, it might require some counseling by the personnel people to identify a more appropriate placement of the subordinate within the organization. The supervisor cannot do this counseling, for even if he had counseling skills, he would not know where other jobs exist in the organization or vacancies are anticipated. The Designer should likewise avoid counseling at this point, even if he has the skills, for the same reason.

7.   What is the availability of the learners?

If all agree on this list and the needs, what are the constraints in the situation? These will have to be explored further in the other events, but are included here as part of the decision-making process.

The supervisor who will assign the subordinate to the learning (if it is to be off the job) must indicate the shortest and longest times that that person can be spared. Also, if there are any factors that make certain days or times less desirable than others, they should be noted. In an extreme case, the list may indicate vast needs, but the supervisor will only allocate one hour a week for three weeks. If so, this suggests a different problem than the one under scrutiny. It could also mean that the supervisor is not committed to training as a response, although nothing has been said previously.

For education, this is the point where a decision may be made to have the new employees enter into a learning assignment before they proceed to the job assignment. That should be decided at this point as it will influence the design work and the decisions for the other events.

CONCLUSION

If there are positive decisions about the preceding questions, the Designer can then proceed to "Determine Objectives."

REFERENCES

1.   At the time this is being written, there is no single book on "Quality Circles" (QC) that tells the whole story. There are many people who are given, or take, credit for the concept. Mr. Ichiro Miyauchi is a Japanese QC expert and he defines the QC as a small work group which meets regularly to perform quality control activities *voluntarily* (his emphasis) within the same workshop. (As reported in the *APO News,* February, 1981, p. 6.)

2.   The article referred to is, "Training People Before Hiring: Sounds Funny but Saves Money." *Training: The Magazine of HRD.* January 1977, pp. 28–29, 32. Obviously the article referred to education not training, but the editor did not consult the author before dreaming up that title for the article.

3.   For material on case studies, and other learning strategies, see the chapter on "Select Learning Strategies."

ADDITIONAL PRINTED RESOURCES

None is listed here for there are few books that are devoted only to the action under this event. There are several books, which are listed at the ends of other chapters, that contain a chapter or at least some material about needs.

6

Determine Objectives

We now come to the event (see Figure 6-1) that has caused more controversy and conflict than any other aspect of designing training programs. Before 1960, learning programs used objectives but with a wide range of flexibility. There was the work of Bloom et al. [1] which constituted a significant attempt to clarify the area of learning objectives. Then, in the early 1960s, we felt the impact of Skinner and those who followed his approach to objectives [2]. Their insistence was on "specific behavioral objectives," and no deviation was allowed.

Over the years, the inevitable mellowing and cross-fertilization has taken place. There is no question about the need for objectives, but there is also no one form or method that satisfies the requirements of all people and all programs.

By the end of this event, the Designer will be able:

To identify the elements that must be considered in determining objectives for the program and for the individual learning experiences.

To list the specific program objectives and learning objectives related to the design under consideration.

Before proceeding further we need a brief discussion of terms. Some have endeavored to distinguish between terms such as program and course. In the past, I have been among them. I must concede that there is so little agreement that it would be counterproductive to attempt it in this book. Generally a course is considered a single learning experience which stands by itself, with a determined beginning and end. A program is usually a series of courses.

This definition may suffice for colleges and universities, but it cannot be directly applied to the HRD field. Indeed, it is questionable if that distinction would be helpful. Therefore, as we proceed with the CEM, the term *program* will be used to identify the learning experience being designed. Whether it will consist

THE CRITICAL EVENTS MODEL

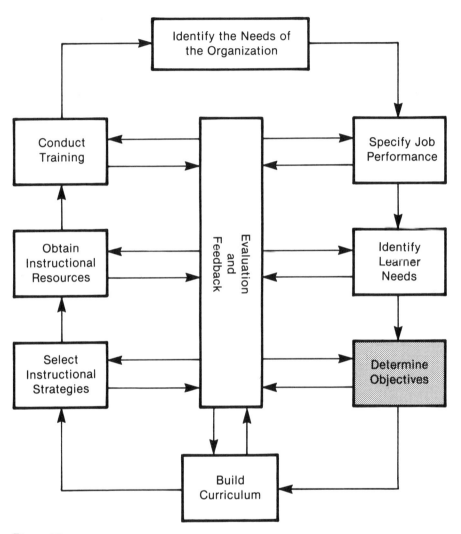

Figure 6.1

of more than one learning experience cannot be determined until a later event of the CEM.

For this event, two areas must be explored and decisions must be made. The first regards the overall program and how it relates to solving the previously identified problem. It can be said that the general objective is to have a program that will solve the problem. More specifically, the second area and decision relates to the specific learning experiences. That is the point at which the objectives will move to the more specific.

WHAT ARE OBJECTIVES?

An objective is the statement of what is to be accomplished by an activity. We could engage in lengthy polemics concerning objectives, goals, and purposes, and some have done this. Perhaps, at times, it is important to make the distinction. Of more value to the Designer is the understanding of what an objective is, how it is developed, and how it can be used.

A training program does not start with objectives. Before we can explore objectives, it is necessary to have successfully completed the previous events of the CEM. At the end of the previous event, we were able to develop a list of needs. These were *not* objectives, but our objectives arise from the needs identified during the previous event.

Objectives are only words put together by people. As such, they are subject to the usual misinterpretations that arise in any human communication. It has been said that meaning is in people, not in words. We try to get agreement on what we mean by reducing our thoughts to words (as I am doing in this book). If you and I could dialogue together on each phase of these events, I am sure we would have less trouble in communicating. We have not yet reached that stage of technology for general use, therefore we still rely on books like this one. As our technology increases, it is not unlikely that "readers" will be able to interact directly with "authors." Meanwhile let us deal within the present limitations.

Some contend that the process of developing objectives can be more significant than the end result—the written objectives. To "Determine Objectives" we go through a processes involving people and data. It is not a straight line process but an evolving one, with many twists and turns. The Designer should not be put in the position of having to write the objectives, and then have to try to defend them. "Determine Objectives" should not be viewed as an adversary proceeding.

It is deceptively easy for the Designer to take the needs identified in the previous event and then write objectives. These become the Designer's objectives and not necessarily those of the organization or the learner. At some point, the Designer must take the available data and actually write some objectives to test out understanding and seek agreement. This should not be done too early in this event, for pushing to premature closure can produce hostility which may block effective agreement on objectives.

When considering objectives, the Designer looks ahead in the CEM and recognizes that the form and content of the written objectives will dramatically influence whatever follows. Specific behavioral objectives are helpful in evaluation, but can wreak havoc with curriculum or instructional strategies. Objectives written in specific behavioral terms do not generally allow for the serendipity and spontaneity that some people require in a learning situation.

Decisions about the form of the written objectives must reflect a variety of factors, including the learner, the organization, the material to be learned, and the extent of the performance change being sought. Underlying all of these is the value system and concepts of the Designer, as influenced by all those factors. There are many learning theories, and we will be looking at some of them in the next event. Even here, however, the Designer must have some idea of the learning theory that might be most appropriate.

A major use of objectives is in evaluation. Indeed, the more specific the objectives, the easier to evaluate the learning and performance. The objectives should be written with evaluation in mind. The Designer must conjecture, "How will we be able to determine if that objective has been reached?" We will not have to actually face this decision until the "Conduct Training" element of the CEM, but it must be considered at this point.

DEVELOP PROGRAM OBJECTIVES

To develop program objectives, the Designer starts with the needs identified in the previous event. The first step is to organize these needs into a priority listing.

Priorities

The development of a listing of the needs, according to priorities, starts with agreement on what is a priority. There are many ways to look upon such a categorization, and the Designer must know the needs of the individual and the organization in order to establish categories of priorities.

It is unlikely that all the needs that have been previously identified can be satisfied in any one program. This does not mean that the needs are not valid, but that there are constraints that limit the possibility ·of meeting all the needs. However, all the previously identified needs are valid if the prior event was successfully completed, but since not all the needs can be satisfied, priorities become essential.

One way of listing priorities is by *time*. The whole design process started with an organizational problem for which HRD could be a response. How soon must that problem be solved? If it is in manufacturing and the process is producing defective output, time is of the essence. Unless the production line can be closed down, every item produced could be defective. It is important to provide the necessary training as soon as possible so as to decrease or eliminate rejects.

Another priority listing might consider the use of *resources*. What would it take, in the way of company resources, to provide the training program? We have already discussed the cost-benefit aspect. Here we are concerned with when the resources can be made available? Each organization has its own cycle of cash flow, for example, and the need for cash for training could determine the priority classification.

Availability of personnel could influence the priority classification. If the proposed program is for salespeople, and they are out in the field, certain of the needs might have to be delayed until those people are available.

Within any given organization, other items determine priorities. The Designer must determine these before devoting too much time to needs that could have a low priority. Rather than attempt to present specific classifications, let us generally explore other factors that could influence or determine priorities.

The question might arise as to how often a specific performance, related to a need, is required. It could be a need, but one where the performance is demonstrated only rarely, or will not be required at all until some future time.

The possible learners could also become a priority consideration. We have pointed out the problem of availability. There is also a factor of sensitivity. If there is a vote for a union on the horizon, this could be the wrong time to provide some kinds of training or education. If the company is issuing statements to the public and the press about its deteriorating market position, that could influence which needs are best met at this time.

Factors outside the organization also influence priorities. If the organization is under attack from consumer groups, government agencies, or competitors, the range of needs that can be satisfied would be different from a situation where there is no such attack. Previously I have emphasized that the Designer must know the direction of movement of the organization to keep the training and education relevant. The Designer must also be aware of those external forces that could cause a shift in priorities of needs.

Training, generally, means that the individual must be away from the job. Although we could consider some individualized learning on the job site, this is not yet common enough to be given great consideration, but it is a factor that must be explored. If there is a priority, but the individual cannot be away from the job, the Designer might consider using individualized instruction. If so, this should be explored at this point, for it will influence the objectives as well as all the other events of the CEM that follow. Given the limitations of individualized instruction, the priorities may have to be altered.

After priorities have been determined, the needs should be listed to reflect the priorities. Note that it is not the objectives that are listed, for they have not yet been determined. First, the needs are listed. Then, it may become apparent to the Designer that not all the needs can be met and that perhaps it is wasteful to devote time to writing objectives for all the needs when it is obvious that they cannot all be included in the proposed program.

In refining the needs, prioritizing and examining, the Designer may find that some needs can be combined. This should be done cautiously, so as not to weaken the priority listing. Where needs are very similar or overlapping, the grouping process can be helpful in making program decisions. When we move to the learning level, we will have to revert back to the original needs listing.

Process

The Designer should never determine objectives in a vacuum. It is relatively easy to sit at one's desk, carefully writing objectives, but there is always the risk of producing irrelevant statements. Determining (and writing) objectives is a process in which the written material is the result. If the Designer alone writes the objectives and passes them around for review and reaction, it puts the other members of the organization into a conflict mode. Not all conflict is bad, but this one could be. The Designer is not the only one with a vested interest in the final objectives. Therefore others in the organization need to be involved in the process of determining the objective.

The most crucial people are the supervisors. The supervisor is the one who must make the learner available, and is frequently the one who must devote some resources (usually financial) to the the learning. It is most important as the supervisor is the one who is directly concerned with the ultimate performance change which results from the learning.

In a sense, the same can be said for managers. They are concerned, by definition, with the performance of the supervisors in their area. If the objectives are for the purpose of changing performance, some managers will want to be involved. For training, involving the managers is important to make sure that the objectives are consonant with other planning that the managers are doing.

In one company, at this event, the objectives were concerned with a selling strategy that would create a high demand for a particular item the company was selling. The planned training was to provide the sales staff with more skills and knowledge about the product, market, and so on. The objectives were carefully drafted with the assistance of the district sales managers as well as the sales supervisors. Fortunately, in this case, the Designer urged that the objectives be reviewed at the next higher level of the organization.

This recommendation was not usually made, although the Designer had urged similar action in previous design work. This time somebody listened. The draft objectives were sent to a higher level for review and came back with a resounding negative response. After blood pressures returned to normal, the Designer, managers, and supervisors asked for reasons. It was simple, after explanation by the higher levels. There were to be some significant changes in market strategy of the organization. Until the higher levels had clarified their strategy, it would not be appropriate to design and conduct the training being considered.

Upper management had not yet reached full agreement on the changes or how they would be implemented. Until that time, everything was in a hold position. This had not been communicated earlier, as management did not want to risk leaks. At this time, however, management had to take action to delay the training program until their decisions were made and communicated.

A common problem, particularly in the mid-1960s to mid-1970s, was in education programs for minority groups. The general program objective was to provide learning to enable selected minority groups to move to higher level positions in organizations. These objectives were infrequently stated in such specific terms. The managers and higher level officials made broad commitments in speeches and interviews. Designers, caught up in the sweep and pleased to be asked by managers and executives, wrote program objectives focusing on minorities moving ahead in the work force.

For the supervisors, such objectives came as a shock. Supervisors discovered, when they reviewed the objectives, that they were to provide for the promotion of their better minority employees. This meant, to the supervisors, losing a good employee and having to deal with a replacement who would be an unknown quantity.

As program objectives have very often been overlooked or ignored, supervisors did not pay too much attention. The confrontation came when the minority employee completed the education program and sought the promotion. The supervisor, not having accepted the program objectives, had looked upon the learning as a way of increasing present performance. The problem could have been avoided if the supervisors had been involved in determining the program objectives.

At this point in determining program objectives it is not necessary to involve the potential learner, though there is no harm in doing so. Considering the possible disruption and cost incurred in any design process, the Designer should take a conservative approach.

Some benefit is to be gained by involving the potential learner. It relates to whether the employee knows what to do and has the skill, but is not performing as desired because the standard for performance was not adequately communicated. If the Designer has been checking this out from the start of the CEM, this step could be redundant at this time.

SKILLS, KNOWLEDGE, AND ATTITUDE

There are a variety of ways to begin to convert needs into objectives. One generally accepted pattern is to explore the skills, knowledge, and attitudes (SKA) that relate to the needs and the requisite learning. Though there is not complete agreement on this approach, it is so generally used that the Designer should be cognizant of it.

If you look for SKA in many of the books on educational psychology or related disciplines, you will find other words. The relationship is:

skill   = psychomotor
knowledge = cognitive
attitude   = affective

Generally they are referred to as the three domains of learning. Some purists may wish to argue as to which are the more appropriate terms, but little can be accomplished by such a discussion. Rather, the Designer must recognize the three areas/domains and watch for them in the literature, as well as being concerned with them when developing objectives.

The word "learning" is generally difficult to define, but let us explore it here for purposes of clarity. It must be contrasted with performance. *Learning* is the process of *acquiring* some new skill, attitude, or knowledge. *Performance* is *using* the skill, attitude, or knowledge. The obvious difference is between acquisition and utilization. Not all learning is acquired with a use in mind, yet it is probable that all learning in some way influences performance. In training situations, we are concerned with the direct linkage between learning and performance.

Can performance change without learning? This is a difficult question to answer. Theoretically this is not possible. Individuals cannot perform that which they have not learned. The problem is that we are not sure exactly how learning takes place, or what a person has learned in the past. Therefore we may suddenly find new performance, without an identified prior experience, because the learning had taken place at some earlier but unidentified time.

How about behavior? Generally the terms *behavior* and *performance* are used interchangeably. In more recent years, the emphasis has been on the word "performance," particularly as signifying something observable. At one time, this was the definition used for behavior, or termed behavior. You will find managers who say, "I don't care how the employee behaves, I am interested in performance!" It would be of little use to begin a semantic argument over the use of the words. In essence, both the manager and the Designer are seeking the same end—the performance that relates to what the employee is doing on the job.

The relationships are depicted in Figure 6-2. The total container represents the potential that every individual is born with. As has often been said, very few of us use a significant level of our own potential. Into this potential, flow two different kinds of learning. One is experience, which comes from living and adapting to our environment and to the forces with which we are constantly in contact. The result of these contacts is *incidental learning.* We do not start out with needs and objectives, but we do continually learn.

The other source is composed of the activities we undertake with the express purpose of learning, and this is *intentional learning.* Training, education, and development are all aspects of this (though in the CEM we are concerned mainly with training, somewhat with education, and not at all with development). Within each individual, the two kinds of learning are continually mixing and interacting.

The result is the *possibility* of a change in some kind of performance. Many factors influence that possibility. A major factor is the personality of the individual—that internal force that limits what one will let himself do or do differently. The external force is the culture which either encourages or discourages certain kinds of performance. These factors act as a spigot, turning performance on and off. Therefore the individual can learn, but may still not be able to perform because of the factors in the spigot.

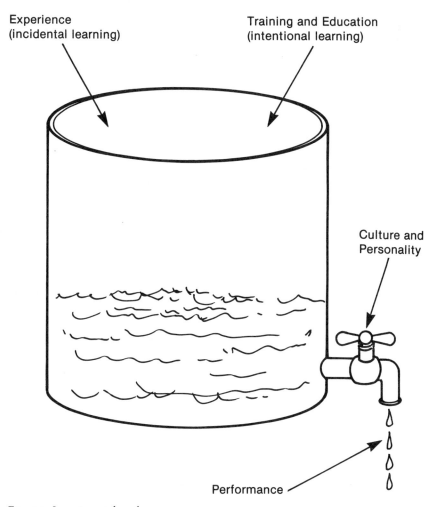

Experience
(incidental learning)

Training and Education
(intentional learning)

Culture and
Personality

Performance

Fig. 6.2 Learning and performance.

Given this, we will now look at SKA in terms of providing intentional learning.

Skills

Skills are generally thought of as an area that relates to blue-collar or production line workers. This is erroneous. An executive who cannot write a good letter lacks skill in letter writing. There is a skill element in delegating and in other performance required of executives and managers.

Learning a skill requires practice. It is impossible to learn a skill by listening to somebody talk about it, by seeing a demonstration, or reading a book. Skill, by definition, implies action of some kind.

It is easier to write learning objectives for skill-related learning than for the other domains. As skills are observable, they can be stated more specifically than the other two categories of learning.

Knowledge

Most learning involves some kind of knowledge. Knowledge itself does not change performance, though it may have some influence. If there were a direct relationship between knowledge and performance, it would be easy to change the latter. Merely have people learn the "right way" or the "truth," and they would all perform in the acceptable manner. Reality teaches us that such is not the case. Knowledge may be power, but it does not necessarily change performance. I cannot subscribe to the old cliche, "to know is to do."

This does not mean that knowledge is not important. Quite the contrary. Most of us want to know the why of an expected performance. We are not robots and do not want to be treated as such. There are times when we seek more knowledge than we can ever use. Such thirst should not be discouraged but must be balanced against the problem, expected performance, the needs of the learner, and the resources available.

In the next event ("Build Curriculum") we will be faced with the specific question of what knowledge needs to be included. At this event, we are focusing on how knowledge relates to the learning objective.

Attitude

This is the most controversial area of learning. There are *behaviorists* (Skinner, et al.) who insist that as you cannot observe or measure attitudes, they cannot be learned. The *behavioral* people, (Lewin, Rogers, et al.) contend that attitudes are crucial to most of human performance. It is not necessary to take a fixed position on either end of this debate. Rather, there is a spectrum, a range of possibilities. I tend to believe (the result of my values and attitudes) that attitudes are important even though not always observable. There has been some interesting work done on identifying and even measuring values and attitudes, if the reader is interested in pursuing this further [3].

Of more immediate concern is the direct relationship of attitudes to performance. The question is frequently posed as, "Shouldn't we change attitudes in order to change performance?" This is one of those questions that does not have a single, simple, direct response.

There are valid, and strong, arguments on both sides. Some insist that learning must precede any change in attitude, to bring about performance change. Others, equally adamant, contend that performance can change and then people will learn to rationalize their attitudes to conform with the new performance. Both are right! Each of us can probably cite examples to substantiate either possibility. Neither position can stand entirely on its own. When we are dealing with attitudes, we are encountering an area that is much more deeply part of the individual than is the case with either skills or knowledge.

It does not mean that we should ignore attitudes. They are essential to performance, unless we want to adopt the stance that the supervisor can say, "I don't care whether you like it or not, just do it." At one time, that was the essential behavior of the supervisor or foreman. In the world today, such behavior on the part of the supervisor would be severely criticized and even punished.

When exploring the needs that relate to attitudes, the Designer must proceed cautiously. Some people react in forceful and even violent ways when their basic attitudes are subjected to scrutiny. This was evident during the decades of the 1960s and 1970s when, for the first time, minority groups were introduced into factories and offices that had previously never known a Black or Hispanic. Women, as a minority, can attest to some of the treatment they received when the managerial suites were opened to females, in greater numbers than ever before.

Programs in those volatile areas could not rely only on knowledge. They had to address attitudes, though the objectives may have been stated in other terms. Many programs were offered as "a means of complying with the law." People were not asked to change their attitudes, but were required to change their performance to comply with the law. As we now know, not all such efforts met with success.

DEVELOPING LEARNING OBJECTIVES

As some point, the needs must be converted into objectives. As we have seen, the first step is to write the broad program objectives. These must then be reduced to more usable items, frequently referred to as *specific behavioral objectives*. We will do some of that, in this book, but there are many sources one can go to in order to develop competency in writing such objectives. More important is the process and thought that goes into producing the learning objective. The writing is the end result.

Mediation

Learning objectives do not exist in a vacuum. The actual objective must reflect certain realities of the learning situation. One aspect is how the learning will be delivered. Given advances in technology, we now refer to machine-mediated learning and instructor-mediated learning.

Machine-mediated instruction achieved its greatest impetus with the introduction of teaching machines. This is usually dated in the early 1960s, but I recall a conference of the American Society for Training and Development, in the mid-1950s, where teaching machines were being demonstrated. Of course they were primitive, but they did exist. In the 1960s, partly because of increased interest by the military, the market grew and the machines became more sophisticated. General acceptance was delayed until the development of the microprocessors, portable computer terminals, and other devices that made machine-mediated instruction more available. For the most part, we now have machines that are related to computers, though it is still possible to have free-standing learning machines.

When the learning is machine-mediated, the objectives must be very specific. One reason is that the machine can only do what is programmed into it, and the program must relate to previously agreed upon objectives. Once the machine is being used, there is a limit to flexibility. The more sophisticated machines can allow for branching and other alternatives, but we are still limited to those alternatives that have previously been entered into the machine.

Although the decision on the delivery system (that is, mediation) will not be made until later in the design process, some thought must be given to it at this point. If machines are to be used, the objectives must be as specific as language allows.

Where the program is to be *instructor-mediated*, the objectives need not be quite so specific. It is not suggested that there be no objectives, or poorly written objectives, but the level of specificity is not as crucial. When the instructor is a professional, overly specific objectives might even prove to be a hindrance. If nothing else, the self-image of the professional instructor requires some influence over the learning situation, and some flexibility in meeting the objectives.

There is one form of instructor-mediated learning that requires objectives that are more specific, though limited. This is a system referred to as Peer-Mediated-Learning (PML). As is obvious from the label, it is using an instructor who is not a professional but who will have responsibility for conducting the learning experience. This approach has many benefits, but also some limitations. If PML is to be used, the objectives should be very specific, but also very limited. Unless we want to try to make the peer a professional, which defeats the reason for using peers, we cannot expect the peer to have the flexibility inherent in the performance of a professional instructor.

If it is possible, at this point in the CEM, to have a decision on the mediation approach to be used, it will faciliate writing the learning objectives. If such a decision is not possible at this time, the Designer must proceed to write objectives based on what appears to be the possible form of mediation. It is essential that the Designer indicate the probable forms of delivery, for without identifying that aspect it is not possible to know the level of specificity required for the learning objectives.

Writing Learning Objectives

We now come to actually writing the learning objectives. Note that there has been a good deal of discussion and exploration before we come to the actual writing—and there will be still more. Too many people think that the major activity is to sit and write, to find the exact words, and then the learning objectives will be meaningful and helpful. That is not the case. The written learning objective is the end result of a good deal of work and interpersonal activity.

A useful learning objective will be stated in terms of the desired outcome, not what has to be done to achieve that outcome. The objective should not describe content or practice. For the kinds of learning programs we are concerned with in this book, we can say that the learning objective must indicate the performance of the learner at the end of the learning experience.

There are lists of categories for the cognitive (knowledge) and affective (attitude) domains. The list for the psychomotor (skills) is still being developed. It is good to know, and at times can be useful but on a practical level, very few Designers go into that much detail. The relevant books are listed in the bibliography and the Designer is encouraged to go to them repeatedly. Experience has shown, however, that many Designers get frustrated because they have neither the time nor the requisite academic background to make these lists useful. This is not to deprecate Designers, for the same could be said of the "curriculum advisors" in school systems who are not using the domains at a more than superficial level.

A way of focusing the emphasis on the end result of the learning is to start the list of learning objectives with a preamble which states, "By the end of this learning experience, the learner will be able to . . . ."

This emphasizes that the focus is on the learner, not the instructor. It also underscores the requirement to look at the completion of the learning experience and the performance that is expected at that time.

Three components should appear in an objective:

1. Performance
2. Condition
3. Criterion

Performance is stated in terms of what the learner will be able to do by the end of the learning experience. It is easier to state what the instructor will do during the experience, but that is not the purpose of the learning activity. The expected outcome is the change of performance by the learner, not by the instructor. This does not mean that an instructor may not learn during the experience, but that is not the objective.

The objective is stated in terms of the observable and measurable whenever possible. As the focus is on performance, the objective should not contain any statement about content, instructional strategies or any other factors that indicate how the learning will take place.

The second component is *condition*, which specifies the limitations or constraints under which the performance is expected to take place. Note that these are not the limitations of the learning situation, but of the terminal performance. Terminal is the final performance in the learning situation, before actual use on the job. That is when a significant evaluation step must occur, as we will see later in the CEM.

If the condition statement reflects an understanding of the job, it limits the loss through transfer of learning when the learner takes the new performance back to the job site. The condition should state the actual tool or tools to be used in performance. The Designer, in effect, is checking out with the supervisor if that is the actual condition under which the job is performed. It avoids the situation where the learner says, "If I had this tool back on the job, sure I could do it the way they want."

It keeps the learning center relevant (in tools and equipment) as related to the job site where the performance will take place. It also recognizes any limitations that actually exist in the job area as contrasted with what the textbooks say should be happening.

A condition might be that, "the learner/manager conducts the performance appraisal on company time in a private but informal locale." Many managers would immediately scoff at such a condition as being realistic. They would prefer to take some employees out to the local bar or a restaurant after work for the appraisal conference. To take an employee away from the work situation, during hours, may be disruptive to the work. If it is done on company time, where is the private but informal locale? Many offices are using open space arrangements and other features which eliminate private space.

For one organization, that condition may be exactly what is happening, but for a different organization it may be completely unrealistic. That is why a Designer cannot borrow objectives, particularly the condition component, from outside the organization. The condition statement must represent, as closely as possible, the conditions under which the actual performance is to take place.

This will present a problem later, when we evaluate the learning, in that the learning situation, by its very nature, is not the work situation. Therefore we will have to be very careful about what we are actually evaluating. Without this written condition, however, evaluation becomes difficult, if not impossible.

Another factor to be considered in the condition statement is time. When the performance is time constrained, this should be reflected in the written statement. For production-related learning, the time component is easy to identify and to put into writing. For service-related learning, this is sometimes possible. An example would be a statement which contains the performance requirement of being able to serve "six tables during designated peak hours and nine tables in nonpeak hour times."

For managerial performance, time may be difficult to establish, except for some tasks. A time condition for a manager might be to be able to prepare a periodic written report "within two hours after the initial data have been provided." We all know that the management of time is crucial for managers, but until we have better standards, the condition objectives for such programs remain difficult to write.

The third component is *criterion*, or stating what is acceptable performance. Under the first component we were only looking for performance, and under the second component the conditions under which that performance should occur. Now we look at how well the learner is expected to perform. Presumably we are looking for 100% performance, where it is measurable. The question is whether 100% performance is necessary. Before we ask whether the learner can produce that level of performance, there is a prior question: Is 100% necessary? What is the leeway, the plus or minus, which would still be acceptable performance for the individual and the organization?

It is a waste of resources to bring people up to a level of performance that is not required. This is a difficult area to determine, even for measurable jobs. Quality manufacturing dictates a zero defect policy and for some manufacturing processes this is not only desirable, but essential. For others, a certain deviation from tolerance is permissible.

When we are dealing with jobs that are less measurable, such as managerial and some service jobs, criteria are much more difficult to state. The Designer should not err by writing criteria that are not acceptable to the organization. During the design process, actually the Designer may highlight a problem in the organization—the lack of criteria for performance of some jobs.

Criteria are part of both quantity and quality. Therefore the written objective should contain both elements, to the degree possible. This is the component that provides the greatest area of confrontation for some jobs. Perhaps this is the reason that some managers shy away from written objectives for learning. Such objectives require a specificity that has not previously been stated. It is not unusual to find, at this time in the CEM, that the problem identified earlier can be readily solved by being specific about the quality and quantity expected on a job.

There is another possible side effect about which the Designer should be aware. If supervisors, managers, and other personnel feel insecure about being specific on quality and quantity, hostility can arise at this point. This hostility frequently takes the form of opposing all HRD because the program cannot show a cost-benefit result. In other words, the Designer cannot quantify because the supervisors and managers have not quantified. Some managers and supervisors are realistic enough to realize that they cannot oppose learning generally, but they can stay as far away from the HRD operation as possible to avoid having to be specific.

It is not a totally bleak picture. Those individuals can be encouraged to see the benefit of stating the condition part of the objective in specific job-related terms. The situation must be approached cautiously so that it does not imply criticism of them.

Other supervisors and managers will welcome the help of the HRD people in surfacing a lack of specificity of which they were not aware. For these supervisors and managers, this part of the event can prove very helpful, and of course they will see the Designer and HRD as a help to management.

A useful tool for all three components is in the use of verbs. The Designer will find that if each component is stated as simply as possible, but always starting with a verb, writing objectives becomes a positive activity. Figure 6-3 presents a list of some of the common verbs that can be used. Selection of the particular verb that is acceptable to all is one way of assuring that the written objective will be useful—and used.

EVALUATION AND FEEDBACK

After the objectives have been written and discussed, the E&FB will take place. Of course, there may well have been some E&FB during the event, but it is also important to conclude the event with specifics.

We start by looking back at the objectives of this event, which were that by the end of this event the Designer will be able:

To identify the elements that must be considered in determining objectives for the program and for the individual learning experience.

To list the specific program objectives and the learning objectives related to the design under consideration.

The first objective is related to the priorities and similar factors that the Designer will have explored. The second produces the written objectives.

Analysis

For analysis to take place, the written objectives must be shared with at least the supervisor, as well as the managers and learners if possible.

Stimulus Responding	Motor Chaining	Verbal Chaining	Multiple Discriminating	Concepts	Principles	Problem Solving
associate	activate	cite	choose	allocate	anticipate	accommodate
gave a word for	adjust	copy	compare	arrange	calculate	adapt
grasp	aline	enumerate	contrast	assign	calibrate	administer
hold	close	letter	couple	catalog	check	adjust to
identify	copy	list	decide	categorize	compile	analyze
indicate	(dis)assemble	quote	detect	characterize	compute	compose
label	(dis)connect	recite	differentiate	classify	conclude	contrive
lift	draw	record	discern	collect	construct	correlate
locate	duplicate	reiterate	distinguish	file	convert	create
loosen	insert	repeat	divide	grade	coordinate	develop
move	load	reproduce	isolate	group	correct	devise
name	manipulate	(re)state	judge	index	deduce	diagnose
pick up	measure	transcribe	pick	inventory	define	discover
place	open	type	recognize	itemize	demonstrate	find a way
press	operate		select	match	design	invent
pull	remove			mate	determine	realize
push	replace			order	diagram	reason
recognize	stencil			rank	equate	resolve
repeat	trace			rate	estimate	study
reply	tune			reject	evaluate	synthesize
respond	turn off/on			screen	examine	think through
rotate				sort	expect	troubleshoot
say				specify	explain	
set				survey	extrapolate	
slide				tabulate	figure	
signal					foresee	
tighten					generalize	
touch					illustrate	
turn					infer	
twist					interpolate	
					interpret	
					monitor	
					organize	
					plan	
					predict	
					prescribe	
					program	
					project	
					schedule	
					solve	
					translate	
					verify	

Source: Job Analysis for Human Resource Management: A Review of Selected Research and Development. U.S. Department of Labor. Manpower Research Monograph #36, 1974, page 33, (as adapted).

Fig. 6.3 Useful verb list for writing objectives.

The program objectives should be stated in terms that related to the original problem or purpose that triggered the CEM. The Designer may wish to actually restate the original problem, as agreed upon at the conclusion of "Identify Needs of the Organization." Although some of the same people will still be involved, time has passed and this particular program may not be the high priority for others that it has been for the Designer. It is also possible that there have been some changes in personnel since the initial event was concluded, so it is important that everybody is still in agreement on the original problem.

The Designer should present the learning objectives for analysis by providing written statements. One technique is to list them all, one after another, on the same page and then follow this listing with an individual page for each objective, double spaced. Having all the objectives on one page can appear overwhelming. The separate pages provide for the analysis and thought that is required at this part of the event. The double spacing enables the Designer to communicate that the words are not set in concrete or some other immutable form. Rather, they are being presented as the best thinking that the Designer has been able to gather during the event and are still subject to modification and change. The recipients of the analysis can do this by writing between the printed lines.

Learning objectives should be listed in some priority order. If possible, the Designer should have had supervisors and others contribute to this ranking during the event. The process of ranking is time consuming, as it requires several iterations, so it is best done before reaching E&FB. It there has been no other alternative, and ranking could not be done earlier, it must be done here. If it was done earlier, this would be the place to have the ranking reviewed.

In the analysis, the Designer indicates how each objective relates to what had previously been agreed upon under "Identify Learning Needs." Each need should have an objective, or a reason indicating why no objective was written for that need. If any objectives have been written which do not relate to a specific need, and this is possible, the Designer should indicate the basis for including that objective.

The Designer may also indicate the possible result of not meeting an objective. What performance would not change, or what need would not be met? It is unlikely that all objectives can be met, unless there are unlimited resources. Therefore what is the relative cost (not only in financial terms) of not meeting an objective? It is difficult to think negatively, but this could be helpful during the analysis phase of this event.

Feedback

As before, we must first consider who should be involved. The crucial person, once again, is the supervisor. The Designer may wish to provide the supervisor with the objectives and analysis for review prior to any meeting. The Designer cannot expect the supervisor to read and react immediately. The supervisor needs time to think about the objectives and perhaps even test them out. As the objectives relate specifically to how the job is done, the supervisor may prefer to review the objectives at the job site.

The supervisor may also find it helpful to review the objectives with the concerned employees. It would be more appropriate for the supervisor to do this than the Designer. As the objectives relate to the components of performance, conditions, and criteria, they also relate to how well the employee is actually performing. This is an important supervisory concern, rather than an activity for the Designer.

If possible, managers should also be involved, but the Designer should not be overly concerned if some managers indicate a lack of interest at this point. Some managers need not or cannot be concerned with the specifics of job performance, for to do so would be to function on a supervisory level. Managers should, however, be concerned with the program objectives, as they relate to the broader implications of jobs concerned with organizational goals, though the specific learning objectives might not be a concern of managers. For reasons of organizational politics, a Designer might choose to share the objectives with managers, but should not push for any direct response.

A complaint heard all too often is that there are too many meetings. Unfortunately the successful design experience requires meetings, but the Designer is cautioned to have them only when necessary. At this point in the design process, it may not be necessary to have a face-to-face meeting unless there are apparent areas of disagreement on the objectives.

If more than one work unit is involved, it could be necessary to bring together the supervisors of the various units. A meeting might be unavoidable, but before calling such a meeting, the Designer should determine that the benefits outweigh the negative response which might result from having to attend another meeting.

The one item that could require a meeting is the rank order of the learning objectives. The need could vary from one unit to another, depending upon a variety of factors including personnel, work schedules, production schedules, and locale. If a program involves more than one unit, the rank order of learning objectives will have to reflect a compromise that is best obtained through a face-to-face meeting.

Decisions

As a result of the E&FB some decisions can be made:

1. Are the program objectives acceptable?

The major focus here would be on agreement that the original problem still exists and in essentially the same form as earlier stipulated. If there has been any change of which the Designer is not aware, it must surface before proceeding further.

When several units are involved, it is possible that the program objectives are still valid for some but not for others. In a large organization, as the program objectives become clear, it can also become apparent that there are other units of the organization that could benefit by also being included.

2.   Are the learning objectives acceptable?

This is a more difficult decision to reach. The Designer should avoid having the supervisors and others involved turn this decision back to the Designer. This is sometimes done by saying, "Well, the objectives are too technical and contain all kinds of jargon, so why don't we leave it to the Designer?" This must not happen. If the supervisors do not feel comfortable with the objectives, there is a problem here and a land mine is being planted that could produce a crisis at a later time.

3.   Have all the needs been reflected in the objectives?

The answer to this could be in the negative and still be acceptable. As this event has been worked on, there could have been an earlier agreement that some of the needs were not as essential as they appeared to be. If this happened, it would have been indicated in the analysis, but should be agreed upon here.

4.   Is the priority of learning objectives acceptable?

The importance of the priority listing becomes apparent when the Designer moves to "Build Curriculum." At that time, it will probably become necessary to limit the number of objectives because of time and other factors. If the priority ranking is not agreed to now, the Designer will have to do additional work in the next event.

5.   Do the objectives relate to "Specify Job Performance?"

The purpose of the learning program is not only to meet needs, but to relate to job performance. Although, logically, through following the CEM, these should all be congruent, there is always the possibility that something went a bit off-track during the process. It is important to check continually. Therefore, at this time, it should be agreed that if the stated objectives are met, they will be congruent with the job performance that has been specified earlier.

6.   Can the objectives best be met internally or externally?

This is a difficult question to answer at this time, but it is one that must be asked. Once the objectives have been agreed upon, it is possible to have some general idea of the program needed. Perhaps learning programs or packages already exist on the open market that can meet the objectives. If so, the Designer can then move right to "Obtain Instructional Resources." If not, the next event would be "Build Curriculum." There is also the possibility of some combination.

CONCLUSION

Continuing on the assumption that the learning program will be essentially designed in-house and that the decisions have been positive, we can now proceed to "Build Curriculum."

REFERENCES

1. The basic book in the field was *Taxonomy of Educational Objectives*. Handbook I: Cognitive Domain. Benjamin S. Bloom, et al. (New York: David McKay Company, 1956). Since then Handbook II: Affective Domain has appeared (1964).

2. There are many sources and references for Skinner. Perhaps one of the most interesting, to get a feel for his theories, is *The Technology of Teaching*. (New York: Appleton-Century-Crofts, 1968). Be sure to read the acknowledgments, in front, as the various chapters do not appear in chronological order and therefore can be confusing.

3. See *The Nature of Human Values*. Milton Rokeach. (New York: Free Press, 1973). This book contains not only theory, but practical materials which can be used when exploring values.

ADDITIONAL PRINTED RESOURCES

Broadwell, Martin M. *The Supervisor as an Instructor: A Guide for Classroom Training*. Second Edition. Reading, Mass.: Addison-Wesley, 1970.

Loughary, John W., and Barrie Hopson. *Producing Workshops, Seminars, and Short Courses: A Trainer's Handbook*. Chicago: Follett Publishing, 1979.

Mager, Robert F. *Goal Analysis*, Belmont, Calif.: Fearon, 1972.

Mager, Robert F. *Preparing Instructional Objectives*. Second Edition. Belmont, Calif.: Fearon, 1975.

Pipe, Peter. *Objectives—Tools for Change*. Belmont, Calif.: Fearon, 1975.

Tracy, William R. *Designing Training and Development Systems*. New York: American Management Associations, 1971.

7

Build Curriculum

We are now at the point in the CEM (Figure 7-1) where the focus is on what is to be learned, and the sequence of the learning, which is a definition of the word *curriculum*. It is a word that has obviously been borrowed directly from school-based learning, but it is the word that best communicates what the Designer accomplishes in this event.

By the completion of the event, the Designer will be able:

1. To develop a specific list of the items to be learned in order to meet the previously determined objectives.

2. To list the order in which the learning is to take place.

There are other definitions of curriculum, but it would not contribute anything to our process to become involved in that semantic discussion. Perhaps, in the years to come, as the HRD field develops its own identity, a new word will emerge which will communicate more exactly what we mean today by the word curriculum.

CLARIFYING TERMS

Even within the field of K-12 learning (kindergarten through senior high school) there is confusion and a proliferation of terms when discussing curriculum. How much more so, then, can we expect to find that in the field of HRD? As people in HRD enter the field from a variety of disciplines, each brings his own terminology. Therefore, by defining a few terms now, those that are crucial to the curriculum building event, perhaps we can improve our communication and mutual understanding.

THE CRITICAL EVENTS MODEL

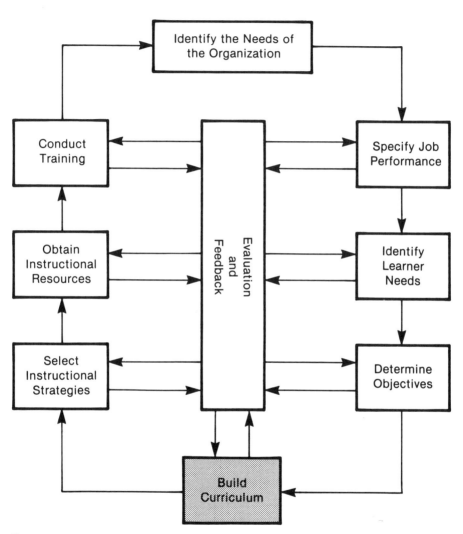

Figure 7.1

The term *syllabus* is sometimes used and can have several meanings. Generally the syllabus is the listing of the content which is to be learned. It contains the main topic headings, subheadings, and may possibly go to several levels of specificity. Indeed, the syllabus is the place where the listing of content should get as specific as possible. It does not indicate how the learning is to take place, only what is to be learned. The syllabus sometimes indicates the flow of the units. In that sense, it almost becomes synonomous with curriculum, and some people do use the terms interchangeably.

Another element are the *lesson plans,* and the term is used in the plural. Lesson plans set forth, very specifically, how the instructor will guide the learning situation. When a lesson is learner-centered, the lesson plan indicates what the learner will do. It is the actual road map to help the instructor and learner reach the determined objectives.

At a later point in this chapter, we will return to lesson plans in more depth, for that is one of the items that must result from the successful completion of this event.

One item is missing at this time and that is *instructional strategies,* or how the learning will take place. This is not an oversight but an important distinction. People in HRD have been accused, and rightly so, of being faddish and gimmicky. There has been a tendency to look for the latest media (or multimedia), the star speaker or presenter, the "hot" item, as shown at some of the recent conferences, conventions, and exhibits. There is nothing wrong with using any or all of these but the first decision is *what* is to be learned, and then we can explore *how* the learning is to take place. Instructional strategies address the how. They are important, so much so that a whole event ("Select Instructional Strategies") is set aside in the CEM, but not until we have completed "Build Curriculum."

This approach is based on the dictum of the architects who say that "function determines form." The function is the curriculum, and the form is the instructional strategy. Therefore we now proceed to clarify the function, or to build the curriculum.

Given the objectives that resulted from the previous event of the CEM, it is now possible for the Designer to start identifying what must be learned to reach the stated objectives. The curriculum, as built by the Designer, deals with skills, attitude, and knowledge. How this is stated is, in part, a reflection of the beliefs of the Designer and the nature of the subject matter. Some Designers prefer to list the curriculum in terms of SKA, while others are just as comfortable blending the three domains.

The objectives now serve as a checklist. Each of the stated learning objectives should be readily identifiable in the curriculum. Conversely there should not be any part of the curriculum that does not relate to an objective. The Designer can readily construct a matrix that illustrates this relationship, if needed.

THEORIES OF LEARNING

The curriculum, as built by the Designer, reflects a theory of learning. Some purists insist that the entire curriculum must reflect a unified theory, while more eclectic Designers feel comfortable in using different theories at different points of the curriculum. By the time an individual becomes a Designer, he has developed an identification with some of the theories that do influence his behavior.

At this time, all we have basically are *theories* of learning. There are many ways to look at a theory, but essentially it is much like the concept of a model which was discussed in Chapter 1. A theory is a way of explaining something which is essentially abstract, but for which we build a plausible explanation so we can use it. As such, theories are subject to change as we are able to move away from the abstract or find other explanations for previously accepted theories.

We do not have any options. We still know so little about how people learn that we cannot deal with *laws* of learning. At one time, what we now call theories were presented as laws, but the more the researchers worked on the laws, the closer we moved to replacing them with theories.

Given the range of theories, how do we get some kind of handle so we can understand and use them? Malcolm Knowles has been helpful in presenting *organismic* and *mechanistic* models [1].

The organismic approach is based on the concept of the learning environment as a living and changing element. This does not mean that there is no form, but rather that it is a changing and constantly altering situation. The emphasis in the organismic model is on process rather than product.

A common reference point is the use of the word *"behavioral"* when referring to the various theories in the organismic model. Some of the theorists associated with this model are John Dewey, Kurt Lewin, and Carl Rogers.

The mechanistic model is characterized by the stimulus-response approach. Learning is viewed as conditioning, with a strong emphasis on the quantification of the learning. Those who follow this model are often referred to as *behaviorists*. Theorists associated with this model are Edward L. Thorndike, I. P. Pavlov, and B. F. Skinner.

The field of learning theory is by no means this uncomplicated. Within the two models there are many theorists with differences in emphasis and approach. Some theories do not fit readily into either category. For the Designer, the problem is one of understanding enough about the various learning theories to be able to make distinctions and to use them effectively. It is not necessary to quote or cite some of the different and differing theorists, but the Designer must know enough about learning theory to know what has been researched and theorized in the past. There are proponents and opponents of every learning theory that exists. The Designer may not want to choose sides, but at times must make decisions as to which learning theory is most appropriate for a specific learning experience.

VARIABLES TO BE CONSIDERED

A curriculum cannot be built without recognition of some significant variables. These are factors, some of which are difficult to stipulate specifically, but all of which have an impact on the way the learning will be delivered. Although the ultimate delivery ("Conduct Training") is still ahead of us, we must consider some aspects of it at this time.

One variable is the *learner* who has had prior learning experiences before the one under consideration. The Designer cannot possibly know about all the learning experiences, but likewise, cannot ignore the culture of the learner or his prior experiences when designing the present one.

The following example comes from a university setting. In the mid 1960s, I was working in Ethiopia and had sent some Ethiopians to the United States for training. On their returns, I followed up to see how they would apply their learning. One returned participant had learned about programmed instruction (PI) in the United States and wanted to introduce PI into Ethiopia. This particular participant was associated with the Haile Selassie University (since renamed) and had identified a specific problem. Instruction was in English, but there were students who were inadequate in that language and, therefore, were a problem to themselves and the university. The participant planned to provide English instruction, through PI, to help increase English proficiency of the students at a nominal cost.

I expressed caution due to the previous experiences of the students. Coming from tribal societies, I reasoned, it was unlikely that they would be familiar with a self-instructional mode or the self-discipline required to complete PI successfully. My objections were overruled and the program instituted. A large number of students were gathered in a big hall, the PI material was distributed, and they were instructed to proceed. The material was of a high quality, previously tested and validated, and completely self-instructional.

Within a few days the campus erupted into a riot, something that was unknown at that time on a campus in Ethiopia. The students complained that the new instructional form was degrading. In other classes they had live instructors, but here they were forced to deal with faceless paper and they considered that an insult. The nature of the learner had been ignored. PI ultimately worked, but after a modification was introduced. Instructors were assigned to the large hall to sit there, on a platform, even though they did no instruction. This satisfied the cultural need of the learners.

Even in developed countries, Designers can expect to face similar issues though perhaps not as clear cut and dramatic. We still have a great deal to find out about learning styles, but we do know that some people are more visual, while others are more verbal. This will strongly influence a later event ("Select Instructional Strategies"), but it also has implications for the present event. The curriculum may have to be modified to be congruent with the self-image of the learners. Some topics may either have to be omitted or deemphasized for a particular group of learners.

The nature of the *instructor* must also be considered. If we are concerned with machine-mediated instruction, we will have to limit the curriculum as regards skills and attitudes, as has been previously discussed. Of course, as we gain more experience with machine-mediated instruction, it may become evident that we can include those two domains as easily as we can the knowledge area.

If the instructor is a subject matter specialist, there is more latitude allowable in the curriculum than when the instructor is not as well versed in the subject matter. At this time, the Designer can opt to include all the relevant subject matter and then see what conditions this creates to be considered under "Obtain Instructional Resources." The vision the Designer has of the instructor at this time influences what is to be included in the curriculum.

A third consideration is *geography,* or the relative distance between the instructor and the Designer. Some programs, once mounted, allow for almost no contact between the Designer and the instructor. With packaged programs there is usually no contact at all [2]. With some programs that are designed by a central HRD unit and then sent out to various parts of the company, contact is very limited. In the retail gasoline business, for example, central units design programs, which are then conducted in field offices or at the service stations themselves. The curriculum content is different, depending upon who the Designer envisions the instructor will be and how much contact the Designer and the instructor have while the program is being conducted.

SELECTING CONTENT

This is the part of the CEM where the Designer must recognize that he is not expected to know content. This can be difficult for a Designer to deal with. Each of us has ego needs, and it is sometimes difficult for some of us to acknowledge that there are areas we do not know. This is one of those times when it is essential to make this statement loud and clear. The Designer has something special to bring to the design process, but knowledge of content is not that unique contribution. The Designer should have high level of competency in design, using the CEM or other appropriate models, and should focus on design.

A particular trap becomes obvious when the content appears to be so generic that everybody should know it. This includes areas such as supervision or management and subareas such as motivation, leadership, and delegation. It can be difficult for the Designer to communicate to some managers that content knowledge in those areas changes, and though the Designer might endeavor to keep up to date, there are others who make those areas their specialty. They are more suited to be content people.

There are infrequent instances when the person who has been hired to design may also have subject matter expertise. There are still those organizations, as in the accounting field, that prefer to select an accountant for design work. If that has been the choice and the Designer knows that the job entails competency in both design and content, there is no conflict. Such people are rare, but it is possible for an organization to identify and select such people. It is not possible to put a value judgment on such a decision, whether it is good or bad. There are too many variables that must be considered, including whether or not the organization views design as an entry point for content people who will then move into the line organization.

Designers can get caught up in the subject matter to the point where they become encouraged to become specialists in content. In one situation, my wife and I worked with an organization in Malaysia which was concerned with cultivation of oil palms. We designed appropriate learning experiences, though both of us come from urban backgrounds. About six months after we returned home, we received an invitation to become members of an international consulting organization in the field of agriculture. We responded that we appreciated the invitation, but that our field was learning, not agriculture. They responded by noting that the program had received such glowing comments from those in the country, as well as from UN and other international agricultural experts, that we must know more agricultural content than we realized. We once again wrote, expressing our appreciation for their kind remarks, but noting that we preferred to be known as specialists in learning design and, therefore, could not accept their invitation. It was tempting, but we felt that such membership would communicate inappropriately to potential clients.

PEOPLE INVOLVED IN CONTENT

The Designer can, and generally does, rely on others for the content area. These other people are called Subject Matter Specialists (SMS), though the term Subject Matter Expert is also used.

There are various considerations for which the Designer can turn to an SMS. A major one is budget, which can dictate whether the Designer is restricted to internal people or can go outside the organization. Just because the Designer has the budget is no reason to go external, but it does provide the Designer with more options.

Internal People

In the earlier events of the CEM, the Designer may already have identified those people who could serve as internal SMSs. Supervisors are one such group, though they may not have the time to devote to this activity. Some supervisors might designate one of their subordinates to serve as an SMS.

Other internal SMS resources could be employees who have previously been in the same or similar learning experiences. Though by no means professionals, they could serve as an SMS in relating proposed content to the actual job.

Large organizations have R&D departments and other staff resources who might likewise provide an SMS. Small organizations might have such resources, but it is less likely. In some large organizations, an appropriate SMS might be working in another part of the organization, so arrangements are required to obtain the necessary inputs.

A variety of arrangements is possible. If the need is minimal, the Designer can just visit with the SMS and discuss the content required in this event. Other arrangements can allow for more time for an internal SMS to work with the Designer. All the arrangements should legitimize the use of internal SMSs by the Designer.

Another possibility is a *part-time assignment.* That is, the person is assigned to be an SMS for a specified number of hours or for a designated number of days. The SMS still remains with his original work unit, but meets with the Designer on an arranged schedule. When the SMS is involved in production, such an arrangement is essential, so that the supervisor knows when a job must be covered and for how long. This arrangement is similar to common work assignments found in a matrix organization.

It may not be possible, at the outset, to know the full extent of the assignment. The Designer should negotiate with the supervisor for a minimum time allotment, with the understanding that some additional time might be necessary. Depending on how such internal assignments are handled in the organization, the Designer could be required to provide the budget to cover the loss of time or the cost of a replacement for the employee used as an SMS by the Designer.

When the SMS is a high-level person, such as a manager, the arrangement can be more fluid. The manager could agree to be an SMS, but not prepare to allocate specific time slots. Managers, it is generally accepted, cannot control all of their time. They must be available to be responsive to problems. Planned meetings between the manager and the Designer may have to be canceled at the last moment due to a crisis or a call from the executive suite. This can be frustrating to the Designer, but if managers are used for SMS, this is part of the "price" that must be paid.

Another common arrangement is a *temporary assignment* where the SMS is released from the regular job and actually moves into the HRD unit. Such an assignment may be for several days, even several months, but usually it is for a stated period of time. Budget can be a factor, for the HRD unit may have to consider the SMS as a temporary employee for that period, with the salary or wage being charged to the HRD unit. Some companies' policies allow for such internal transfers without any charges, but this is becoming less common. The trend is towards making each unit of an organization, particularly in large organizations, an identifiable financial center for either cost or profit [3].

During the temporary assignment, it should be made clear that the SMS has not been drafted into the HRD unit and that there is no intent that this person will remain in the HRD unit. Sometimes an SMS opts to remain in the HRD unit, if there is a place for that person. This practice must be avoided, however, or the HRD unit will develop the reputation of being a "pirate." The result will be that, in the future, other units of the organization will not detail their best people as SMSs, for fear of losing them. The quality of SMS people will decline, with resultant damage to the design process.

External People

As used here, the term *external people* refers to all those outside of the organization who could be called upon to assist in selecting content. These people are frequently referred to as *consultants* though the more appropriate term would be *vendor*. There are essentially two groups: those who provide services and those who provide goods. But, of course, some provide both.

If the Designer is considering purchasing a program, seeking a vendor of goods is appropriate. Some of these vendors have packaged programs which have been widely tested. It is possible for the Designer to get the vendor's "track record"—to share in the experience of others who have used that vendor. We will return to these vendors later in this chapter when we discuss the question of "Make or Buy?"

The vendors of services can be extremely helpful at this point, for they can serve as SMSs. The Designer should select those who can function as content consultants, rather than as process consultants [4]. The content consultant should be able to provide input of specific content from which the Designer can select what he needs.

There are various kinds of external content people who can serve as SMSs. A frequently used group of people is professors from colleges and universities. One of the specified behaviors of such people is to keep in continued contact with the state of the art of their particular field. In addition, they are often required to do research of their own. This is supplemented by the research being done by their graduate students. Being in that position, the professors are an extremely important resource for content. (Note that this is not being said by me as a professor, for I spent many years as a practitioner before joining a university faculty. This discussion, therefore, should not be seen as self-serving.)

As with any group, generalizations can lead to error. Just because a person carries an academic title and is employed by an institution of higher learning does not mean that person is up to date on the latest in the particular field. There are academics who stopped learning after they got tenure or upon completion of their own doctoral dissertation. The Designer must exercise the same care in selecting an SMS from a university as from any other external source.

Personnel, within vendor companies, can be a valuable resource, if caution is exercised. The Designer must distinguish between the vendor organization that will provide an SMS and the specific individual who will serve as an SMS. It is not unknown that a company that provides an SMS for the Designer may also be looking for a long-range relationship, such as providing a whole program. The Designer must exercise the usual caution of any purchaser, but should not allow this stance to deprive him of the rich resource which is available from vendor companies.

The ebb and flow of organizations that could provide external SMSs is so great that to include a list here would be to offer the reader a resource which would be obsolete by the time this appears in print. There are, however, some possible sources from which the Designer can call out the necessary external content specialists [5].

There are other external people and resources but they do not generally see themselves as serving in the SMS role. Professional societies and organizations, related to the specified content area, sometimes provide publications as well as people who can serve as SMSs or provide content. This is common in fields such as engineering and accounting. In those fields there are ongoing study groups, commissions, and other formal activities that are directed towards the content of the field.

A companion group is the trade organization, and sometimes it is difficult to differentiate between the trade and professional societies. The trade groups devote a significant portion of their resources to continually updating the content of their particular field.

Suppliers to an organization can also be an external resource for contributing content. When suppliers provide a machine or device (for example, computer, telephone, office equipment), they will also frequently offer training and education opportunities for the employees of the customer. In some cases, the program they provide will eliminate the necessity for any further design work. In other situations, the Designer will still have to continue designing but can use the content already identified by the supplier.

A source that is frequently overlooked because it is inexpensive and sometimes considered suspect, is the federal government! The Government Printing Office has a warehouse of materials that have been researched and published, (using tax money) and are available at ridiculously low prices. Many of their pamphlets and books contain excellent material for content in specific fields, such as occupational health and safety, and some of the newer technologies, such as the nuclear field.

TYPES OF CONTENT

The world of content is quite broad, even when tied to specific objectives. Here, too, as with needs and objectives, it is important to develop some priorities. Differing from the other areas, however, it is possible to provide a model for organizing content based on priorities.

All the content, related to the objectives, can be organized under one of four categories:

1. Essential

2. Helpful

3. Peripheral

4. Unrelated

Placing the various content components into one of these categories is no easy task. The Designer will find, however, that the process of doing this will assist in clarifying the content and even sharpening the previously agreed upon objectives.

Essential

In this category is the absolute minimal content that the curriculum must contain if the learning experience is to meet the previously stated objectives. The question to ask constantly about content in this category is: Can it be omitted? If the answer is affirmative, the content can still be valid but more appropriately placed in a different category.

In seeking to identify the items to be placed in this category, the Designer can anticipate a common human behavior. It is expressed by: "When I was learning to do that job, this is what I had to learn, and look where I am now. Therefore anybody learning to do that job should be taught the same things." Of course, the statement may not be made so openly. It may just be implied or hinted. This is most evident when dealing with supervisory and managerial programs. It was very frequently heard, at one time, in some of the technical fields, but given rapid changes in content one does not now hear that opposition stated so often. It would be unusual for an engineer today to insist that learning how to use a slide rule is essential, though it was a basic skill a decade ago.

Helpful

The next category, helpful, refers to that content which supplements the essential. The content in the essential can stand by itself, but if conditions permit and there is sufficient time and other resources, the helpful content can be included.

One way of identifying the helpful is to ask the question: Could the performance change without this content? An affirmative response tells us at least that it is not essential, but we have to probe further to determine if it is helpful.

Let us take the case of a maintenance person who is being trained to replace fluorescent lights. The essential will contain content related to positioning the ladder for safety, how to remove the guards (if there are any), the procedure for removing the light, putting in a new one, and so on. Each of these steps can be specified and each is important and necessary. The content related to those steps is essential.

Under helpful could be items such as how fluorescent light compares to traditional incandescent light in terms of handling the bulbs, the use of the fluorescent starter, the reason for the guard or diffuser, and so on.

The maintenance person can certainly replace the light knowing only the essential. The helpful provides content which is indirectly related to the performance expected, but content which will help the maintenance person understand more about the job.

Peripheral

The peripheral content can also be tested in terms of whether the performance can change even if the peripheral content is not included. It is difficult to establish a firm demarcation between *helpful* and *peripheral*. At best, it is a judgment call.

Given the example discussed earlier, the maintenance person replacing a light, peripheral content might consist of some items such as the comparative lumens expected from each source, comparative costs for their operation, and advantages and disadvantages of each form of illumination.

The Designer will find that different SMSs, as well as supervisors and managers, will have their own pet areas of content that they contend must be included. Some will be essential, and some may also be helpful. The Designer should not be surprised if there is also some peripheral. This stems from the concept of, "That is what I learned, therefore that is what should be learned." The inclusion of this material may be more a political decision than a design decision.

Unrelated

One can readily question why they should even be in this category. If the content is unrelated, isn't it obvious that it should not be included? Perhaps. The unrelated arises in various ways but one of the most common is the tendency of some to feel that if the content was good for somebody in another organization, we should have it also.

The unrelated poses a problem because it will generally arise from outside the usual design process. It will be communicated by some higher level person who heard that another organization taught that content, so why don't we? Unfortunately the Designer may have so much difficulty responding to that question without getting into specifics that a posture of benign acceptance is adopted. You can't win them all, and there are times when compromise is necessary. One approach is to include such content, but under this category. If this content is included in the final curriculum, at least everybody will know the category and treat it accordingly.

PROCESS OF CATEGORIZING

The Designer may wonder: Why bother to categorize? The answer is complex but let us explore some of the aspects.

When items are written down, in an outline or list form, we tend to give the same weight to each item. Obviously not all the content will have the same importance to the learning and the performance change desired. As we will see later, sequencing is one way of providing emphasis. Categorizing is another.

Frequently there will be more content than can be taught or learned in the limited time available. The Designer must choose what to include and what to exclude. The omissions should be the result of a positive decision, not oversight. By categorizing, and retaining this information, the Designer is able to show the wide range of content that was considered, compared to the limited content that was finally included.

Categorizing is essentially the responsibility of the Designer. This is in direct contrast to almost all of the earlier work in the CEM where responsibility more frequently rested on the supervisor or manager. In this event, the Designer functions as a professional and must make the appropriate decisions. Of course, it is helpful to seek the advice and reactions of the supervisor, but the Designer is cautioned not to place too much of a burden on the supervisor. If the previous events in the CEM have been completed successfully, the assignment into categories can be done by the Designer with the assistance of the SMS.

Placing the content into categories will take time. There may be many iterations before the Designer and the SMS feel comfortable and confident that the categories (of content) contain clear and defensible elements. There will be continual testing and exploration of the content items. The content must be stated so clearly and specifically that it is possible to instruct almost directly from that content. There will be the need for a transition into teaching form, the lesson plans, but that will take place later in this event.

In previous events, the Designer had the option of using E&FB during this event. Here it is mandatory. Before going further, the Designer should check back using questions, regarding each content item, such as:

- Will this content, if learned, meet the previously stated objectives?

- Will this content, if learned, meet the previously identified needs?

■   Will this content, if learned, lead to the performance specified?

■   Will this content, if learned, solve the previously identified problem of the organization?

Obviously an affirmative response is required to each of these questions, particularly for the *essential* material. For the other categories, the response will be a weaker affirmative, and probably a negative in the case of *unrelated*. If any *essential* content does not receive a clear affirmative response, the Designer should reexamine the content and then process it back through the actions to determine at what point a deviation occurred.

SEQUENCING

The first component of the curriculum is the content. The second is the *sequence*, or in what order the content should be presented to the learner. There are no absolutes, but there are some generalizations that the Designer considers when making the decision about sequencing.

One approach is the *general to the specific*. In this situation, the learner is first introduced to the overview, and then the content is presented that moves toward the specific. This seems simplistic, but it reflects some assumptions about the learner and a commitment to a learning theory. In this sequence, the Designer is using the *Gestalt* approach which is based on the learner needing to see the whole picture before proceeding. It is the learning theory approach based on the concepts of Lewin, Rogers et al. (behavioral). This approach sees the learner as needing a focus on the total learning situation before getting to the specifics.

The opposite approach is also possible, the *specific to the general*. This sequence is based on the behaviorists, such as Skinner. It is contended that the learner need not know the end result, but if the learning program is appropriately constructed, the learner will reach the end result, the general, by going through the well-planned specifics. This sequence is important when the end performance of all the learners must be identical.

Implanted in both sequences are some assumptions about the learner. The Designer should not be misled. Some critics of the latter (behaviorist) approach contend that it dehumanizes, while critics of the former approach (behavioral) argue that it does not produce any performance changes that are observable and/or measurable. There is an element of reality in both arguments, but this draws us away from the crux of the learning situation. If there is any generalization that can be made it is this: there is no *one* way of sequencing that is best for all content and for all learners.

Sequencing should reflect the content and the learner. It has been found that learners who have high social needs (for example, interaction with others, oral communication) tend to benefit more if the sequencing is from the general to the specific. Indeed, such learners sometimes reject some of the specifics and consequently have difficulty with programmed instruction. (We still are not sure how they react, in general, to PI when presented on a computer.) This high social need is not better or worse than the low social need, but it is different. The sequencing must consider the social need of the learner.

Another approach is from the *concrete to the abstract*. The learner starts with content that is solid, observable, or beyond dispute. This is contrasted with the *abstract to the concrete* which starts with generalizations which then lead to more solid components. This latter form of sequencing is sometimes used with content that is philosophical or based on broad generalizations. In this approach, the learner can be more crucial than the content. Where there is a crosscultural learning situation, this sequencing must be used with extreme caution.

We also have to explore the concept of *context* which alerts us to high-context and low-context societies. Perhaps this can best be seen through a language experience I had and I am sure is shared by others who studied Japanese. The more polite one gets in speaking Japanese, the more vague the statements. (We will not digress here for a discussion of the reason for this.) Often, when studying, we were not sure exactly what was being said because of the use of "honorifics" in the language. Our language instructor would reply with, "You have to know the context." That is, you have to know the specific situation in which the oral com munication is taking place. It is a situation which to some of us could be quite ambiguous. If we come from a low-context society, we want things spelled out. We rely on laws, printed statements, contracts, and other items that are indicative of a low-context society.

Do not place a value judgment on this, but recognize the difference. This was experienced during the 9th Conference of the International Federation of Training and Development Organizations (IFTDO) in Rio de Janeiro in 1980. My wife and I had a group of graduate students from George Washington University who attended the IFTDO Conference with us. Each evening there was a social function, as evidenced by tickets in the booklet we received at registration. The ticket was exchanged daily for a more specific coupon for that evening's activities. Neither the ticket nor the coupon stated specifics. We (from a low-context society) wanted to know exactly what would happen that evening. Our hosts (from a high-context society) would merely shrug their shoulders and wait for the evening. Obviously a social experience may not be a learning experience, but the learner approaches both with the same concept of context.

There are other variations in sequencing, but they are essentially all based on some kind of dichotomy similar to those just discussed. Examples are: known to unknown, particular to the general, and observation to reasoning. In each case, the reverse can also be used as a content sequence.

Before starting to sequence, the Designer must have the content clearly stated and written. Sometimes the content itself will indicate the sequence, whereas at other times the learner will be the governing factor. Usually it is an accommodation to both.

Sequencing can also be affected by the type of delivery system to be used. The most common way of offering learning, in work situations, is to use several days, one following after the other. The reasons are many, but the most obvious is that it is easy to schedule and causes less disruption to the normal work procedures than some other alternatives. When distance is a factor, the single continuous learning experience is less costly, as travel costs are incurred for only one trip.

Another alternative is *spaced learning*. In this mode, the content is separated into various components, depending upon the frequency of the spaced learning. Instead of one continuous learning situation, the learner returns to the job at stipulated times and then returns again to the learning situation. This recycling can occur once or many times.

Why should a Designer consider spaced learning? In the more traditional mode, the learner leaves the job, comes to the learning situation, and then returns to the job. During the entire learning time, the learner is in an artificial situation. In learning to be effective, a high-risk environment should be provided so that the learner can try out new performance without risk of punishment or negative criticism. It is a situation that allows the learner to "fail successfully." Such performance cannot be permitted at the actual job site.

The Designer faces the challenge of planning for reentry and providing for relevance. In the more traditional delivery modes, the learner is faced with taking the new performance and immediately applying it to the job. If there is then a question, the learner does not have the opportunity of confronting the instructor and peers with "I tried it the way we learned it, but it didn't work." Spaced learning provides for small increments, application on the job, and feedback or relearning in the learning situation.

When the Designer has alternatives, spaced learning can be considered. There are several variations. One is relatively easy to provide for, that is when all the learners are in the same physical facility or travel time and cost are not a consideration. Group instruction is conducted for a specified number of hours during the day, perhaps two hours, over a period of several days. At the end of each two-hour period, the learners return to their regular jobs.

A variation of this is to have the sessions conducted for a specific period of time. Once again let us suggest two hours, but for only one day a week, for several weeks. Once again, the learners return to their regular jobs after each session.

Another variation not so commonly used is to have a block of perhaps three days (the actual days will depend upon objectives and content) and allow the learner to return to the job for a stipulated period of time after the first learning sequence and then return to the learning situation. I have used this sequencing in a program we call "Creative Thinking for Managers." The spaced learning was chosen because we knew that we were asking managers for performance much different than usual. Generally managers are rewarded for results, not for trying. Creative thinking does not promise results, but it emphasizes the attempt.

We had executive approval for the program using spaced learning. The group came together for three days during which the learners engaged in various exercises and experiences to help them focus on thinking creatively. The last afternoon of the third day was devoted to planning for back home application during the interim between the two spaced learning situations. The learners then returned to their regular jobs for a month. During that time, they were to try to use the material at least once and more often if possible. They were not to create artificial situations, but rather use the creative learning techniques in some real situations during that back-on-the-job period of the spaced learning. When the learning group reconvened, the first activity was to process what happened when they tried to use creative thinking in real work situations back on the job. After that, additional material was presented, based on the feedback, plus some material used earlier for this unit.

Obviously the sequence of presenting the material is different for spaced learning than for a continuous program. The content will still be the same, as the objectives are identical for both continuous and spaced learning.

With the content determined and the sequence selected, the Designer can almost proceed to the next step of converting that material into lesson plans. Before that activity, the Designer pauses for another important decision.

MAKE OR BUY?

The Designer can proceed with the CEM (make internally) or obtain an appropriate program that already exists (buy externally). Given the ego needs that many of us have, it is easy to see why some Designers tend to continue in the design process without exploring an apparent and reasonable alternative. As the HRD market expands, an increasing number of specialized companies are offering various forms of packaged programs for sale.

The exploration of packaged programs should not take place until the content and sequence have been determined. If packaged programs are looked into at an earlier event of the CEM, the content and sequence probably will be distorted to relate to the package rather than to the previously developed data in the earlier stages of the CEM. This does not mean that the Designer should not consider trade-offs in revising curriculum and sequence if the appropriate package is identified. Rather, the process proceeds as described up to this point, and now the Designer looks at packages.

Packages are only one part of the total resources available to the Designer from outside the organization. There are modules, units, and components, all of which could be coupled with the internal resources to make a total program. There is nothing wrong with a Designer buying some external resources as a way of supplementing the internal capability.

The Designer might opt to buy the whole program from an external resource. When the need is a general one in the work force, such programs are frequently developed. The external vendor seldom devotes the necessary resources to develop a program that will have only limited use. Programs of a general nature are available for training supervisors and managers. Dupont, for example, has found a market for its packaged programs on maintenance. An expanding product that is becoming available in many forms of packaged programs are learning programs related to computers.

When the Designer has identified an external program that is closely related to the desired content and sequence, the first step is to determine availability and restrictions. That is, what are the conditions that come with the package? The Designer asks questions such as:

- Can the program be bought outright?

- Are there any restrictions on the use of the material?

- Must subsequent use be authorized by the vendor?

- What is the cost for subsequent use?

- Can the learning materials be reproduced by the Designer or must supplies continually be purchased from the vendor?

Some programs can be "purchased" but then require that the Designer use only "certified" instructors. When this is the case, the vendor may supply the certified instructors or have a parallel program which certifies the instructional personnel of the Designer.

It is unusual that the material purchased on the open market will meet the needs of each Designer without modification. There are two approaches to this. The Designer can take the purchased material and modify it to be congruent with the content and sequence previously determined. (This reemphasizes why the content-sequence task should be completed before exploring purchasing.) Such modification may not be as easy as it sounds. If the vendor has done a good job, the content and sequence should represent what the vendor believes are general needs in the purchasing public. It is not probable that they would be the needs of each individual purchaser. Modification can easily destroy the content and certainly do damage to the sequence. Despite this, modification is possible and is sometimes more satisfactory than the Designer doing the entire task.

Another approach is to take the previously determined content-sequence and modify it to be congruent with the material to be purchased. At first, this appears to be distortion, but it is a realistic and even beneficial procedure. If the program is readily available, the cost can be much less than what will be required for proceeding with the CEM, considering such factors as staff time and the cost of development of instructional materials. The Designer might select out of the content-sequence that part which can be immediately satisfied by the purchase of the available learning program. Then, the remaining content-sequence can become a separate learning experience.

This alternative is easily stated, but not so easily done. Dividing the content is no easy task, and the sequence may have to be severely altered. It is a situation where the Designer makes a professional judgment. In some instances, there may be pressure on the Designer to use some well-advertised or generally accepted external resource. Although it means even more work than just continuing internally, it may be politic for the Designer to purchase from the vendor and then make the necessary adaptations.

A question frequently asked is: "Which approach is less expensive?" This is an extremely difficult question to answer. It also depends upon when it is asked. All too often the Designer is confronted by this question immediately after "Identify the Needs of the Organization." At that early point, it is not possible for the Designer to do more than provide a very loose approximation. As the CEM proceeds, the Designer comes closer to being able to provide comparative cost data. As this event of the CEM, the Designer must be able to justify the relative cost of proceeding internally (that is, make) as contrasted with external purchase (that is, buy). Even now, all the cost data will not be absolutely determinable for the make aspects. As the Designer continues to deal with a variety of people, there is little control over the exact amount of time the completed design will take.

On the buy side, the money figure an be determined fairly accurately. That is, the purchase price can be calculated. If the Designer is concerned about "cost per learner," it may be more difficult as the final decision as to the total number of learners has probably not yet been made. At this time, the Designer must once again estimate.

Since many HRD units are understaffed (or at least consider themselves to be in that position), Designers frequently opt to purchase as this requires financial resources rather than human resources. The Designer frequently finds it easier to obtain funds than staff. Therefore the temptation is to purchase and not to use staff to continue with this event or the next event of the CEM. The Designer can skip to "Obtain Instructional Resources," which in this case is the money, and then go right into "Conduct Training."

Most Designers, for a variety of sound reasons, will still opt to continue the internal design, so we will proceed with the CEM.

LESSON PLANS

Before proceeding to produce lesson plans, the Designer is advised to do some E&FB. There is no point in using time to write the lesson plans if there has not been agreement on content and sequence. The evaluation, at this time, will not be in depth, but only to determine if the content is relevant to the data gathered during the previous elements. This will be checked again during the final E&FB for this event.

The lesson plan takes the content and sequence and translates that material into a form that is a plan for the learning situation. The major element that will *not* be included is exactly how the learning will take place. That relies, in part, on "Selecting Instructional Strategies," which is the next event. The reasons for this distinction will become apparent during the discussion in this chapter, and much more so when we actually move to the next event in the following chapter.

The Users

The actual form of the lesson plan will be influenced by various factors. A major one is *past history*. It is not suggested that the Designer should merely repeat what has been done in the past, but if the organization (that is, the HRD unit) has had an agreed upon form that has been used generally, the Designer is advised to first examine that form. There can be many good reasons why that form evolved and is generally accepted. The Designer can still recommend changes, but recognizes that changes can produce resistance. Is it worth the effort to try to change the form, unless there is a good reason?

An important variable is the *instructor*. If it is contemplated during the course of designing that the instructors will come from the line, the lesson plan will have to be much different than if instruction is to be provided by people from the HRD unit. A nonprofessional instructor needs a different lesson plan than a professional one requires.

In a program I designed for line people, the lesson plan was limited to:

- Ask—and the specific question was written out.

- Tell—and the specific instruction was written out.

- Distribute—and the handouts were keyed into the lesson plan with specific instructions for distribution.

- Notes—which were comments from the Designer to the nonprofessional instructor in terms of answers that could be expected, and classroom management situations.

If the instructors were professionals, the fact that the material was so explicit could be considered an insult. It certainly would conflict with the self-image of a professional instructor. The nonprofessionals were eager for such material and responded very favorably to that kind of lesson plan.

Even nonprofessionals might offer resistance to the preceding detailed lesson plan if there has been a prior training program to familiarize them with the lesson plans. Indeed, there would probably not be a need for such detail if the training program for instructors was carefully designed.

When the Designer cannot determine exactly who will be doing the instruction, it is wise to err on the side of more detail rather than less. Obviously it is easier for the instructor to use only part of the lesson plan, than to be forced to construct a lesson plan. Not all instructors have that competency, nor should they be expected to have it.

JIT

One form of lesson plan is the famous *Job Instruction Training* (JIT) which first emerged during World War I and became generally accepted during World War II. It was designed to provide nonprofessional instructors, usually line personnel, with a quick and easy formula for providing instruction at the job site. It is still used today. It is so simple that at first it seems naive, yet it contains the necessary elements for a successful learning situation. The steps are:

Preparation
Presentation
Application
Verification

Given the wide use of the JIT approach today, some people use different words for the four steps, but the steps are generally accepted.

Preparation is what the instructor must do to get ready for the learning situation. This includes becoming familiar and comfortable with the lesson plan, or other material provided. It also means checking out the physical facility, the equipment necessary for the particular session, and the required materials. Although originally not included, today there is also concern for preparation of the learner. This includes making sure that the learner has been informed of the time and place of the learning and that adequate provision has been made for work coverage while the learner is in the learning mode. This is necessary even if the instruction takes place adjacent to or on the job site. For the period of instruction, no matter how brief, the learner is not expected to be performing the regular tasks of the job or producing the expected output.

The next step is *presentation*, which includes those activities that are the initial part of the learning process. It can include any number of learning strategies and is concerned with the initial learning. It does not mean only lecture. It usually means, when used in production performance, a demonstration of the correct method or procedure. It also includes questions, discussion, and a variety of other presentation possibilities. The emphasis is on the activities of the instructor.

This is followed by *application*, which is when the learner uses what has been learned during the presentation. In the area of psychomotor skills, where JIT is used most extensively, this means that the learner actually performs the task, or that part of the task which has been presented earlier. It can also include a role-play, simulation, or any other learning strategy that provides an opportunity for the learner to actually use the material learned, while still in the learning situation.

JIT concludes with *verification*, which today is more commonly called evaluation. In actual practice, some of this will have taken place during application for before the learner can conclude the learning, it must be tried out and the learner be able to produce or perform at the acceptable level. In verification, the instructor and learner agree that the learner has the necessary level of performance to be qualified to work alone on the job.

JIT is one way to organize a lesson plan, but it is more applicable to the psychomotor area and omits some of the factors that an instructor must provide for, and which the Designer has the responsibility for building into this stage of the design process and lesson plans.

GENERAL FORM FOR A LESSON PLAN

There is no one best form for a lesson plan. Rather, it must reflect the interaction of content, sequence, type of instructor, type of learner, and the norms in the organization. It is possible, however, to indicate some of the general items that should appear in a lesson plan, as shown in Figure 7-2.

A lesson plan is prepared for each unit or segment of the learning experience. The units can be stated in hours or in one day. Generally when the experience is for more than one day, a separate lesson plan is prepared for each day. This recognizes the flow that is necessary during a day and the linkage from one day to the next.

The lesson plan should not be immutable, but that will depend to a good degree on the learning concepts built into the plan and on the experience of the instructor. The Designer is obligated to set forth, in a general description of the learning experience, the degree of latitude which should be exercised to enable the learner to meet the objectives through the learning experience.

Objectives

The objectives contained in the lesson plan are those that have been developed as a result of the previous event of the CEM. If the Designer finds it necessary to change the objectives in any substantial way, the writing of the lesson plan should

Program Title: _____

Objectives of this lesson:

Preparation:
1. Physical environment
2. Equipment and materials
3. Instructor
4. Learner

Time	Major Topics	Instructor Activity	Learner Activity	Strategies

Fig. 7.2 Lesson plan.

be delayed until there has been a recycling, through E&FB, back to the previous event.

The objectives, as indicated earlier, are stated in terms of the factors of performance, conditions, and criteria. By this time, the objectives should be so clear that an instructor can pick them up from the lesson plan and immediately understand them. Indeed, there are times when the instructor must do exactly that, for he may not have had any prior training and the Designer may not be available to explain the objectives. Of course, well-written objectives do not need any explanation.

Preparation

Some instructors must do all the preparation themselves, while others can rely upon aides or personnel whose sole function is to prepare the learning setting. No matter how it is done, the lesson plan should have clear and unambiguous directions about what is needed to prepare for the learning experience.

Four factors should be considered. The first is the preparation of the *physical environment*. This includes the availability of the room, its condition, the set-up (when a special arrangement is required), and control (to reduce external interference).

The second factor relates to *equipment and materials*. It is not possible for this part of the lesson plan to be completed during this event, as the specific learning strategies have not yet been selected. At this time, the Designer can only note a heading such as "equipment and materials" so that it will not be overlooked later. Upon completion of the next event ("Select Instructional Strategies") it will be possible to complete this part of the lesson plan.

The third factor is the *instructor*. The preparation will vary, but it is expected that every instructor will have access to and will study the lesson plan, prior to the start of the actual instruction. This part of the lesson plan should indicate which specific activities need to be implemented by the instructor prior to meeting the learner.

For example, a program was developed for the Metropolitan Police Department of the District of Columbia where the instructors were all from an external organization. The lesson plans were developed in detail and specified that each instructor was required to ride a shift in a police car before instructing. For me, it was a fantastic learning experience, one that I will never forget. By no means, did it make me an expert on police work generally, and not even just what is involved in riding in a patrol car in an urban area. It did help me understand something of the work life of the learner, as well as how the police viewed people from outside their organization, no matter how well meaning those people were.

The fourth factor is the preparation of the *learner*. We should not expect that an individual can be withdrawn from the regular work situation, thrust into a learning environment with little or no notice, and still retain a level of trust and interest.

All of these factors will be addressed again in some of the following events. Particular attention will be paid to these factors when we reach "Conduct Training."

Time

The lesson plan lists the *expected* duration of each element of the lesson. The Designer realizes, of course, that individual differences in the instructor and the learners, as well as other factors, influence the exact time devoted to any element of the lesson plan. The times indicated are only guidelines.

Time must be indicated. It is unfair to require that the instructor determine the duration of the various units, when the instructor was probably not involved in the CEM. The time suggested for each unit communicates to the instructor something of the emphasis to be given to that part of the curriculum.

The listing of time also communicates to the instructor regarding flexibility. Time should never be listed in units of less than 5 minutes. It is unrealistic to make the time allocation that specific unless the entire lesson is scripted where each thing is written out and has been timed beforehand. Such lessons are less frequently used than they were years ago, but occasionally one still finds a lesson plan with time gradation of 2 and 3 minutes!

At the other extreme, a unit within the lesson plan should not take more than one hour. When projected visuals are used (for example, 16 mm film, video cassettes) it is rare for one to last more than 30 minutes. Indeed, a longer period than that is questionable, from a learning viewpoint, unless there is some kind of intervention by the instructor and reaction by the learners.

Within those general parameters (no fewer than 5 minutes, no more than 60 minutes) the Designer indicates how much time each unit might take. The actual listing of the time is a reflection of the organizational culture or norms. In a military organization or in organizations located in some countries outside the United States, the 24-hour clock is the accepted norm. Therefore the time on the lesson plan should be in similar notations. It would not list 9:00 A.M. as the starting time, but 0900 hours. This becomes confusing to those outside the organization, when after noon, 1:00 P.M. becomes 1300 hours. If the instructor comes from within such an organization, the time listing obviously reflects that organization's normal use of clock hours. When the instructor is from outside, it is a good idea to inform the instructor in advance how the listing will appear on the lesson plan.

Some lesson plans do not give a specific clock hour, for the experience may be conducted at different times in different parts of the organization. The lesson plan will generally start with 00:00 signifying the start of the clock no matter what the actual time of day or night. If the first unit is for 10 minutes, the next listing would be 00:10. If it goes beyond one hour, there would be a listing of 01:20 which designates that this would be one hour and twenty minutes after the start of the program.

Provision is also made for planned breaks for refreshment, lunch, and so on. The lesson plan shows if the intention is a 5-minute break, or a 15-minute break. Of course, the actual break given by the instructor in the learning situation can vary, but it is the responsibility of the Designer to indicate in the lesson plan what provision has been made for the breaks.

It may seem picayune to pay this much attention to time. If the Designer is also going to be the instructor, it is unnecessary to be this detailed. When the instructor will have little or no contact with the Designer, it is essential to indicate the time in sufficient clarity so the instructor does not have to improvise more than is required in any learning situation.

Main Topic

This column on the lesson plan has several purposes. For the Designer, it is a direct link back to this event of the CEM. The major headings in this column reflect the content and sequence which have been agreed upon earlier. The column serves as a checkpoint for the Designer.

For the instructor, this column provides an overview of the flow of the lesson. The major topic headings indicate the overall content that will be covered, and the sequence. As the instructor has probably not been included in the CEM, this column communicates the curriculum directly to the instructor.

It is possible to put subtopics under the main topic, but they should be kept to a minimum. They should only be included if it is necessary to provide a user of the lesson plan with more specifics about the content that will be covered.

Instructor Activity

In this column is listed what the instructor will do during the lesson. The detail will, once again, depend upon the qualifications of the instructor. Professional instructors might resent too much detail, while nonprofessional instructors require all the detail that can be of help to them.

At this point in the development of the lesson plan, not all the specifics can be written down. This will have to wait until the next event, though it is possible to include some specific material, such as questions. If the instructor is expected to ask questions, this is indicated in the appropriate part of the lesson plan. Asking questions is much more difficult and sophisticated than many instructors realize. Therefore the Designer can opt to actually write out carefully developed questions rather than just indicating that this is the point in the lesson where questions will be asked.

The Designer has to anticipate all the other tasks required of the instructor, and tasks do tend to change throughout any given lesson. This column will also relate directly to the column on "Strategies," which will be discussed later.

When the instructor has options, the Designer indicates this in the lesson plan. If there are options, the Designer lists them and the possible outcomes that can result from one option as compared to others. The options might relate to the competency and experience of the instructor, the nature and experience of the learner, the availability of materials and equipment, or the physical environment where the learning might take place.

Learner Activity

Learning is a very active situation, and it is important that the learner and the instructor be equally active. Even a lecture, essentially a one-way communication, has active components (for example, taking notes, phrasing questions).

It can be difficult for the Designer to indicate specifically some of the learner activities, as that will depend in a large part on the actual learners. The Designer can only identify and list some of the possibilities of learner activity.

Activities will be in direct relationship to the objectives, the curriculum, and the potential and expected performance. The learner should at least respond, but should do more than only respond. The learner is encouraged to be pro-active and to initiate some activities (for example, develop a learning contract, relate the lesson to actual job situations). To encourage the learner to merely respond is to seek only reactive behavior which, for many adults, can be defeating in a learning situation.

Strategies

There are learning strategies that apply to both the instructor and the learner, but for convenience we refer to "instructional strategies." The variety is extensive as will be seen in the next chapter. The actual selection will be made during the next event. That is necessary as, until this entire event is concluded, the total picture is not in place, and therefore it is not possible to indicate which might be the most desirable instructional strategies.

At this point in the development of the lesson plan, the Designer can make suggestions. For example, this column might suggest that a case study is desirable at a certain point. The exact case study will not be selected or written until the next event. Right now, all that is required is the suggestion in the lesson plan that a case study be provided at this point. These suggestions are important, and the Designer does not wait until the next event to write down the suggestions. There are times, of course, when the Designer can be very specific, even though this is less desirable. For a particular main topic in the lesson plan there may be a film that the Designer knows is directly relevant. It can be helpful if the Designer makes a note of that on the lesson plan at this point, but also reserves the right to make changes during the next event if another film appears more appropriate. In a sense, the Designer is committing that part of the lesson plan to use a film, with the assumption that the film to be selected will be relevant. Here, too, the Designer should reserve the right to change even the suggestion about a film, when the lesson plan is reviewed in the next event.

Evaluating

There is no specific column in the lesson plan for evaluation, for it is a pervasive activity that should take place at many points during each lesson. Evaluation should not be left until the completion of the lesson, although that is one point at which there must be specific evaluation.

When discussing evaluation, we always start with objectives. It is not possible to evaluate if one does not have objectives. In the suggested lesson plan, note that *objectives* is the first heading.

The Designer indicates *what* is to be evaluated, and then *how*. Obviously the what will refer to the objectives, but they may have to be restated for purposes of evaluation. When evaluating, we seek those factors which are at least *observable* and, when possible, *measurable*. Some contend that if there is no measurement there can be no evaluation. Perhaps they have a point, but they must face the question, "If there is no measurement before the learning, how can there be any after?" If the performance does not presently have any measurable criteria, the Designer can encourage management to introduce quantification of performance. If management will not do that, the Designer cannot build in an evaluation using measurement. Of course, the Designer can build in a quantification of the *learning* that has taken place as a result of the lesson, but this cannot be extended to indicate that the measurement applies to *performance*. The Designer can construct an evaluation of the learning as a result of the lesson and is required to do so. Care should be taken so that such evaluation is not extended to indicate that a similar and direct change can be expected in job performance.

Evaluation is generally equated with tests. In most situations, this is unquestionably the relationship, but it is also possible to evaluate by other means. Let us start, however, with tests.

There are two major types of tests. One is the *standardized test* which can be purchased from an outside source. There are companies that specialize in construction and they will be able to provide the protocol regarding their tests. That protocol indicates the important factors of: standardization, reliability, and validity. Given the data on these factors, the Designer can determine if the standardized test is appropriate to the objectives.

When a learning package is purchased from an external source, as discussed earlier under *make or buy*, the Designer should request the test that should accompany the package. It will be a rare situation however, when the Designer can actually find such tests. Much more has to be done to encourage vendors of packaged learning programs to provide tests that have an established protocol. As the consumers (that is, the Designer) do not usually demand this, the producers/vendors are not encouraged to supply the tests and protocol.

The second major source of tests is the *Designer.* It may be the instructor, but this has many pitfalls. For one, has the instructor been selected because of an ability to develop a test? Generally this is not one of the requirements, particularly when instructional personnel come from line operations. Designing test instruments is a sophisticated activity that requires more than being able to phrase questions. The Designer has the responsibility for providing the appropriate tests to the instructor. This means that the Designer must have the skill of test construction, have somebody on the HRD staff with this competency, or bring in an external resource for test construction as related to specific objectives.

Analyzing test results is an equally difficult task. When a test is constructed by a professional, it should be organized in such a manner that the results are immediately available and usable by the instructor and the learners. This does not exclude the use of statistical manipulation to better understand the results, but such analysis must either be made explicit and simple, or the material should be left to the professional in the HRD unit for analysis.

An all too frequently repeated cliche is, "If the learner hasn't learned, the teacher has not taught." This is unfair and dangerous. From a general viewpoint, it puts the emphasis on the instructor, rather than on the responsibility of the learner. From the viewpoint of evaluation, it can cause distortion. If that cliche is accepted as policy, it forces the instructor to "teach to the test." That is, to provide only that instruction which is directly related to the items on the test.

Theoretically this should not provide a conflict, though actually it does. On the theoretical level, as the test should be a reflection of the objectives, it should mean that the instructor is "teaching to the objectives." This is valid only if the test has been so carefully constructed that there is a direct relationship between the test and the objectives. For some psychomotor (skill) activities, this can be done. For the knowledge and attitude areas, it is much more difficult if not impractical.

Tests are not limited to the traditional written form. There are other ways to test. All should be based on some criteria, though once we move away from the written or performance test, this becomes more difficult.

A simulation can be used not only for learning, but for evaluation. In a simulation, the learner is asked to perform in an artificial situation, but one that is as closely related to reality as possible. A major difference is that the learner can perform below standard in a simulation without undue cost to himself, the organization, or his peers.

The assessment center technique can be used for evaluating learning, but to do this the Designer must change it from the usual form, which is concerned with selection. Even case studies and role plays can be used for evaluation but then the analysis of the activity must be different than it is when those strategies are used for learning. Similarly other learning strategies can often be used for evaluation.

We now come to the question of *when* to evaluate. The general rule is, frequently. There should be evaluation points throughout a lesson, particularly at crucial points. These are times in the lesson when a main topic has been completed or when a full understanding of a main topic must be ascertained before proceeding. These are sometimes referred to as *formative* evaluation points, as evaluation is conducted while the learning is in process and the formation of new ideas and performance is emerging. From the results of a formative evaluation, the instructor may proceed with several alternatives. When such formative evaluation is designed into a lesson plan, the Designer is required to indicate the alternatives and provide appropriate material. Formative evaluations can be offered at several points during a lesson and are expected to influence the remainder of the learning experience.

At the end of a lesson, there should be a *summative* evaluation. Generally such an evaluation will not have any direct effect on what has already taken place in the lesson just completed. It can, however, serve as an indicator to the instructor as to whether or not to proceed to the next lesson, or if some review and repetition of prior learning is required. Once again, the Designer builds in some appropriate alternatives concerning the summative evaluation. One alternative may merely be that when learners fall below a given point on the summative evaluation, the instructor calls for help from the HRD unit.

At this point, the preliminary lesson plan has been completed, but before proceeding to the next event, we must cycle through the E&FB event which is at the conclusion of each event of the CEM.

EVALUATION AND FEEDBACK

The tasks under this event having been completed, we need to ascertain if the event has been completed successfully. The objectives for this event were that, by completion, the Designer will be able:

To develop a specific list of the items to be learned in order to meet the previously determined objectives.

To list the order in which the learning is to take place.

The products are the lesson plans which reflect the accomplishment of the stated objectives. The Designer has the option of using either the content and sequence or the specific lesson plans.

Analysis

The Designer must determine which approach to the analysis would prove most helpful. That decision is influenced by the nature of the content and the form of the lesson plans. The question is: Which approach will communicate better to the people who will be involved in the feedback? Another option, of course, is to offer both (content and lesson plan), but this may require more time for review than is available.

If time and personnel allow, the Designer follows the pattern used in developing the lesson plan. That is, the Designer starts with the content and indicates how each element within the content relates to the previously determined objectives. Where there is a direct relationship, this can be readily stated. For some content, further explanation may be required to justify its inclusion.

The sequence can likewise be stated. The reasons for sequencing may be more difficult to set forth, and as the Designer has relied on some particular learning theory there is a temptation to discuss learning theory in the analysis. The problem is that most of the readers of the analysis are not concerned with learning theory, and indeed need not be. That is why they have called on the Designer, who is the professional in the field of learning theory.

There is a way to bridge this gap, in the analysis. The Designer can state specifically the assumptions which have been made about the nature of the subject matter and the kinds of learners expected. This latter, particularly, will surface the opinions of the supervisors and managers concerning the employees they intend to send to the learning situation. The supervisor and managers likewise have some assumptions about the learners, and it is important that these be compared with those stated by the Designer in the analysis.

Bringing together the content, sequence, and assumptions about the learner (the application of learning theory) is extremely important. There must be a real congruency among these three elements. There will be a temptation for the Designer to write lengthy documentation on the relationship of these three elements, but restraint must be exercised. Only as much should be included in the analysis as will be helpful and will facilitate the decision making that is the concluding activity in the event. This relationship should be set forth as clearly as possible, and even indicate alternatives, if such are the case.

One alternative relates to time. The analysis should contain indications of those content elements that might be dropped if the time must be decreased from what is set forth in the analysis. It does not mean that those elements are unimportant, and they should certainly have related to the objectives. Previously, however, it would not have been possible for the Designer to indicate exactly how long the learning requires. At this point, this can be indicated specifically. When faced with the time requirements, the decision-makers may express satisfaction with the curriculum, but ask that it be done in less time.

A reduction in time must mean a reduction in content. Time constraints should not be met by "asking the instructor to move faster." Anticipating questions about time, the Designer indicates in the analysis the effect of time decisions on different main topics of the lesson plan or on the content areas. It may mean that some topics are dropped from this learning experience but will be included in a different learning experience to be offered at a later time.

There may be, during feedback, a suggestion that more time is required, particularly when skill development is concerned. The Designer need not indicate that possibility in the analysis, and probably cannot. But, the Designer should be aware that this can happen after the analysis has been reviewed and feedback is received.

When a make-or-buy decision has been made, the Designer indicates this. In the analysis, it is important to specifically state the basis for the decision. Although the appropriate people may have been involved in the earlier decision, they may want another chance to review what has happened, now that a larger part of the program is observable through the lesson plans.

It may be discouraging to the Designer, after complying with an earlier decision and developing the lesson plans, to find that now the same people are suggesting a buy option. It may not be a reflection on the competency of the Designer, but rather that once the specifics are available (through the lesson plans) the same people may have a different point of view.

Something similar can happen when the decision was to buy. When the Designer brings the purchased program into the analysis in preparation for feedback, there may be some second thoughts. Of course, this can be even more expensive than recanting the previous decision, but the important question is: At this time, what is the appropriate decision about make or buy?

Feedback

As before, the criteria for inclusion in giving feedback is related to those people who can be helpful at this stage of the CEM. Previously it was suggested that the employee (potential learner) be included. In this event, the reasons for inclusion are not as strong as before. Though it may not be detrimental to have some potential learners involved in the feedback, there is also some question as to the benefits relative to the time required. If potential learners were involved in the previous events, they may not be necessary here. The decision to include potential learners may be based more on the politics and culture of the organization than on learning theory.

The supervisor is required as before. If the supervisors do not have an opportunity to be involved in feedback, the very success of the program can be in jeopardy. Among other apparent reasons for such involvement is the major decision that must be made as to the time that can be allowed for the learning. If the supervisor is going to be asked to send producing employees away from their jobs, time is a crucial factor. The feedback session may almost be the point at which the supervisors make the time commitments that will enable the Designer to have some feeling of confidence in the ultimate success of the learning experience. If the supervisors react negatively, compromise may be in order.

Managers may be involved here for numerous reasons, and primarily because the need for additional resources begins to surface. The managers will very likely not want to be concerned with the content, sequence, or lesson plans. These are operational factors that they traditionally and wisely leave to others. The decision on time, or other resources, can be a managerial decision, so their involvement would be helpful. In most situations like this, however, there is room for negotiation.

It is appropriate to consider involving the SMSs, particularly if they are internal people. That provides for further verification by the Designer that the inputs from the SMSs have been understood and used. It is not necessary that every bit of their input should have been included, and it is not necessary that every SMS used be involved in the feedback. Certainly it is appropriate that provision be made for some communication with some of the previously involved SMS people.

Decisions

The event should conclude with some specific decisions by those involved in the feedback, as related to the following questions:

1. Does the content meet the previously determined objectives?

The objectives were stated specifically at the conclusion of the previous event. In the interim, there have been a variety of people who made inputs to the content. All of them should have seen the objectives, but there may have been a variety of interpretations. During discussions and arguments, it is possible that the objectives have become obscured. Now is the time to return and verify that the content is related to the objectives.

2. Will that content satisfy the identified needs of the learners?

This is much the same as the previous question but reflects the common problem with communications and the use of words. The content should relate directly to the needs, specifically those that were selected for further consideration. Another way to ask this is: "If the content is mastered, will the need of the individual learner be met?"

3. Does the content relate to performance?

Following the same line of inquiry, we are seeking to decide if the content is really what the job is all about. There must be a direct match between content and specified job performance. If not, the differences need to be explained or rationalized. Ultimately this question must receive a positive response.

4. Does the content relate to the previously identified need of the organization?

As noted earlier, the need of the organization for the learning program was to solve a problem. The content may not have a direct relationship to the problem, but at the same time, the content should not be creating additional problems. Where the content can contribute to solving the problem, and this is readily discernible, there will be no hesitation in receiving a positive response to this question. Where the relationship is not so obvious, additional discussion may be required before a positive response can be received to this question.

    5.   Is there agreement on the make-or-buy decision?

This point should have been settled earlier, but it can always come up again. The Designer forestalls this by including this question in decision making at this time. If there is still any strong feeling against the decision made earlier, this is the time for it to surface. Indeed, the Designer would want it to surface before going further. The purpose of this question is to seek reaffirmation, not to continue a previous discussion. If it provokes discussion here, perhaps the previous decision was not as binding as it appeared to be.

    6.   Will potential learners be made available for the period indicated?

This is where the supervisors must reach agreement. At this point, it will be possible for the supervisors to begin planning for coverage for the time when the learning program is implemented. If there will be any difficulties, these should be voiced when making this decision.

CONCLUSION

If the final decision is to buy a packaged learning program, the Designer does not have to become involved in the next event, "Select Instructional Strategies," as these should have been part of the purchased program. Depending upon the specific package purchased, it might even obviate the necessity for "Obtain Instructional Resources," and the Designer can now proceed to the final event of "Conduct Training."

    Assuming, however, that all of the preceding decisions have been in the affirmative and the decision is still to continue in-house development of the learning experience, the Designer now moves to "Select Instructional Strategies."

REFERENCES

1.   Many of the learning theories pertinent to adults have been brought together in *The Adult Learner: A Neglected Species,* 2 Ed. by Malcolm Knowles. (Houston: Gulf Publishing, 1978).

2.   A useful innovation is a list of packaged programs in *The Trainer's Resource: A Comprehensive Guide to Packaged Training Programs* by Human Resources Development Press, 1981.

158   BUILD CURRICULUM

Recognizing how rapidly the listing of packaged programs changes, they also provide update supplements.

3.   For a discussion of HRD as a budget center, cost center, and profit center see *Corporate
Human Resource Development* by Leonard Nadler. (New York: Van Nostrand, 1980).

4.   A discussion of the differences between process and content consultants can be found
in *The Client-Consultant Handbook* by Chip Bell and Leonard Nadler (editors). (Houston: Gulf
Publishing, 1979).

5.   There are various kinds of buyer's guides. The American Society for Training and
Development issues one annually. *Training* magazine issues a yellow pages as part of one of
its issues each year. There are several packs of mailing cards which you receive once you are
on the mailing lists of HRD organizations. Of course, annual meetings of various organizations also provide exhibits which are a source for learning about new programs.

ADDITIONAL PRINTED REFERENCES

Adult Reading Habits, Attitudes, and Motivations. Indiana University, Viewpoints on Teaching
and Learning, 1979.

The Psychology of Adult Development and Aging. Washington, D.C.: American Psychological
Association, 1973.

Apps, Jerrold W. *Study Skills: For Those Adults Returning to School.* New York: McGraw-Hill,
1978.

Bischof, Ledford J. *Adult Psychology.* New York: Harper & Row, 1976.

Hamblin, A. C. *Evaluation and Control of Training.* New York: McGraw-Hill, 1974.

Havelock, Ronald G., and Mary C. Havelock. *Training for Change Agents: A Guide to the Design
of Training Programs in Education and Other Fields.* Ann Arbor Mich.: Institute for Social
Research, 1973.

Hill, Winfred F. *Learning: A Survey of Psychological Interpretations.* San Francisco: Chandler
Publishing Co., 1963.

Ingalls, John D. *A Trainer's Guide to Andragogy: Its Concepts, Experience, and Application.*
Washington, D.C.: Government Printing Office, 1973.

Kalish, Richard A. *Late Adulthood: Perspectives on Human Development.* Monterey, Calif.: Brooks-
Cole, 1975.

Knowles, Malcolm. *The Modern Practice of Adult Education.* New York: Association Press,
1970.

Mager, Robert E. *Developing Attitude Toward Learning.* Belmont, Calif.: Fearon, 1968.

Mayer, Nancy. *The Male Mid-life Crises: Fresh Starts After Forty.* New York: Doubleday, 1978.

Verduin, John R., Harry G. Miller, and Charles E. Greer. *Adults Teaching Adults.* San Diego:
Learning Concepts, 1977.

8

Select Instructional

Strategies

The previous chapter frequently referred to delaying the selection of instructional strategies until after the curriculum had been built. Therefore the objective of this event (Figure 8-1) is that the Designer will be able:

To select instructional strategies that are appropriate for the curriculum, the learner, the instructor, and the organization.

To revise the lesson plans to reflect the decisions about instructional strategies.

The emphasis first on the curriculum and then on the instructional strategies is based on a concept stated about 150 years ago by an Italian architect who said, "Form follows function." We could develop a tortuous alliteration for our field, but to avoid any ambiguity let us put it in direct terms: "Instructional strategies follow the curriculum."

This is not an easy rule to abide by, for the selection of instructional strategies is far from an automatic procedure. There are some general guidelines, which we will explore, but there are so many variations that it is generally impossible to list a particular element of the curriculum and automatically state that there is one way (that is, instructional strategy) to learn that element.

NOMENCLATURE

Complicating the situation further is the virtual explosion of instructional strategies. It is easy, therefore, to become embroiled in semantic confusion.

When looking at any particular learning activity (for example, case study, overhead transparency, or simulation), the temptation is to try to put a label on it. There are still those who argue about what a particular learning experience is

THE CRITICAL EVENTS MODEL

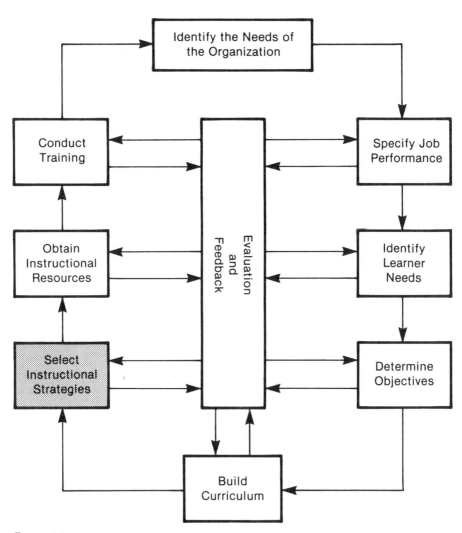

Figure 8.1

using: methods, techniques, devices, media, material, equipment, and so on. Some people in the field have endeavored to define and develop those and similar categories, but they have not been successful. There is still a lack of agreement. Rather than become involved in the defining task, some of us have chosen to describe all such activities as *instructional strategies*. This is done for two reasons.

First, there is no evidence that producing categories will be helpful. If anybody can show that categorization would be of use to designers and others, many of us will rush to support that endeavor. If you look at the available literature, you will find attempts to produce categories and classifications, but no hint as to the benefits of such endeavors.

The second reason is more positive. By using the word "strategies" we are reinforcing the proposition that any learning situation involves the use of a combination of methods, techniques, devices, and so on. We are also communicating, we hope, that a strategy is a way of reaching some objective, but it is not the objective itself.

The history of HRD is replete with examples of strategies that have gotten out of hand because they took on a life of their own. In the early 1950s, brainstorming was introduced through the work of Alex Osborn [1] and rapidly gained acceptance. In some of the highly developed programs using brainstorming, designers used learning aids, including whistles, lights, reinforcement cards, critical cards, and other supplementary materials. In one instance, with which I am personally familiar, an HRD person developed a program using supporting materials, with brainstorming, that was truly magnificent. As a result, however, his behavior became highly predictable. No matter what he was asked to design (he was internal to the organization), there was always a curriculum piece that required brainstorming. Obviously, after many years, this became laughable. Unfortunately he had a position of power and his staff felt they could not give him the necessary feedback. His unit suffered, however, simply because managers began to seek external design assistance rather than have another brainstorming session.

A similar experience can be recounted with "sensitivity training." Perhaps my biases should be set forth so the reader does not misunderstand. I became involved in that type of learning in 1954 and I subsequently became a member of the National Training Laboratories (NTL), the leading exponents of that form of learning. I have conducted labs, T-groups, and similar related learning experiences. Unfortunately, for many years since its inception in 1948 [2], there have been those who saw sensitivity training as the response for all human behavior problems. Today such limited response is no longer the vogue.

There are many other examples, and one relates to programmed instruction (PI). It had its major initial impact in the early 1960s and was touted by its exponents as being *the* way to learn. Until they retreated from that position, they encouraged hostility from those who were critical of that strategy. Obviously there are many more examples, but the point has been made. No single strategy suffices for all learning situations.

There is another aspect of nomenclature that we must address. This refers to the terms: *teaching, learning,* and *instruction.* Generally the term *teaching* is used to designate the activities of the person who is directing the learning experience. This can be a teacher, professor, instructor, group leader, facilitator—and the list can go on. *Learning* is used to signify the activities of the learner in the situation, who likewise has many designations such as trainee, student, pupil, or participant.

Note that such a division suggests a gulf between the teacher and the learner. It negates an often used approach in which roles may be reversed for a brief period. It overemphasizes one-way communication from the teacher to the learner.

I propose to use the term *instruction* (or instructional) to refer to the process that occurs during a learning experience. Therefore the reference to *instructional strategies* encompasses all the various teaching-aid learning activities as well as the supporting mechanisms that are used by all involved in the experience. Perhaps an equally valid argument could be made for calling these *learning strategies,* and if that term is more acceptable to some readers I can only ask that they make the translation in their minds. It would be cumbersome to continually refer to "learning/instructional strategies."

FACTORS INVOLVED IN SELECTION

The selection of appropriate instructional strategies becomes more challenging with each passing year. The availability of sources is rapidly increasing as the market for HRD continues to expand. New producers continually enter the field. That is good, for it provides more possibilities, but it does complicate the selection process.

The continuing impact of new technology must also be considered. In the early 1950s, I conducted a study and discovered that for classroom teachers, the 16 mm projector was considered the ultimate in technology. Today that machine has been wonderfully simplified, but there are other technologies that are more threatening, or challenging, depending upon the competency and experience of the Designer. The field has expanded to the point where the Designer may not be the appropriate person to make a decision about a specific instructional strategy, but instead calls upon a specialist who has a wide range of experience with a variety of instructional strategies.

There is an inherent trap that the Designer endeavors to avoid, when utilizing an expert in the field of instructional strategies. One organization, which must remain nameless for ethical reasons, found that it was developing instructional programs that required numerous slides. It was a large, multisite, multinational organization, and the need for the slides was directly related to programs that were produced, in a packaged form, to be sent all over the United States, as well as various parts of the world. It seemed logical, at the time, to hire an instructional strategies person who had competency in the area of slides. They did this, but within months discovered that they needed two people and more equipment! As their slide operation grew, it soon became evident to some that they had experienced that not unusual phenomenon, "If you give person a hammer, it will not be long before it is decided that everything in sight must be hammered!" In the organization, not only was everything reduced to slides, but it meant the exclusion of almost every other mode of presentation from the packages. The HRD director had to actually dismantle this part of the operation before Designers could begin to explore alternative learning strategies.

A question that is asked frequently is: "What criteria can I use to select an appropriate instructional strategy?" The assumption buried in the question is that there is a direct one-to-one relationship, when in fact this does not exist. A mixture of variables must be considered (as listed in Figure 8-2). The Designer must identify where a particular unit of a program exists on the scale between any two factors.

For example, will the particular instructional unit (part of a lesson plan) be individual or group? When the Designer can identify this component, there is some

---

Considerations for Selecting Instructional Strategies

instructor centered _____ learner centered

individual_____group

abstract subject matter_____concrete subject matter

self instructional _____ group learning

didactic_____experiential

low learner experience _____ high learner experience

short time to apply _____long time to apply

long time for learning _____ short time for learning

low instructor competence _____ high instructor competence

low student motivation _____ high student motivation

Figure 8.2

focus on the appropriate instructional strategy. Obviously individual or group is not the only factor that may be considered, so the Designer will have to use most of the list in making selections.

Though this is time consuming, the end product is certainly worth the effort. As a Designer develops a level of competency in using the list, the task becomes easier, but by no means should it be ignored or overlooked.

Final selection is based on a combination of factors, and some require much more insight than just checking a list—any list. Let us look at: learning psychology, administration, culture, the instructor, and the learners.

Concepts of Learning Psychology

One selection approach is to study learning psychology and determine what various writers have to say about selecting the appropriate instructional strategy for a given objective. This information is presented by writers in several ways, but a common one is the cone of experiences. There are various renditions of this, depending upon the writer. The cone can represent a continuum from the simple to the complex, from direct experience to wholly vicarious, or any other continuum the writer wishes to select. The difficulty with this approach is that it assumes that there is a continuum, and that concept is debatable. It also puts selection on a one-dimensional plane that excludes the variables of the material, the previous experience of the learner, and the style of the learner, and it usually completely ignores two other factors that will be discussed later in this section.

The cones have some worth, for they organize the instructional strategies into usable patterns. The problem is with the Designer who seeks *the* answer from the cones or continuums as the variables are complex. A single instrument will not permit the luxury of a quick and easy selection.

Administrative Practices

Once we leave the area of learning psychology, the selection picture becomes even more confused. Perhaps that is why most Designers tend to consider only that aspect, for learning psychology provides some printed material and references that can be used. Little has been written about the factor of administrative practices in selecting instructional strategies.

Overriding almost any other administrative considerations *is the one of budget.* If the HRD Designer is working with a limited budget, the possibility of selection is curtailed, for many of the strategies require financial expenditure for materials. When equipment becomes a consideration (for example, video-cassette recorders), a not insignificant budget may be required.

It is not that the organizations will not make funds available, although in some situations that might be that case. More often the difficulty is one of timing. When budgets are being prepared, it is not always possible to forecast probable future expenditures for equipment related to a program that has not yet been designed. The HRD director will try to make provisions for some expenditures in that category when preparing the annual budget. The difficulty is that some HRD directors do not have control over their own budgets. Even when they do, it is difficult to sell a budget item when the need is not apparent. This leads the HRD director to try stockpiling when economic conditions are favorable, but the items that may have been stockpiled frequently do not meet the needs of the program being designed.

Selection reflects administrative practices of the organization in the area of the budget. The Designer should not take a negative stance. Just because it has not been budgeted does not mean that materials and equipment for intructional strategies cannot be obtained as every budget process provides for some flexibility. If the Designer can demonstrate the need strongly enough, funds might still be made available.

Another aspect of budget is timing. Every organization has a cash flow sequence. There are certain times of the year, a particular month or week, when cash is more or less available. The HRD director must remain sensitive to this when seeking funds for unbudgeted instuctional strategy items.

Where the HRD director and the Designer are the same person, this sensitivity should be obvious. As HRD units become more active and grow in size, a gulf can develop between the HRD director and the Designer. In that situation, it is the responsibility of the Designer to keep the director informed. Unfortunately it may not be until this event in the CEM that the Designer can identify the budgetary requirements for a particular instructional strategy.

Much the same can be said about facilities. There are some instructional strategies that require special facilities. This can be as basic as a room that can be darkened if slides are to be used. It can be more sophisticated if technology is involved, such as closed-circuit TV, or group-oriented strategies requiring appropriate space for small break-out groups. There is a growing tendency among large corporations to build or lease their own facilities. Generally they are not labeled as HRD facilities, the more common term being conference center. In some cases the company will actually build a center. The February 1981 issue of *Meeting News* carried a story that indicated that companies planned to spend $3 billion in 1981 to rent facilities, and that was in an uncertain economic climate.

In addition, there are more than 50 facilities, just in the northeast region of the United States, that cater specifically to HRD activities. The Sunbelt can claim a growing number of such facilities that were built primarily to provide an appropriate learning environment.

To these company-owned facilities and the specially built conference centers can be added most of the hotels and motels in the United States that are frequently used by companies for some of their HRD activities [3]. Some of the facilities have very sophisticated equipment, while others provide only chairs, tables, and bare walls.

The Designer must know what is available, or possible in the way of facilities, when selecting an instructional strategy. The HRD director must be involved, if the budget and facilities are different from what had been provided previously. Though it may not be possible to obtain additional budget, or different facilities this year, the HRD director might want to anticipate needs that have budget and facility implications for next year.

Culture of the Organization

Culture is always a difficult dimension to determine. By its very nature, culture is "what everybody believes" but is not actually stated. If it has been written down in a manual, directive, or similar document, it becomes legal or administrative practice. This does not mean that everybody follows it, but at least everybody knows what it is supposed to be. Culture is not written but generally represents accepted behavior in the organization. As such, it is not always possible to tell when one has acted counterculturally until penalized by the people or the system.

The most frequently repeated phrase, when one encounters cultural practice, is, "We have always done it that way." Or, the contrary, "*Everybody knows* that is not done in this organization." An example of this, but only one of many, is from the Marine Corps. At one time, in the late 1960s they used sensitivity training (see the list that follows for a description) as an instructional strategy. For reasons that are not germane to this discussion, sensitivity training fell into disrepute in that organization. The cultural norm developed that sensitivity training was not to be used in the Marine Corps. To the best of my knowledge, no edict or dictum was issued, but the message was loud and clear. As the learning that can be achieved by sensitivity was still needed to reach stated objectives of some of the Marine Corps training, it became an example of "old wines in new goatskins." The strategy was renamed and was continued, as needed.

In many organizations it is generally assumed (cultural behavior) that executives and managers should be sent to external programs rather than to those provided internally. There could be programs conducted by other organizations or, at the very least, conducted off the regular work site. There may not be an issued policy or a written statement (that takes it out of cultural behavior), but I have encountered many organizations in which this was one of the first inputs I received when designing a program for that level of personnel.

History, within an organization, creates cultural norms. One such organization was a large oil company in which the managers were brought together twice a year from all over the United Stated for training purposes. Frequently managers working overseas were also scheduled to attend, and the training was coupled with home office consultation. What I had not been told about were the various rituals that accompanied this activity. In later discussion, the in-house HRD person remarked that he did not see the need for telling me about the presession activities, as he would take care of that. Unfortunately these presession activities involved some interesting rituals. For one, newcomers to the group were not introduced. It was later explained that fighting one's way into the group was one indication of being able to survive at the management level. The week-long session started with a "social." Actually it was what college students would call a "beer bust." The intent was to visibly consume as much liquor as possible while still maintaining one's balance and composure. This "social" started before the opening evening session, continued for several hours, and was then interrupted for a content session. After the completion of that session, the participants were expected to once again join in the libation and festivities. The "evaluation" was the ability to engage in this activity the first evening, and still be prompt for breakfast at 7:00 A.M. the next morning, and be active in the first day's session.

Other organizations have equally unusual cultural behaviors that are expected at training sessions. It is hoped that not too many require the cultural behaviors just described. Many of the cultural behaviors relate more to dress, times of day that are used or must be avoided, and even times of the year that are more or less desirable. There may be a "requirement" that each session start with a predetermined ritual or event. The list of cultural behaviors can be quite lengthy but is crucial in determining how a session can be organized and which are the appropriate instructional strategies.

The Designer, if internal, is expected to know these cultural requirements. Generally, however, only members of the particular group know the appropriate cultural behaviors. If the Designer is not a member of that group, study and open communication are required to identify the cultural factors that influence the selection of instructional strategies.

If the Designer or the instructional strategies developer is external to the organization, he needs the skills necessary to identify and provide for the cultural factors. This is not easily done, for by definition, cultural behavior is not written down. This emphasizes how important it is for an external person to have a reliable internal counterpart.

Instructor

References have been made to the instructor, and once again that person becomes crucial to the Designer. If the program is intended to be entirely machine-mediated, with no live person in attendance, the emphasis is on the technology, not the person. The Designer need only consider who will deliver the learning program in physical terms, such as set up, arrangements, and so on. This will be discussed further in the event "Conduct Training."

Even when a learning experience is essentially machine or technology oriented, there may still be a live person in attendance. Though the term instructor can still be used, the person will function more as a coach. As a result, much different behaviors are required than when that person serves as the instructor.

The more prevalent mode in most learning situations is the use of a live instructor, using some of the various strategies that are set forth in the following. The learning experience is under the "control" of the instructor, even though self-directed or learner-directed strategies are being used.

It is essential that the Designer have at least an image of who that instructor might be. (Although phrased in the singular, "instructor," there is also the obvious consideration that most learning programs require more than one instructor.) Even more to the point, the perfect condition would be when the Designer knows the instructor and the competencies that instructor will bring to the learning situation. One limitation in selecting appropriate learning strategies is the competency and inclination of the instructor.

If the instructor to be used is a professional, the range of possible instructional strategies available is much broader than when a nonprofessional is being used. This should not be read as being disparaging to the nonprofessional, as such instructors are extremely significant when a knowledge of the subject matter is important. The nonprofessional can also be more effective when an objective calls for a leading company figure, such as the Chief Executive Officer or a vice-president. These nonprofessionals may feel uncomfortable with some of the technology available (including something as comparatively simple as slides), but the presence of that high-level nonprofessional may be essential to meeting the objectives of the learning. The culture of the organization demands it.

Another nonprofessional is the line person who is a peer. I have used supervisors to train other supervisors. Having the sessions conducted by one of their own can have a stronger learning impact than when the session is conducted by a professional who is comfortable with the instructional strategies but has never walked in the shoes of the learner.

Some professionals feel more competent with one instructional strategy as compared to another, and they show that. A professional instructor might have no problem with using projected materials (for example, films, slides, overheads) but balks when required to use the video-cassette recorder. It is even possible to conduct training programs for the professionals in the use of a new technology or an old method (for example, role-playing), but if the instructor does not feel comfortable with that particular strategy, it may be necessary for the Designer to make modifications.

If the Designer has selected a particular instructional strategy, but thinks that there may be some resistance or discomfort on the part of the instructor (professional or nonprofessional), there is another alternative. The next step of the CEM, "Obtain Instructional Resources," contains provisions for meeting this possible need. It includes "training of instructors" as one component, so we will defer a discussion of this alternative until the next chapter.

Learner

As has been stated so often, a crucial element in the learning situation is the learner. If the learner rejects or fights a particular instructional strategy, the Designer may consider selecting an alternate one. It is not suggested that the instructional strategies be limited only to those that are familiar and/or comfortable for the learner. There are times when discomfort is a part of learning. Discomfort can even create a need to learn, but if the discomfort level is too high, the learner is apt to block, fight, withdraw, and call upon a variety of other psychological mechanisms, rather than learn.

The Designer can consider "bridges." These are learning experiences that are used to prepare the learner for the next learning experience. If the learner has never engaged in role-playing, the Designer can build into the lesson plans some warm-up experiences that will allow the learner to experience a low-risk example of role-playing before using this strategy with the content of the particular session.

The Designer should not underestimate the learners. Though to the best of the Designer's knowledge they may never have experienced a particular strategy, the learner may have had that experience outside of the work situation. Many community organizations (churches, and so on) use some of the more sophisticated instructional strategies that formerly were almost the sole property of profit-making organizations. The impact of technology, particularly on some of the younger people in the work force, has provided them with some experience that is beyond the ken of the Designer. The use of computers for learning is a prime example.

Reference was made previously to learning styles, and once again that aspect becomes important in selecting an instructional strategy. To date, we still have much to learn, so it is not possible to provide exact listings that indicate *the* instructional strategy for a *particular learner.* Also, when learning is done in group settings, the instructional strategies must reflect the group rather than a single individual. As work on learning styles moves ahead, this paragraph will have to modified, but that may be a long time in the future.

Back to the Lesson Plans

Considering all the variables just discussed the Designer now returns to the lesson plans and selects instructional strategies. The selection process may indicate that some of the curriculum elements must be offered in a fashion different than originally contemplated.

The factors just discussed can require a significant alteration in a lesson plan and the Designer may have to backtrack through the CEM. Given the requirements imposed by a particular strategy, are there elements of the content that must be changed, or is there an impact on sequence? Frequently there is none, but the Designer should explore this possibility as part of this event.

INSTRUCTIONAL STRATEGIES

Volumes have been written about the range of instructional strategies, but few books have ever achieved any significant general acceptance. The reasons are not clear enough to allow for a discussion of this phenomenon and it is doubtful if it would be helpful to the Designer. What is obvious is that there are some core instructional strategies that never seem to change (for example, lecture) and others that shift under the impact of constantly emerging technology (for example, computer conferencing).

In the listing that follows, I have endeavored to include those instructional strategies of which Designers should be aware. It is not claimed that the list contains every single strategy there is, but neither is it merely just a few of the more commonly used strategies.

There is no attempt to classify these strategies as, so far, no classification has evolved in this field that has proven generally useful. Also, some semantic problems are related to labels, perceptions of some strategies, and so on. This is reflected in the "related" item under each strategy. Given space limitation, the brief description under each strategy will probably not provide all the information that a particular Designer may want. The listing, however, provides the Designer with help in going to other sources, data banks, and publications.

Action Maze: A highly structured written variation of the case study in which the problem unfolds, one incident at a time, as a consequence of a series of decisions made (or action taken) by the learner.
  Related: case study, simulation, game.

Alter Ego: Used to facilitate communications whereby one person observes the learner in a situation and provides immediate or delayed feedback to the learner on how he is communicating or behaving.
  Related: coaching, counseling.

Annotated Reading List: A list of readings on a particular subject characterized by a short description, explanation, or evaluation of the entry.
  Related: handout, bibliography.

Apprenticeship: A means of learning a craft or skill by which the learner (apprentice) works with an experienced worker on the job.
  Related: OJT, vestibule learning, coaching, JIT.

Audience Reaction: Used with a guest speaker in order to provide for interaction with the learners. A small group of learners is selected, not more than five, who sit with the speaker and ask questions or make comments.
  Related: listening team, interview.

Audio Tape: Using a machine, sound is recorded on specially prepared tape. Earlier models used reel-to-reel, but the most common today is the cassette which comes in various sizes depending upon the playback machine. Recordings are easily made, and professional recordings are available, particularly with tapes by leading professionals or thinkers. Can also be used for providing simple routine instructions.

    Related: video-tape, recordings.

Audio-Visual: Refers to the whole range of instructional materials, using sight and/or sound to aid or reinforce learning.

    Related: films, filmstrips, overhead projectors, opaque projector.

Bibliography: A list of books that relate to the topic of the learning experience. Can also be extended to lists of other nonprinted resources. Should indicate sufficient information so the learner can obtain a desired resource.

    Related: annotated reading list, handout.

Brainstorming: Encourages the generation of ideas without any evaluation. Can also be used in conjunction with problem solving and various forms of creativity. Emphasis is on ideas, not on solutions, provided in a free-wheeling and non-judgmental atmosphere.

    Related: creative thinking, think tank, synectics.

Buzz Group: A class is divided into small units, usually of no more than six learners, meeting simultaneously, to react to a topic or charge given to them. Emphasis is on ideas as time is usually limited to 10 minutes or less. Provision must be made for feedback.

    Related: group discussion, workshop, workgroup.

Cable Television: Franchised transmission of multiple (50 or more) nonstandard channels over coaxial cable to individual homes or institutions for a fixed monthlyfee.

    Related: closed-circuit TV, video-tape.

Case Study: An oral or written account of an event, incident, or situation used to develop critical thinking skills and to gain new perceptions into concepts and issues.

    Related: action maze, in-basket, incident process, role play.

Chalkboard: Vertical surface which can be written on with chalk (and easily erased or modified) to be viewed by groups.

    Related: magnetic board, flannel board.

Clinic: A session, or part of a session, where the learners react to some common experience they have earlier shared. Can also be used when part of the group has an experience they would like the others to react to. The instructor serves as a resource person and carefully observes to avoid losing the objective of the session.

> *Related:*   workshop, workgroup, laboratory, group discussion.

Closed Circuit TV (CCTV):   Cable TV within one or more buildings owned by the institution; used to broadcast prepared tapes or live presentations.

> *Related:*   video-tape, cable television.

Coaching: One-on-one, intensive learning through demonstration and practice, characterized by immediate feedback and correction.

> *Related:*   counseling, alter ego, interactive modeling.

Colloquy: A modification of the panel, using six to eight persons—half representing the audience, half serving as resource persons or experts.

> *Related:*   panel, audience reaction team, listening team.

Computer-Assisted Instruction (CAI):   Highly structured and self-paced, a series of learning segments is presented by a computer; the learner is asked to make a response. The computer electronically processes the response and provides immediate feedback to the learner.

> *Related:*   programmed instruction.

Conference: A group of people discussing a common problem or need. Not all conferences focus on learning objectives. Generally uses a variety of strategies during the conference.

> *Related:*   forum, symposium, workshop.

Confrontation, Search and Cope (CSC):   A three-part experience in which the learner is faced with a problem or a need (confrontation) and is then responsible for searching for a solution (search) and applying the solution to the problem (cope).

> *Related:*   DPT, laboratory.

Contract: Written document developed by the learner and reviewed by the instructor. Contains the objectives, methods of reaching them, and evaluation. Although time consuming, it can result in improved learning for each learner who develops a learning contract. Contracts can be renegotiated during the course of the learning.

> *Related:*   peer-mediated learning, confrontation, search/coping, home study, correspondence.

Correspondence: Self-directed learning characterized by written interaction between the learner and facilitator and implemented through the mail.

> *Related:*   home study, contract.

Creative Thinking: Generates fresh patterns, new relationships, unconventional kinds of thinking.

Related: think tank, brainstorming.

Critique: Participants analyze the strengths and weaknesses of a learning experience and make suggestions for improvements.
Related: coaching, laboratory.

Debate: Two individuals, or teams, take opposing sides of a clearly specified issue. They can compete based on a grading system, or present the opposing views for an audience or other participants. Requires a high level of oral ability and stage presence.
Related: panel, colloquy.

Delphi Technique: A method of organizing larger groups of materials or people into smaller groups by a system of narrowing choices.
Related: small groups.

Demonstration: A presentation that shows how to perform an act or procedure. Can be done by direct presentation or through a prepared video-cassette. Should be brief, allow for interaction with the learner, and then can proceed to the next point.
Related: observation, behavior modeling, mock-up.

Diagnosis, Prescription, Treatment: Learner needs and weaknesses are uncovered by some instrument (diagnosis); a course of action or a plan of study is developed to meet the need (prescription); the learner follows the prescribed treatment in order to correct the diagnosed weakness (treatment).
Related: confrontation/search/cope, peer-mediated learning.

Dialogue: A conversation between two individuals in front of a larger group. Could be invited resource people or class members discussing an assigned topic. They need not present opposing views, but should be exploring the topic in some depth from their prior learning or experience.
Related: discussion, interviewing, dyad, debate.

Discussion: A relatively unstructured exchange of ideas among members of a group on a topic of mutual interest.
Related: dyad, dialogue, colloquy.

Drill: Repetitive, structured practice, which can be written, oral, or motor, to reinforce previous learning.
Related: exercise.

Dyad: Another name for a pair, or when two participants work together or talk together. The dyad can remain in the room, or move to another convenient place. Usually some form of feedback is required when using a dyad.
Related: peer-mediated instruction, discussion, dialogue, buzz groups.

Exercise: A structured learning experience, usually using some instrumentation or guide sheets. May be used to introduce a new topic, for skill practice, review, or evaluation.
Related: games, drill, learner-response system, workbook.

Feedback Mechanisms: A response system (mechanical or nonmechanical) that provides feedback on learning to both facilitator and learner.
Related: audience reaction team, CAI, learner-response system, programmed instruction, teaching machine.

Field Trip: A carefully arranged group visit to an object or place for on-site observation and learning. It should not be used for recreation. Field trips require careful planning, coordination, and an analysis of the learning upon return.
Related: demonstration, guided tour.

Film: Visual and audio presentation characterized by motion; can be purchased or produced in-house. Most common is 16 mm, though 8 mm (home movie type) is also available as well as 35 mm (theater).
Related: video, filmstrip, audio/visual.

Filmstrip: A continuous still film that is advanced one frame at a time; can accompany a speaker or a synchronized audio tape.
Related: film, video, audio/visual.

Fishbowl: A discussion group that is divided in two—the inner circle which discusses and an outer group which observes. Member of outer group may "tap in" or exchange places with a member of inner group.
Related: discussion, laboratory.

Flannel Board: A flannel-covered board, used for presentations to groups in which materials are prepared to stick to the boards.
Related: chalkboard, newsprint, magnetic board, flipchart.

Flipcharts: Previously prepared material, usually permanent, that can be mounted on an easel; the pages are turned to disclose the material.
Related: newsprint, easel, flannel board.

Forum: Another type of question and answer period. Is used after a formal presentation, when the entire group is encouraged to ask questions of the presenter(s). Interaction is between the participants and the presenter(s).
Related: discussion, panel, symposium.

Games: An activity characterized by structured competition to provide the opportunity to try out previous learning.
Related: simulation, exercise.

Handout: Printed materials distributed as part of a learning experience. They should be made available at the appropriate time before, during, or after the session. Ample copies are provided so that each participant has an individual copy.
Related: annotated reading list, bibliography.

Home Study: A learning activity that is largely self-directed; facilitator-learner interaction is accomplished by mail.
Related: correspondence course.

In-Basket: A simulated, reinforcing exercise in which the learner responds to a collection of memos, directives, and problems that force the learner to prioritize, make decisions, and handle the difficulties that might be faced on the job.
Related: case study, action maze.

Incident Process: A variation of the case study where the learner is only given some basic data and then must probe the instructor further to obtain the additional data required to complete the assignment. The instructor must have carefully prepared data sheets which are immediately available to the learner when the appropriate question is asked.
Related: case study, simulation, game, exercise, action maze.

Interactive Modeling: A means of learning new behaviors by observing model or ideal behavior, trying new behavior, and receiving feedback; the cycle is repeated until the new behavior is learned. Sometimes called behavior modeling.
Related: role play, demonstration.

Internship: Supervised practical experience, used for advanced learners who are entering new roles (internship: white collar; apprenticeship: blue collar).
Related: apprenticeship, OJT, practicum, JIT, vestibule learning.

Interview: A strategy for using a resource person without a speech. The resource person is asked questions, while the learners listen. The questions can be spontaneous, or given to the resource person earlier to allow for preparation.
Related: audience reaction team, colloquy, dialogue, panel.

Job Instruction Training (JIT): A form of on-the-job training, characterized by supervisory responsibility for training of new employees.
Related: coaching, apprenticeship, OJT.

Job Rotation: A change of jobs for a specified period of time, with learning as the objective.
Related: OJT, coaching.

Laboratory: An environment equipped for experimentation and testing by the learner. Can be used for a variety of objectives including cognitive, affective, and psychomotor.

Related: T-groups, sensitivity (as one kind of laboratory).

Learner Response Systems: Mechanical devices used by students to enable them to provide immediate and individual feedback to instructors on their learning.
  Related: feedback mechanisms, programmed instruction, teaching machine.

Lecture: A one-way presentation in which a speaker addresses other participants. Can be supplemented with other strategies. Is much maligned as some lecturers do not know how to focus a strictly oral presentation so that it is a stimulating learning experience. Must be limited in time and content.
  Related: forum, audience reaction team, interview.

Listening Groups: Participants are divided into several groups, each of which is assigned the task of listening to and observing an assigned part of a speech, demonstration, panel, and so on.
  Related: audience reaction team.

Magnetic Board: A magnetic device used to display prepared materials that are magnetized. Allows for showing movement, relationships, and so on.
  Related: chalkboard, flannel board, newsprint.

Mock-up: A full-sized replica built accurately to scale, but not the real object.
  Related: model, simulator.

Model: Usually used to present a physical item, but in a different form than usual in order to facilitate learning. Can also be used to present ideas, and show the flow of a series of actions. Is not the real thing, but represents the real thing or idea.
  Related: mock-up, diagram, flowchart.

Newsprint: Large sheets of paper mounted on easels to be written on with felt tip markers or crayons (may be called flipchart pads).
  Related: chalkboard, flannel board, magnetic board.

Nonverbal Learning: A learning experience that does not use any spoken communication. Must use speech to give instructions and process the learning after completion of the nonverbal experience.
  Related: exercise, laboratory.

Observation: Learner observes and reports on an action or incident.
  Related: demonstration, field trip.

Opaque Projector: A device capable of reproducing an image of greater size than the original, from a nontransparent master, such as a book.
  Related: overhead projector.

Overhead Projector: A device capable of reproducing an image of greater size than the original from a transparent master. Masters (called slides or transparencies) can be commercially produced or instructor made. Special marking pens allow for flexibility and if nonpermanent can be easily erased.

Related: opaque projectors.

Panel: A group of several persons having a purposeful conversation on an assigned topic in the presence of participants.

Related: discussion, debate, colloquy, dialogue, symposium.

Peer-Mediated Learning (PML):   Learners are grouped with their peers and facilitate each others' learning under the guidance of a group leader who provides them with specially prepared materials.

Related: internship, observation.

Practicum: A study program which allows the learner to pursue a special project under the guidance of an instrument.

Related: tutorial, internship, apprenticeship.

Programmed Instruction: Subject matter presented in a series of small carefully graduated, sequential steps, so that the student achieves mastery of the material presented and is self-paced.

Related: teaching machine, CAI, feedback mechanism, computer-assisted instruction.

Project: A specially assigned task in which the participants work independently on an assignment, such as a term paper or a book review.

Related: field trip.

Puppets: Less than life-size figures through which the learners can express ideals and thoughts which might not be possible in direct conversation.

Related: skit, role play.

Question: An inquiry designed to test, stimulate thought, or clarify.

Related: discussion.

Reading Assignment: Assigned readings in textbooks, manuals, periodicals and other printed media, followed by written report, class discussion, or other positive activity.

Related: textbook, bibliography, annotated reading list.

Role Play: Interaction among two or more individuals on a given topic or situation. Often used to provide practice for learners on previously presented material. Has many variations including multiple role play and role reversal.

Related: interactive modeling, simulation, case study, laboratory.

Seminar: A form of learning where each learner in the group is expected to be at a sufficient level to actively participate. The instructor serves as a resource person

with the seminar members being reponsible for the interaction during the seminar.
Related: workshop, clinic, discussion.

Sensitivity Training: Not only "training" but also "education," it involves a group which is deprived of leader, agenda, and norms. As the group struggles to fill those gaps, members exhibit behaviors which are then used as the basis for learning.
Related: laboratory, T-groups.

Slides: A transparency capable of being enlarged and projected onto a screen. Can be synchronized with an audio tape, or support a speaker.
Related: filmstrip, audio-visual.

Skit: A short, rehearsed dramatic presentation, involving two or more persons, usually acted from a prepared script, and dramatizes an incident which illustrates a problem or situation.
Related: role play.

Still Pictures: Photographs usually offered in a sequence to illustrate a point or show the learner a view which would not ordinarily be seen.
Related: diagrams, field trip, observation, flipchart.

Study Guide: Provides an organized progressive learning experience, in written form, leading towards predetermined objectives. Useful for individual learning, though can be used with groups.
Related: workbook, handouts.

Symposium: A series of related speeches by several persons qualified to speak with authority on different phases of the same topic, or closely related topics.
Related: colloquy, debate, dialogue, interview, panel.

Teaching Machine: A mechanical device (simple or complex) that carries a programmed learning activity which provides immediate feedback to individual learner responses.
Related: CAI, PI.

Team Building: A concept that uses various instructional strategies to promote effective group interaction.
Related: exercises, role play, laboratory.

Telecon: Prearranged conference by telephone.
Related: CCTV.

Test: Any means measuring skill, knowledge, intelligence, or aptitudes against some standard.
Related: question, exercise, feedback.

Textbook: A manual of instruction; a book containing a presentation of the principles of a subject, used as a basis for instruction.
   Related: workbook.

Think Tank: An ongoing group of people, with the task of generating fresh ideas, using a combination of strategies.
   Related: brainstorming, creative thinking.

Tutorial: Tailor-made reading sequences developed to help engage in self-directed inquiry, with periodic consultation on the individual's progress and problems.
   Related: directed study, DPT, contract, correspondence.

Simulation: A learning environment constructed to allow the learner to experience the desired performance without incurring the risk associated with the real-life situation.
   Related: game, role play, vestibule learning.

Video-Cassette: A specially treated ribbon (tape) capable of retaining pictures and sound which have been recorded on its surface. Originally reel-to-reel but now more common in cassette form. Can be color, or black and white. Cassettes can be produced in house or purchased commercially on a variety of topics.
   Related: film, audio-visual.

VTR (Video Tape Recorder):   An electromechanical device, capable of recording and/or playing back a video-tape. Also referred to as VCR (Video Cassette Recorder).
   Related: film.

Vestibule Learning: Off-line, instructor-led training, designed to bring the learner up to production standards before assuming on-line responsibilities.
   Related: OJT, JIT, apprenticeship, simulation.

White Board: Similar to a chalkboard but is white rather than some darker color. Comes in a variety of sizes and can be mounted or portable. Uses a washable, nonpermanent marker which is easily removed with an eraser or damp cloth. Colored markers are available.
   Related: chalkboard, flannel board, newsprint.

Workbook: A book of questions or written exercises which provides space for the learner to write answers.
   Related: drill, exercise.

Work Group: Members work toward stated objectives and produce a tangible product.
   Related: discussion, laboratory, performance team.

Work Shop: A group learning experience with the purpose of producing a product by having the participants highly involved.
>   *Related:*   seminar, conference.

Work Study: Learners work on a job related to their studies part of the time, and study part of the time. Designed to reinforce learning as soon as possible in a work situation.
>   *Related:*   cooperative education, internship, apprenticeship

EVALUATION AND FEEDBACK

Once again the Designer must consider E&FB though, as will be seen, the emphasis is much different than in previous events. The objectives of this event were:

> To select instructional strategies that are appropriate for the curriculum, the learner, the instructor, and the organization.

> To revise the lesson plans to reflect the decisions about instructional strategies.

Analysis

The analysis, for this event, is different than those previously prepared for the other events. This reflects, in part, that the E&FB for this event may not include learners as has been the case in previous events. For this event, the Designer can opt to use external people to react to what has been accomplished.

There are many ways to prepare the analysis. Under certain conditions the Designer lists each instructional strategy and the reason for the selection. By no means is this an easy task, but it can serve to highlight the assumptions made by the Designer during this event. A detailed listing of this kind also communicates to others the basis for selecting a particular strategy rather than some of the alternatives. At a deeper level of specificity, the Designer can also indicate, for example, why a particular film was chosen over some other possible films that might have been chosen. The more detail the Designer provides in this analysis, the clearer will be the completed lesson plan that is the ultimate result.

At this point, the analysis lists the selection and decisions that have been made. The analysis also highlights what is readily available and what must be made or bought. This includes rentals or other temporary procurement. Although no final decision can be made at this time, such information will be required during the next event, "Obtain Instructional Resources." If the analysis contains sufficient data for decision making for the current event, it will also provide the basis for the next event.

The analysis should specify clearly the type of instructors required for the program, as designed to this point. A lesson plan has been produced which reflects the type of instructor who will be expected to use it. Although instructors may not yet have been selected, and the decisions regarding selection will be made in the next event, the Designer can capture the momentum of this event by indicating the profile of the instructors who will be expected to use the lesson plans.

There are times when several instructional strategies may be equally appropriate. The Designer reflects this in the analysis by providing alternative lesson plans with the same content and sequence, but with different proposed strategies.

Feedback

The groups to be involved in feedback in this event will differ somewhat from those involved earlier in the CEM. This requires that the Designer provide for appropriate linkage so that those involved for the first time are not made to feel inadequate. As we know, feelings of inadequacy can produce hostility, and that would not be helpful during feedback.

The Designer may wish to share the lesson plans with others in the HRD unit, if the Designer is fortunate enough to have peers available. Some Designers have developed networks of peers outside their own organizations with whom they can exchange lesson plans for feedback purposes.

When the content is not familiar to the Designer, the lesson plans can be shared with the Subject Matter Specialists who were involved in earlier events of the CEM.

It may be desirable to involve the supervisor in this event. Of course, the supervisor is not expected to be an expert on instructional strategies, but it is possible for supervisors to provide insight into how their people might react to the instructional strategies selected for the learning situation.

The instructor is a crucial element in the learning process, as the instructor is expected to use the lesson plan that has been developed up to this point. It is logical, therefore, to have instructors involved in the feedback in this event. The difficulty may be that it is not possible, at this time, to specifically identify the instructors. The assumption here is that they will be from within the organization but have not yet been identified. If so, the Designer can ask that there be at least a preliminary identification of some potential instructors who could be asked to provide feedback on the lesson plans. The core of the feedback should be on the instructional strategies, not on the curriculum, but it is important that the instructors feel comfortable with the fit between the curriculum and the instructional strategies.

There is another group who might be involved but who, up to this point, have not been part of the CEM. These are the budget and fiscal people. At first, it may seem strange to involve this group, but we are now reaching that part of the CEM where financial resources become significant. Of course, if the Designer has determined that no special financial resources will be needed, involving the budget and fiscal people is superfluous. If there is the possibility of funding problems, this is the time to involve those people.

The B&F people are not particularly interested in all the details, but they frequently want to get something more than a formal request. They want to have some feeling for what they are expected to fund. They should not be overwhelmed with the lesson plans, but the analysis should be marked carefully to indicate those areas in which the B&F people can be expected to have some concern.

Decisions

Many of the decisions that have to be made for this event are in the province of the Designer. They are essentially of a technical nature related to learning and instructional strategies, and that is the area where the Designer is expected to have competence. Other people are still to be involved, however, as their input to the process is essential.

The following are the decision questions that must be asked:

1.   Do the instructional strategies complement the curriculum?

There is no other purpose for the learning strategies than to implement the curriculum that has been previously agreed upon. If there is an inconsistency between a particular instructional strategy and the curriculum, reexamination of the curriculum may be required. Generally the curriculum should not be changed to satisfy the selection of a particular strategy.

2.   If the lesson plans are implemented, will be objectives be reached?

The lesson plans should be based on the objectives previously agreed upon. It sometimes happens, though not too frequently, that the final version of the lesson plans contains some alterations in the previously stated objectives. This is the place for a check on the agreement of the objectives in the final lesson plan and the objectives determined by the earlier event of the CEM.

3.   Do the lesson plans reflect the identified learning needs?

This too is a checkpoint question. It should not be difficult to determine if the lesson plans are directly related to the identified needs. It is equally important to verify that the needs have not changed. That can happen, because there has been a time lapse between the event that focused on "Identifying Learning Needs" and the completion of this event. It is possible that the potential learners have changed, due to job reassignment, attrition, and so on. If so, learning needs may have changed and therefore may not be correctly reflected in the lesson plans.

Time lapse is a factor that has not received adequate attention. The Designer should not be defensive of what was previously accomplished but should recognize that all organizations are in a constant state of flux and change. The Designer may choose to ignore this natural phenomenon but only at the risk of producing a learning program that is outdated before it is offered.

4. If the lesson plans are used, will they relate to current job performance?

The phrasing of this question has been carefully developed to encourage the Designer to relate to the job, as it is *now* expected to be performed. As with the previous question, the time lapse factor is significant. The rapid impact of technology, managerial decisions, and new equipment are only a few of the factors that cause rapid changes in job performance requirement. The lesson plans should be compared to the job performance as it exists at this time to determine if there are any changes that require further examination of needs, objectives, or curriculum.

5. If the training is conducted using these lesson plans, will the problem be solved?

It may be redundant, but it is significant enough to bear repetition, that the major purpose of training is to solve problems or avert possible problems. Therefore the evaluation of the lesson plans must be in terms of the identified problems.

6. Can the selected instructional strategies be implemented?

This is a difficult question, but one that must be asked at this time. The final answer will be in the next event, but at least a preliminary decision is necessary here. If additional equipment, facilities, materials, and funds are needed, there should at least be the recognition at this decision point. The specification of these will be explored in the next event.

In addition to the physical and financial resources, the Designer also questions if the necessary human resources will be made available. At this time, only a general recognition of this area is needed. The specifics will evolve in the next event.

7. Will the selected instructional strategies be available when needed?

Whether one chooses to make or buy, time is needed to obtain selected instructional strategies that are not now under the control of the HRD unit. It can take time to make a good video-cassette, even if the HRD unit has its own studio. Therefore the Designer determines if there is a delivery date for the instructional program that is out of phase with the availability of the instructional strategies.

A buy decision may require even more time, depending upon the fiscal cycle in the organization. Even if the money is in the annual budget, it may not be available at the time when the expenditure is needed by the Designer.

CONCLUSION

The Designer should now have produced lesson plans that are almost ready for delivery. The next event is to "Obtain Instructional Resources" so the program can be readily implemented.

REFERENCES

1.   The initial work in brainstorming is credited to Alex Osborne in the 1950s. Since then, the work has been extended in various ways. There is the Center for Creative Thinking in Buffalo headed by Dr. Sydney Parnes. Variations have emerged. A variety of approaches can be found in *Training Creative Thinking* by Gary A. Davis. (New York: Holt, Rinehart, and Winston, 1971).

2.   Historical background on sensitivity training can be found in *T-Group Theory and Laboratory Method* by Leland Bradford, Jack R. Gibb, and Kenneth D. Benne. (New York: John Wiley & Sons, 1964).

3.   There are three major publications in the meeting field: *Meeting News, Successful Meetings,* and *Meetings and Conventions.* Each publishes an annual directory of meeting facilities with some detail on room size, and so on.

ADDITIONAL PRINTED RESOURCES

Anderson, Ronald H. *Selecting and Developing Media for Instruction.* New York: Van Nostrand, 1976.

Belch, Jean. *Contemporary Games: A Directory and Bibliography Covering Games and Play Situations or Simulations Used for Instruction and Training by Schools, Colleges and Universities, Government, Business, and Management.* Detroit: Gale Research Co., 1973.

Brilhart, John K. *Effective Group Discussion.* Dubuque, Iowa: William C. Brown, 1974.

Dyer, William G. (editor). *Modern Theory and Method in Group Training.* New York: Van Nostrand, 1972.

Engel, Herbert M. *Handbook of Creative Learning Exercises.* Houston: Gulf Publishing, 1973.

Goldstein, Arnold P., and Melvin Sorcher. *Changing Supervisor Behavior.* Elmsford, N.Y.: Pergamon, 1974.

Gordon, William J. J. *Synectics.* New York: Harper & Row, 1961.

Horn, Robert E. (editor). *The Guide to Simulation: Games for Education and Training.* Cranbury, N.J.: Didactic Systems, 1977.

Howe, Anne (editor). *International Yearbook of Education and Instructional Technology.* Chicago: Nichols Publishing, 1980.

Hyman, Ronald. *Improving Discussion Leadership.* New York: Teachers College, 1980.

Knowles, Malcolm. *Self-Directed Learning.* New York: Association Press, 1975.

Laird, Dugan. *Approaches to Training and Development.* Reading, Mass.: Addison-Wesley, 1978.

Maier, Norman R. F., Allen R. Solem, and Ayesha A. Maier. *The Role-Playing Technique: A Handbook for Management and Leadership Practice.* San Diego: University Associates, 1975.

Napier, Rodney W., and Mati G. Gershenfeld. *Groups: Theory and Experience.* Boston: Houghton Mifflin, 1973.

Newstrom, John W., and Edward E. Scannell. *Games Trainers Play.* New York: McGraw-Hill, 1980.

Pfeiffer, William, and John Jones. (They produce an annual handbook of learning exercises which can be supplemented with articles on theory and practice.) San Diego: University Associates (issued annually).

Silvern, Leonard. *Principles of Computer Assisted Instruction.* Los Angeles: Education and Training Consultants, 1970.

Tough, Allen. *The Adult's Learning Projects.* Ontario Institute for Studies in Education, 1971.

9

Obtain

Instructional Resources

The Designer who has followed the Critical Events Model to this point will find that this event (see Figure 9-1) brings together all the work of the earlier events. The stage is now set for the specific decisions that must result from this event. The various people who need to be consulted for this event will have been involved in the earlier events.

The objective of this event is:

To assure that all the necessary resources will be made available for the program that has been designed.

VARIETY OF RESOURCES NEEDED

In organizations where there are large HRD units, at this time the Designer may step aside and the HRD director or a similar person take over. One reason is that Designers are not required to have the planning skills required by this event, though it is beneficial to the organization when the Designer does have the requisite skills. Usually the Designer is selected and assigned to the design task for a variety of competencies that may not include planning coordination.

In large organizations, the coordination of the necessary resources may be seen as a management function, and the Designer is generally not considered to be part of management. Where there is a small HRD unit, it is not unlikely that the Designer will also be required to have management skills and to function as a manager, particularly during this event of the CEM. Though there will be continuing reference to the Designer, it is recognized that this event may be in the province of a manager of HRD.

The variety of resources needed is not unusual and falls within the traditional categories of: physical, financial, and human.

THE CRITICAL EVENTS MODEL

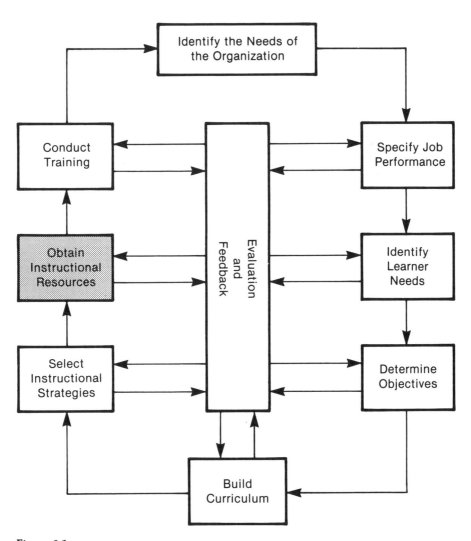

Figure 9.1

Physical Resources

Referring back to the lesson plans, the Designer can now identify the specific *equipment* that is required. As used here, equipment refers to those items that are expected to have a life beyond a single use. What is frequently used is audio-visual equipment. That includes projectors and the software, such as films or filmstrips. The overhead projector and transparencies are also considered equipment.

There is room for argument here. Shouldn't films, overhead transparencies, slides, and similar articles be included as materials rather than equipment? There are good arguments for each classification but the basic point is to be consistent. Whatever classification your organization applies to films, and so on, you should do the same. Also, it should be the same for every program and not waver back and forth between equipment and materials.

The rationale for including films, slides, and so on in this category is that they are generally used for more than one program. There is an element of accountability (or inventory if you prefer). Even films that are rented for a single program may be included in this category, for there is accountability—they must be returned.

The Designer must first identify the exact equipment that is required to implement the lesson plans and then determine availability. If programs are conducted within the organization facility, there is probably a depository that contains the equipment and a unit that controls its use. In general, the equipment should be in the hands of the HRD unit, but this is not always so. In some organizations such equipment is under the control of some other part of the organization, and the HRD unit must initiate requests when the equipment is needed.

In either event, the Designer determines that the necessary equipment is on hand and available at the times needed, according to the lesson plan. When an organization conducts many learning programs at the same time, careful scheduling is required. In organizations with many programs, a specialist is usually responsible for the scheduling and maintenance of the equipment, and the Designer works with that specialist to coordinate the particular equipment needed for a specific lesson. If there is no specialist, the Designer may have the additional function of determining if the equipment is in working order. The obvious problem is that the Designer can check this out before the program begins only to find at a later time that the equipment has been used in the interim and is no longer working. This is an important problem, for it discourages some Designers from building equipment into their lesson plans.

When an off-site facility is being used, the equipment picture is different. There are three possible ways to provide equipment for off-site programs. The first is for the organization to provide its own equipment. Depending upon the size and type of equipment, this may not always be practical. Technology has reduced the size of much of the equipment used in learning programs, but there are still some programs that require special equipment, or a labor squad to bring the equipment to the site.

A second possibility is to rent the equipment from outside the facility. Some conference facilities prefer this, as it is too complicated and costly for them to stock the various pieces of equipment that may be requested. A facility that has been built as a "conference site" can be expected to have the basic equipment of projectors, easels, and so on. This cannot be taken for granted, however. At one major hotel in New York City, one that describes itself as having a conference facility, I had blocked 16 rooms for small group work. Their information stated that each room came with an easel. Later, in the negotiations, I discovered that they had only one easel and the others would have to be rented and charged to my account.

The third alternative is to rent from companies that specialize in rental equipment of the kind used in learning programs. There are many such companies, and if rental is the policy of the organization, the Designer should maintain a list of companies, the kinds of equipment, their rates, and previous experience with delivery and condition of the equipment. Some hotels and motels that offer facilities for learning programs advertise that equipment is available. They may even provide a lengthy list with prices and conditions. However, the supplier may not be the hotel, but an outside firm that has an arrangement and even space in the hotel/motel. The Designer will have to determine if the facility requires that the supplier be used, or if the Designer is allowed to rent from another organization for delivery to the hotel/motel.

Renting, either from the conference site or from an external supplier, has many advantages. The Designer's organization does not have to maintain an inventory of the variety of equipment that may be needed and have funds tied up in equipment that may be used only infrequently. The rental company has the responsibility for maintenance of the equipment and for any repairs that are necessary. A good rental company, and there are many, will be able to provide a wide range of equipment and will change the equipment as technology contributes to the improvement and variety of the equipment.

Materials are defined as those items that are used in a learning program that are expendable. There is no intent that an inventory be maintained, and neither the instructor nor the Designer is held accountable for the materials made available to a program and not returned.

Here too, we can get involved in long debates about classification. Some materials are fairly obvious, such as writing implements, pads, and even chalk. A difference of opinion can arise when we talk of items such as felt tip markers, masking tape, and clear transparencies. Some organizations actually inventory these items and the instructor must account for them. If cost analysis was done, it would probably be determined that it is more expensive to retain the records and to take time to assign accountability than the cost of lost materials warrants. The Designer will have to conform to the practice within the organization, but should try to influence it so that such items are not considered equipment. If instructors have to account for each marker (turning in dried out ones) or clear transparencies (even though misused with a permanent marker), the tendency will be for the instructor to avoid using such materials even though stipulated in the lesson plan.

Some materials must be controlled, but in a different way. If a training program requires the use of a workbook, that is expendable and therefore material. The learner will use the workbook and either it is to be discarded or is designed so that the learner takes it back to the work situation. In either event, it is not to be returned and therefore falls within the classification of a material. Confusion may arise from the need to print numerous copies. This requires inventory control, but only for one purpose and that is to assure that there are sufficient copies when the need arises. The instructor is not expected to return any workbooks.

The responsibility of the Designer is to plan for the materials that will be needed. Even if they are common materials, the kind that are always available, such as pencils, the Designer must provide sufficient notice to whoever provides this (from within the unit) so that stocks are not depleted. If there is more than one Designer/Manager this becomes even more crucial. Designers know what they will need, but there may be an inordinate demand that cannot be met if all the Designers do not funnel their material requests through one channel.

The final physical element is *facilities*. This is generally thought of as classroom space or conference space, depending upon the organization. The Designer must be cautious about the use of these words, as they can communicate something different from what is intended. Facilities is a more encompassing and neutral term.

When an organization has numerous programs, space may be assigned to the HRD unit for conducting those learning programs. The ideal model is to have this space controlled by the HRD unit, so that scheduling does not become a problem. When control of space is not in the purview of the HRD unit, the Designer will have to request space much earlier in the CEM, even before the selection of strategies that can determine the kind of space that will be required.

Financial Resources

It is now possible for the Designer to prepare a specific budget for this program. The exact process will depend upon whether the HRD unit is funded as a budget center, a cost center, or a profit center. No matter what the form, it is still desirable to cost out each program, and this is the time in the CEM when this must be done.

In earlier events, reference was made to costs. Indeed, some costs may already have been incurred for the use of Subject Matter Specialists from outside the organization. Some calculations will have been made in relation to instructional strategies or other make-or-buy decisions. Now is the time to bring all of this together.

A common error made by Designers is to propose the program at the lowest cost. Of course the Designer should not be extravagant, but cost is relative. Does your family want a small mobile home or a big multiroom house with grass and trees? It is not possible to give a single or simple answer to that question. You would probably respond that it depends on need, financial resources, future movement of the family, location, and so on. Similar thinking is required when costing out a learning program. The Designer first identifies the numerous variables and then develops alternative cost plans.

The Designer should not assume that the organization wants the cheapest program. It may want the best, and cheapest and best are neither the same or mutually exclusive. The Designer estimates the most desirable program and the comparable cost. A basic reason for this approach is that the organization relies on the Designer to propose the appropriate program. If the Designer tries to bring it down to the lowest cost, under the assumption that cost is the only factor, a disservice is being done to the organization.

If there has been a history of low-cost programs the Designer can anticipate some resistance when costs go up. The Designer must be able to justify the cost in terms of the market place and the results.

As the financial area is measurable, the Designer must recognize the need to show financial results for a training program. This is not always possible, but the closer the Designer can approach that relationship, the less difficulty he will experience in obtaining the requested financial resources. The final evaluation can, in some cases, be reported in financial terms. The Designer, or somebody in the HRD unit, must be able to think in the financial terms of the organization [1]. There are concepts that must be explored and understood, such as: return on investment (ROI), profit, bottom line, and cost effective. Despite the general literature in the field, the Designer will find that each organization has its own formula or way of looking at the financial expenditures and the measurement of return or results. The Designer will probably turn to the HRD Manager for assistance at this phase of the event.

Budget alone is not enough. *Cash* outlay is also important. The budget only says that it is planned to have the money earmarked for that item; it does not say it can actually be spent. (Note that I am using cash, money, and similar terms interchangeably; all refer to some kind of negotiable instrument.) The Designer may be surprised to find that there are cultural behaviors related to the budget. For example, in one organization where I was employed "everybody knew" (remember cultural behavior?) that a department head was expected to spend only up to 90% of the budget without higher level approval. Generally only 80% would ever be spent, so the higher levels could show the results of their efforts in cost cutting and savings. A Designer who planned to spend the total budgeted amount would not remain long with that organization.

Some items may be purchased from other parts of the organization or may be charged to other parts of the organization. Although these are only internal book transfers, the Designer must determine the appropriate procedure and build this into the budget process that is reflected in this event.

A limitation is that we cannot offer the Designer or the HRD Manager any clear-cut guidelines for what is to be costed or charged either internally or externally. A training program has many costs that can be anticipated, but for which we have no accounting experience. For example, what about the salary or wage of a learner while in training? How should this be costed? There are many possible variations and each organization has its own way of doing this. It can range from charging the "lost production" to the cost of training, to ignoring the whole thing and taking no note of this personnel cost. Similarly the cost of the travel may have to be costed in the training budget—it may be absorbed by the learner's unit or even appear in somebody else's budget.

The basic approach for the Designer is to determine how all the items are presently handled. This requires that the Designer (or somebody in the HRD unit) devote the time needed to identify all the anticipated costs. Then, the items can be specified and decisions made as to what will be charged and how. When the Designer does this unilaterally, there are bound to be problems. The financial people in the organization must be involved, so that funds can be made available and that the appropriate accounting procedures can reflect those costs that have been agreed upon.

An item that is frequently overlooked is the need for repairs and replacements. All equipment, at some time, requires some repair. As indicated earlier, if the HRD unit relies on equipment rented from the outside, the repair cost will not be necessary, but the rental costs must be provided. When the HRD unit has its own equipment, the HRD Manager must be familiar with how depreciation is handled in the organization, and the Designer must be sure that this accounting procedure is included in the cost estimate for the training program.

It is understandable that a Designer, and some HRD Managers, prefer not to become involved in the financial aspects. If the HRD Manager is a general manager type who is only temporarily in the HRD unit, it would not be unusual for this individual to be knowledgeable about the financial procedures in the organization. If the HRD Manager does not have that background, it must be acquired, or there should be someone on the HRD staff who is conversant with the financial procedures in the organization. The least desirable position is to have someone outside the HRD unit responsible for drafting the budget for the training program being designed.

There is also the sensitivity, discussed earlier, of knowing when to request funds. The budget cycle varies from organization to organization, but it is there.

In some organizations, it is specifially stated in manuals and procedure handbooks. Many organizations do not specify all the elements in the cycle, as that is "known" only by those in power. (As has been said often, knowledge is power or at least one form thereof.) If the HRD unit is not in the power structure, good training programs can be deprived of part of the budget or may not receive funds when they are needed.

Human Resources

Learning programs require human resources. Even if the decision is to provide a totally machine-mediated program, it is still necessary, at some point, to use people.

A learning program must have a program facilitator who is generally not the Designer. The titles used for the program facilitators vary greatly, and one is the *Supervisor of Programs*. This person functions much as any supervisor, in that the work is accomplished through the efforts of others. The Supervisor of Programs should *not* be the instructor, although this can happen, particularly in very small organizations. Perhaps it cannot be helped in those situations, but it should be avoided whenever possible. In a large HRD unit, it is possible for a person to be a Supervisor of Programs for one program, while being an instructor in another. It is even possible for the Designer to be a Supervisor of Programs, but these two positions require much different competencies.

The Supervisor of Programs *must* come from within the HRD unit. This emphasis may surprise you as I have generally tended to present alternatives. This is one case where there are few acceptable alternatives. The Supervisor of Programs is responsible for many activities, which will appear in the next event of the CEM. Therefore, when obtaining instructional resources, the Designer indicates the need for the Supervisor and even recommends who, within the HRD unit, would be the best Supervisor for this program.

It is possible that the Supervisor has been designated much earlier in the CEM. Where it is possible to do this, the Supervisor should be working alongside the Designer from the first event. Generally this does not happen, but the earlier the Supervisor can be involved, the more familiar he will be with the program. Too often the Designer completes the work up to this point, and during this event the Supervisor and Designer work together, but after that the Designer is out of the picture. This is the reality, even if it is not the best thing. However, we must work within the limitations imposed by our organizations while still seeking the best use of the resources made available to us.

Another important human resource is the *instructor*. This is not the best term for this person, but it designates that individual who is responsible for delivering the learning experience. Even a totally machine-mediated program needs an instructor to function as a counselor or coach. In all learning programs, at least one person must be designated as the instructor to whom the learner can relate.

There are many kinds of instructors. The Designer identifies the kind of instructor needed for the specific program being designed. As mentioned earlier, in some situations, the instructor may have been identified in a tentative way at an earlier event. Now is the time to designate the requested instructor by name (or names where there is more than one instructor).

The instructor can come from within the organization or be external to the organization. If from within the organization, the instructor might come from the HRD unit, though organizations are finding that it is unproductive to maintain large instructional staffs. There are some unique situations (such as in the military) where internal instructional staffs are preferable. In company-owned learning centers, instructional staff can be assigned from within the company for specified limited periods of time. Many organizations run courses in supervision and management with instruction by HRD staff.

If HRD staff are to be used, the Designer determines during this event whether the required staff will be available. This will probably not be the decision of the Designer, but of the HRD Manager, though the Manager should rely on the Designer for recommendations.

The external instructor comes from a variety of sources. An external SMS, who has been used during the design phase of the program, might be recruited to instruct. For some programs, universities have become an important source of external instructors. There are consulting companies, more appropriately labeled as "vendors," that provide instructional services (and that is why they are not consultants).

It is important that there be some explicit agreement, perhaps even in writing, with the external resource. This is particularly important when using a company rather than an individual. There are numerous instances when an HRD Manager expected to get a particular instructor from the vendor only to be told at the last minute that there would be a substitution. This is most likely to happen when the company has a star or two who are outstanding people and on whom the company depends. There are limits to their time, however, so it is wise to determine exactly who will be doing the instruction.

At an earlier event of the CEM, there may have been a buy decision for a program. Some packaged programs bring with them the possibility of instructional assistance, while in other packages the instructional service is an essential part of what has been bought. If instruction is part of the total packaged program, little need be done at this time except to determine that the financial resources have been provided.

Whether internal or external, there could be the need for what is commonly referred to as "training of trainers." This is the process of preparing an individual to serve as an instructor. Somehow the term "instructor of instructors" has not gained general usage, though it is more descriptive of what is meant. The learning program for instructors is by no means a set and established program; rather it varies depending upon need.

When the instructor already knows the subject matter, all that may be required is a learning program that will develop the competencies needed to instruct that program. This is essential when the lesson plans call for instructional strategies that are beyond the current competency of the identified instructors.

It is also possible that the instructor knows the strategies, but needs work on the subject matter. Of course, this once again raises that perennial question as to whether the organization should select instructors for their competence in content or in process. Naturally the answer is: it depends. There are too many variables in any such situation to give a definitive response. If instructor training is required, there is the need for additional resources and time. Preparing instructors can delay the start of the final event of the CEM, but such a delay is preferable to providing an instructor who is not prepared.

The final, but obvious human resources are the *participants*. It can be argued that they are not a resource in the usual sense, though they are certainly essential to the conduct of the program. At some of the earlier events of the CEM, reference was made to the potential learners. At this point, the listing of potential learners should be made firm. That makes it possible to develop specific rosters, to know almost exactly the quantity of materials needed, to propose a schedule of dates and time, and to do all the myriad tasks related to delivering the program to a specific group.

In some organizations, particularly those using the budget center approach, all the HRD unit may get is the number who will be attending, but not the specific names. Sometimes this is sufficient, but not if precourse work is required or if screening of participants is necessary to provide for either homogeneity or heterogeneity, depending upon how the course has been designed.

Think back to "Identify Learning Needs" and you will recall that this was based on identified potential learners. The Designer must now determine if the "learners" whose needs were identified at that time are still the same learners who are scheduled to attend the program. If they are, then the program is right on target. If there have been changes, the Designer must determine the extent of those changes and whether this requires any modification of the program as reflected in the lesson plans.

Ignoring this step can produce a great deal of conflict. The Designer can follow all the events and design an excellent program only to discover that the participants who arrive are much different from those previously involved in the CEM. It does no good to try to find out who was wrong, for nobody was in error during the earlier design work. If there has been a time lapse from the earlier event to the present, some personnel changes can be expected. It is time consuming, at this point, but the Designer must determine the effect of any personnel changes on the program that is ready for delivery.

An equally significant personnel change can be among the supervisors who were involved earlier. By no means do all supervisors behave in the same manner, yet there is a tendency to think that the job makes the person. Of course it influences behavior, but each person brings different competencies, values, and beliefs to a job. Supervisors have been involved earlier in many of the events of the CEM. If they are not now the same supervisors, the Designer can anticipate some difficulty unless there is a plan to involve the current supervisors before the program actually starts.

CHECKLIST OF INSTRUCTIONAL RESOURCES NEEDED

The activities so far in the CEM have resulted in the lesson plans. The work done under this event is reflected in a much different way, but is parallel to the lesson plans. The following checklist brings together the instructional resources required by the lesson plans. As presented here, there will be relatively little discussion, for that would repeat much of what has already been noted at other points in this book. Some repetition cannot be avoided as we are now bringing together various factors that have been discussed during several prior events.

Scheduling

■ Are the necessary facilities available?

   The specific facilities have been identified earlier. Now, it must be determined if they will be available when needed for the actual program.

■ Who will actually instruct?

   This is the time when the instructors should be designated specifically by name. The purpose, here, is to be able to respond to the following questions.

■ Will the designated instructors be available when needed?

   The dates of the program are required so instructors can be assigned. If they are internal, it can mean that they will have to be released from their present work assignment for the instructional period and allowed adequate time for preparation. If they are external, it may mean that specific contracts or letters of agreement have to be drafted, and perhaps even signed, before there is a certainty that the external instructors will be available.

■ Do the instructors require any prior instruction before beginning their duties?

   If they are internal people, and are Subject Matter Specialists, they may need some form of "training of trainers" experience before they begin instruction. If the instructors come from the HRD unit, they may still require some kind of preparation for the specific program before meeting with the participants. When the instructors are external, preparation may also be required. A frequent error on the part of HRD people is to assume that when they use an external person, that person is ready to "park the car and start instructing." In some cases, that may be true. When it is not, and no provision has been made for some preparation, do not be surprised if the external person is less than adequate. If the external instructor is using a packaged program, very little preparation, internally, is required. If the external person is using his own material, it is important for the internal HRD person to ascertain that it is appropriate, in terms of the total program of which that session (to be done by the external instructor) may only be one part. If the external instructor is expected to use the lesson plans designed internally, provision should be made for preparation and review with the internal Designer.

■ Will the learners be available?

The focus of the program is on the learners. This is the point at which the Designer (or the HRD Manager, or Supervisor) determines if the learners will be available. There should be an agreed upon procedure for selecting the specific learners and determining if they will be available. The actual notification will not occur until the next event, but here the Designer is seeking agreement from the Supervisors that the learners will be able to attend the program.

Equipment and Materials

■ If to be purchased, is there a specific list of the items?

It is now possible to list specifically what has to be purchased. Although budget is another item, the purchase list should reflect what needs to be bought, and the amount of money that will be requested. Also, it may be necessary for the Designer to revise the list, when budget decisions have been made.

A complication can arise when the HRD unit must go out on competitive bid for equipment. (This is less frequently done for materials.) The bidding process may take considerable time and slow down the whole schedule. If your organization requires open and competitive bidding, you have several alternatives. If you are involved in a "crash" program, it may be necessary to anticipate the program equipment needs and request the equipment at a much earlier event in the CEM. The obvious problem is that, as the design process proceeds, you lose your options to make changes in the instructional strategies reflected by that equipment.

If time is available, it is proper to leave the decision to purchase for this point. Whenever the decision is made, a specific list is required. It should relate directly to the lesson plans previously produced.

■   If to be produced in-house, is there a specific list of items?

This applies more to materials than equipment. It is unusual to produce in-house equipment, though this is possible if mock-ups or similar strategies are to be used when the equipment is not available on the open market.

The list of materials will come directly from the lesson plans. Each item should be listed, even down to pencils and paper. Though not "produced" in-house, they are generally available through internal requisition. If not, such materials should have been listed earlier, under purchase.

It is not always possible, in the case of materials, to indicate the exact number that will be required. This is most apparent in something like flip-chart paper (also called newsprint) or various writing implements. You will probably have to provide more than may be required so as not to impede a lesson because of a shortage of materials.

If materials are produced in-house, the HRD unit may have to rely on other elements of the organization for the production. In many large organizations, a graphic arts unit serves the entire company. HRD is only one of their clients and must wait in line, with the others, for such service. You should check with the graphic arts unit, if you have one, as to the lead time they require for the variety of materials you will want them to produce. It may be that, because of time or other factors, you will have to rely on purchase (buy) rather than in-house procurement (make). Therefore an item that starts on this list may have to be moved to the purchase list.

If you intend to use material reproduced from another source, check the constantly changing copyright laws very carefully. At one time, the laws were easy to understand and had not changed for years. In 1979 and 1980 there were vast and significant changes in the copyright laws. As newer technology facilitates reproduction from almost any source, we can anticipate that the copyright laws will keep changing. You have an ethical, as well as a legal, obligation to explore those laws before reproducing the work of others.

■   If to be rented, is there a specific list of items?

This will almost always apply to equipment, not to materials. The borderline becomes unclear when one looks at flipcharts or easels. If rented, will they come with paper, markers, and so on, or is it your responsibility to see that such materials are available? How do you classify a film, as materials or equipment? In either case, if the lesson plan calls for a rented film, it should be listed. For rented materials, there is the combination of concerns related to the financial process as well as availability. In some organizations, even rented equipment must go through a bid process. If so, the cautions indicated earlier under external purchase also apply here.

■ For all equipment and material, have delivery schedules been prepared?

Some equipment and material have to be available at the opening of the learning progam. Others are not needed until some later date. You will have to prepare a schedule, alongside the list, indicating when the equipment and material should be confirmed by the HRD unit, and when they should be available at the learning site.

Budget

There have been previous references to the budget, and this is the point at which all the factors must be considered in producing the budget request. In this event, there may be a formal budget submission, if that is required. Even if there is no formal step required, the budget should be explicitly stated here and retained in the files for future reference.

■ Have there been previous budget estimates?

During "Determine Objectives" and "Build Curriculum," reference was made to preparing budget estimates. If that was done, this is the time to review and update them, based on decisions made during the intervening events.

■ What is included in the budget?

I wish this could be answered specifically, but the response must be: it all depends. We lack agreement on which items should be included when budgeting for training. Direct costs, such as purchasing and renting are all obvious. In-house costs may be determined when there is an accounting system that charges between departments or units. Some organizations include the cost of the salaries and/or wages of the participants. If this is done in your organization, you are expected to comply with it. If this is not the case, do not include it in your budget. Obviously the general answer is to determine the budget items that must be included and to be sure they are listed. If there are budget items that are specifically excluded because of budget practice in your organization, why should you include them? When there are items that do not fall neatly into either category, consult with the budget people who will be reviewing your cost figures. Avoid surprises for either them or yourself. Above all, be consistent. If travel is included in one budget, it should appear in all budgets. When it is excluded, for any reason, that should be stated, so it is seen as a policy decision rather than an oversight.

■ Will the training be cost effective?

This is a frequently asked question, and rightly so. The response, however, is not possible until this event. Now that the learning program has been designed, it is possible for the Designer to determine the cost. Given that cost information, the Designer can compare that with the probable "savings" that might result from changed performance. Then it is possible for the Designer to respond to the cost-benefit question.

If the problem that generated the training request does not have a cost figure on it, the Designer cannot use this budget information to determine whether a "saving" will result. If the problem was the volume of customer complaints and the training is designed to change performance in order to reduce complaints, the training can solve the problem, but a specific cost-benefit ratio is not possible (unless the organization has developed a cost in- dex on complaints). At a later time, when performance has changed, perhaps the people who identified the problem can report how much less time is be- ing required to handle customer complaints. Then, the cost of the program can be compared to the results. Or, perhaps it can be estimated that as a result of the program, there will be x fewer complaints. Then it is possible for the Designer to compare that change with the cost. However, is "customer complaints" only a training problem? We are back to that earlier question of the extent to which training is a solution for problems.

It is possible that, as a result of the training program, customer com- plaints increase. As the employees become more proficient, the word may get out to the consumer or customer and they may bring in complaints that they previously would not have bothered with. Of course, the result could be increased sales, as these formerly dissatisfied customers receive better ser- vice! How does a Designer produce a cost-benefit ratio that can show these factors?

■   Who will be charged for the training?

This depends, in part, on whether your organization has organized the HRD function as a budget center, cost center, or profit center (as was discussed previously). No matter how you are organized, you will have to determine specifically who can authorize charges and whose budget must pay for those charges. That should be made clear at this point, if it has not been done earlier.

■   Do you have alternative budgets?

You owe it to your organization to provide the best program possible. But what if your organization will not pay for the "best" program? One approach is to make it "either this or nothing." That is not the way managers function when making budgetary decisions. Rather, managers prefer to be given alternatives. This can be done with the budget for a training program. You must be able to show the effect of different budgets on the learning situation.

The Designer should be prepared to respond to questions such as, "What would happen if we reduced your budget by 10%?" How do you provide 10% less learning? Your response to a suggested cut should be to indicate those objectives that would have to be deleted, requiring fewer lesson plans, less time, and even a lower cost for instructional strategies.

You must be able to identify those budget items that reflect the alternatives. For example, let us look at using an external facility. Do you take the participants to a local motel or to a conference center? The cost may appear significantly different; however, the cost factor is complex. The conference center may include some equipment in your cost, while the motel may charge extra for equipment. On the other side, the motel may be able to provide food service at a lower cost than the conference center. (Note that I am not implying any of these alternatives are universally accurate; it would depend on the conference center and the motel you compare.)

The number of participants who might attend a program is another variable with budget implications. Increasing the number of participants can lower unit cost, if that budget figure is of concern to you. It can also mean that some people may attend who have no real need. In a large organization, where many programs can be appropriate for large numbers of employees, a budget that shows relative cost based on the numbers participating can be important.

You need alternative budgets, with decision points explicitly shown, so the supervisors and managers involved are able to make decisions. Do not present only the lowest figure, or provide a high figure with hidden "padding." Provide a range with clear statements as to what is gained or lost at each budget level.

EVALUATION AND FEEDBACK

The objective of this event was:

To assure that all the necessary resources will be made available for the program that has been designed.

As we have moved through this event, it has become clear that this is the place where trade-offs are necessary, compromises can be explored, but decisions must be made. This event requires involvement of many people from the organization other than the Designer and supervisors, as has generally been the situation in earlier events.

Analysis

For this event, the analysis will contain the specifics, such as the listing of resources, schedules, and budgets. The analysis consists of much material that goes beyond the earlier emphasis on learning, and the Designer is well advised to seek the professional help of others in preparing the appropriate analysis.

The analysis will include the lesson plans as back-up material and the plans will be referred to as needed. The objectives, curriculum, and lesson plans may need to be reviewed in terms of limitations on the resources being requested. One way of preparing is for the Designer to take each lesson plan and indicate specifically which resources are needed to implement that lesson plan.

If it is determined that resources must be limited, the lesson plan will have to be altered to reflect this. Reduction in the number of lesson plans is actually the last step in the process, but for some people that may be the place to start. If resources are limited, the Designer can ask the decision-makers to indicate which lessons should be cut. Then, the Designer can walk them back through the process and indicate that this means reducing some of the curriculum, which means eliminating some objectives and not meeting some needs. Too few people see the interaction among these items, and the Designer should indicate this in the analysis, if necessary. Different levels of resource availability influence the program, and this can be shown in the analysis.

Scheduling, selection of participants, and identification and preparation of instructors should all be in the analysis. To the degree possible, people should be listed by name. When the decision is made to start the program, the analysis becomes the basic document that can be used immediately.

Feedback

As a result of the wide range implications of this event in the organization, there are many people who should receive the analysis and should be involved in the feedback discussions. The specific individuals will depend on how a particular company is organized, so we can only indicate the kinds of people who should receive the analysis and be involved in the feedback.

The prime person to be involved is still the *supervisor(s)* of the potential learners. The Designer can never lose sight of the focus of the training, which is to solve a problem. The problem rests in the realm of the supervisor and therefore that person is crucial. Also, the potential learners must be sent by the supervisor. Unless the supervisor can see a benefit from the training program, it is unlikely that he will release people from the work situation.

We are once again faced with the difference between training and education, a distinction that has been discussed several times earlier. If the program is for education, the identification of the potential supervisor is more difficult. In some cases, that supervisor has not yet been identified and will not be until some later time when the learner is promoted or transferred. That is one reason why it is so much more difficult to provide education than training within an organization. We will focus on training, however, as that is the area where the CEM is most effective.

Budget people are crucial to this event. The Designer must determine who has control of the budget for this particular training program. If the funding is to come from the supervisor's budget, this is just another item to be considered by the supervisor during feedback. If the budget rests in the hands of people other than the supervisor or the HRD Manager, those who control the budget must also be involved in the feedback on this event. Such people will probably not have been involved earlier, and therefore may need some special material or analysis to understand what prompted the need for the program and the problem that the program has been designed to solve.

At some of the previous events, *managers* (as different from supervisors) have been involved. In the feedback on this event, it is important to once again involve the managers. As managers are involved in planning, they need to know about this program and how it is likely to relate to their planning or expectations. Also, managers generally have more control over resources than supervisors do. As this event is concerned with resources, it is obvious that the involvement of managers is important.

If the program contains heavy demands for instructional resources, the instructional strategies developer should be involved in the feedback. During the discussions, there will have been suggestions as to alternative learning approaches, and the instructional materials developer is in a position to react to the implications of these suggestions. Also, that person can indicate the financial implications of any suggestions that are made. If internal production is required, the presence of the instructional materials developer is mandatory. If purchase is required, the presence of the instructional strategies developer will depend on the kind of involvement he has in the purchasing process.

Decisions

Most of the Decisions to be made at the termination of this event are made by people other than the Designer. It is the function of the Designer to provide sufficient information and alternatives, so that decisions can be made by those others. A psychological problem can surface at this time. The Designer will have spent much time, energy, and professional expertise in designing the program. The people who are reacting to it are more concerned with finances and scheduling. It is very important for the Designer to maintain a perspective and not overreact.

1. Is the cost acceptable?

There is no one response to this question, for that depends on who is responding. The budget people might have one answer, while the supervisor another. The final cost figure may represent trade-offs among the various individuals who are called upon to make the fiscal decisions. During the event, and particularly during feedback, alternative budgets will have been discussed. Trade-offs, revisions, and variations will have been explored. Confusion can be expected, but should not be allowed to remain. The Designer must be sure that by the end of this event there is no ambiguity about the budget, and that the cost is agreed to by those with the decision-making authority.

2.   Will the required physical resources be available when needed?

This relates to budget as well as scheduling. The response to this question must come from all those who would be involved in providing the physical resources, both internally and externally. It seems like the proverbial "Catch 22" or chicken-and-egg dilemma. Which comes first, and what happens next? It may not be possible to finalize the physical arrangements, such as the training site, without the budget commitment. Yet, without some firm figure from the site people, probably reinforced by a deposit or contract, it may not be possible to provide the budget information required.

When this happens, it is best for the Designer to make all of this known, so that appropriate and timely decisions can be made. During a time of rapidly rising inflation, delays can cost an unusual amount of money. For some physical resources, the time of year can be a cost factor. All of this needs to be discussed so that a timely and appropriate decision can be made.

3.   Is there a list of potential learners?

This event should culminate with a list of agreed upon learners for this program. Realistically this seldom happens. Unfortunately the final decision as to the actual learners comes just before the program begins. At this point, the Designer has the responsibility, at the least, for informing all who should know, that the closer they can come to a specific listing of learners, the greater the possibility of a successful program.

Quotas may be established and the Designer informed of how many will be sent from various units of the organization. Numbers alone are not sufficient, for they tell us little about the specific needs of the learners. Despite this, the Designer may have to settle for the barest information. If this is the case, the Designer may have to go back and produce an additional introductory learning unit to ascertain whether the needs of those who come are similar to the needs determined in the earlier phase of the CEM. Another alternative is to introduce a pretest to validate the need for the various lessons that have been designed. Of course, this requires the use of a professional instructor, one who is capable of making the necessary modifications if the data so indicate.

4.   Can specific instructors be assigned?

If the instructors are internal, their supervisors should be able to make a firm commitment as to their availability. This question includes the recognition that there may be the need for some "training of trainers" activity. If so the Designer must also schedule and plan for such learning. It may even require some additional lesson plans just for the instructor training program.

When using external instructors, there must be some assurance that qualified individuals will be available. It is similar to the situation concerning the physical resources, discussed under a previous question. The Designer, (or the appropriate person in the HRD unit) must ascertain whether the identified external instructors will be available and are in agreement with the fiscal arrangements. If it has been determined that the external instructors will need some briefing, or other preparation, who will do it, how, and when? This should all be determined in response to this question, if at all possible. If not, it will mean additional work at the very outset of the next event.

　　5.　Will the training program, with modification, solve the problem?

　　The qualifier, "with modification" refers to any changes that have been made during this event. These changes may require that the Designer back track through the entire CEM to "Specify Job Performance" to be sure that the changes do not make the program irrelevant.

　　Finally, if the program is conducted, will the problem for which it was originally designed, be solved? There can be many reasons why a Designer of a well-designed program may still have to respond to this in the negative. For one, there may no longer be a problem. Other factors may have intervened that significantly alter the situation. A common occurrence is a change in personnel, either subordinate or supervisor, and the problem can either change or no longer be a problem. Additional factors may be changes in materials, equipment, regulations, customer mix, and so on.

　　In essence, the Designer is once again validating that there is a problem and that the final version of the training program is likely to solve that problem. If so, the program should be conducted.

CONCLUSION

In one sense, this event can be the last for the Designer. From here, the program moves into other hands, usually the Supervisor of HRD programs. The Designer should still be involved in many ways, in order to obtain feedback on how the design is working. This can be helpful in improving the present program and in using the CEM to design future programs.

　　In the next chapter, "Conduct Training," we will look at how the program is implemented.

REFERENCES

1.　Too little has been written about this for people in the HRD field. After a national ASTD Conference, where the topic was not clearly identifiable on the program, some members asked me to write about it. Perhaps they were aware of my accounting background? The result was a brief article, "What is Your Financial I.Q.?" which appeared in the *Training and Development Journal,* October 1980, pp. 64–68.

ADDITIONAL PRINTED RESOURCES

Lord, Kenniston, W., Jr. *The Design of the Industrial Classroom.* Reading, Mass.: Addison-Wesley, 1977.

Mills, H. R. *Teaching and Training: A Handbook for Instructions.* Halstead Press, 1972.

Otto, Calvin P., and Rollin O. Glaser. *The Management of Training.* Reading, Mass.: Addison-Wesley, 1970.

10

Conduct Training

This is the payoff! (See Figure 10-1.) All the work that has previously been done now culminates in the learning experience. It is still possible to make variations in the design, but most of it should remain as designed, to this point.

The objective of this event is:

To conduct the training program previously designed.

For some programs, no variations from the design and lesson plans will be permitted, while for others, the lesson plans are expected to serve only as general guidelines, with modifications by the instructor in the actual learning situation.

In the previous event, it was noted that the Designer may have been moving slowly out of the process, to be replaced by a Supervisor of Programs, who is a colleague in the HRD unit. It is also possible for the Designer to continue with the program, but the activities will change from designing to supervising. We will continue to use the designation "Designer" for the person who has responsibility for this event.

If a different person takes over from the previous Designer, there must be coordination between these two individuals. The new person should become familiar with the documentation of the program, including the analysis reports, and the decisions made at the completion of each event of the CEM. Perhaps this suggests that the Designer should continue on as the supervisor even though the two positions require some different competencies.

Whenever the HRD Manager is able to do so, he should double staff the whole CEM, with the Designer taking the lead and the HRD supervisor being one of the people involved. When that is done, the transition to this event can be accomplished with little loss in momentum and no loss of the history of the design process of the particular program. Double staffing may be considered a luxury, and therefore has not been included in previous discussions.

207

THE CRITICAL EVENTS MODEL

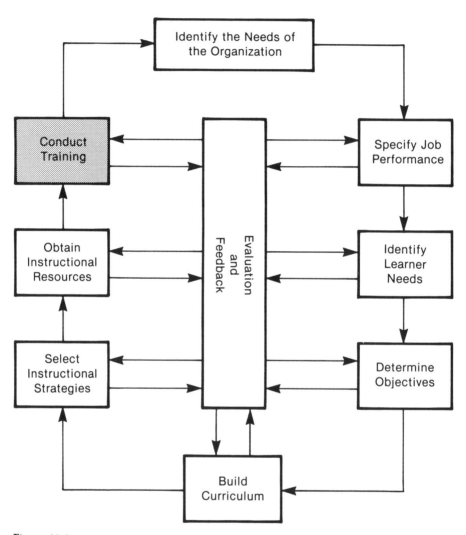

Figure 10.1

THE PARTICIPANTS

As has been said many times, the participants (the potential learners) are crucial to the whole design process. The main reason for providing the training program is to affect the performance of the participants in order to alleviate or solve a problem.

Up to this time, various terms have been used to designate this group. They have been called subordinates, potential learners, employees, and so on, as they were being described in a variety of situations. For this event, the term *participants* will be used.

Selection

The decision as to who will be participants should be in the hands of the supervisor of those participants. This may not always be the case, but first let us explore the desirable and most common, and then look at the variations.

As training is problem focused, and the supervisor wants to solve problems, the ideal participant group consists of those *sent by the supervisor.* In that situation, the supervisor has identified those who need the training in order to solve the problem. This appears simple, straightforward, and direct. Hidden within the decision are a number of problems.

If the supervisor sends only those who need performance change, training can be viewed as punitive. If the participant comes to the learning situation as a form of punishment, the instructor can expect some form of resistance and even hostility. We can assume that the supervisor has explored alternative ways of improving performance, as discussed in earlier events of the CEM, and is finally convinced that training is the appropriate response. One approach is to confirm that the participant accepts that decision and is likewise interested in improving performance.

The selection process is not an isolated incident, but is part of the total style of the supervisor and the climate of the workplace. If the supervisor has been using a style of participative management, it follows that the participants will be involved in the selection process.

Whatever the style, a decision must be made as to who will be the participants. Even in participative management, the supervisor must still make the final decision and allocate the necessary resources.

Considering the possible punitive aspect of selection, a supervisor might opt to send people who do not necessarily need the training. This is not cost effective, for those who do not need the training cannot be expected to improve their performance.

On the positive side, sending several people from the same work unit to the same training program reinforces performance norms. When several people have experienced the same learning, they would all have agreed upon the performance expected. For some this can mean a significant change in performance (they would be the ones with the real need), while for others it would provide reinforcement. Even for the latter group, there could be some improvement in performance but we would not expect it to be significant.

There is also a voluntary type of program, and this would pertain whether the training is provided on company time or off. The term voluntary is more closely associated with the broad field of Adult Education than it is with HRD. Voluntarism is apparent when the HRD unit puts out bulletins listing course offerings, produces what looks like a college catalogue, and has predesigned programs that are available to everybody. The process is usually similar to a university situation in which the participants enroll in courses. The selection is essentially at the volition of the participant.

Why should a supervisor go along with this process? It is certainly not problem centered, from the viewpoint of the supervisor. To withhold cooperation can give the impression that the supervisor is not interested in improving the performance of the subordinates. No supervisor wants to be seen in that light, so the supervisor may sign off on "training requests" even though the program will really be education, or development, with no direct benefit to the work unit.

The voluntary type of program is not completely negative. If the subordinate feels a need, the supervisor should recognize this and explore further. There are voluntary programs that could improve job performance. If the subordinate feels the need, we can expect more learning to take place, with a greater possibility of improving some aspect of job performance.

I am not against voluntary programs offered by employers, but I do caution that they are generally not problem oriented and not training focused. Education and development are important and necessary, but those learning experiences are responses to different problems than we have been concerned with within the CEM.

When the program is offered off company time, the participant may not even need the approval of the supervisor. It is completely voluntary and not expected to be training. Some companies still offer training off company time but that practice is not widespread. The confusion is that some companies offer tuitionrefund or reimbursement to employees for learning programs taken off company time and offered by outside institutions. This is a desirable practice, but very seldom is it training. This does not mean that companies should not continue and expand the practice of tuition refund. It does mean that they should not expect it to solve problems.

Whether sent by the supervisor, or voluntary, the participant must know the objectives of the program and the criteria for being in the learning group. When sent by the supervisor, the participant should be able to focus on the problem that the training program is expected to solve. If this is not known, the participant has little indication of how the training program is expected to influence or change his behavior. Without this mindset, the learning will be less effective.

Needs

When there is a specific list of participants, the Designer should compare those names with those who were involved in the earlier event of "Identify Individual Needs." If they are the same people, there is at least the assumption that the needs are still valid. A quick check is desirable, because of possible changes. This process of checking also alerts the participants to how their former responses have influenced the program they are now going to experience. The participants are more likely to accept the program and participate actively if they can readily see how their prior input about needs is now going to be met.

For a variety of reasons, some discussed earlier, those who were involved in the earlier event may not be the same as the participants who are actually assigned to the training program. The same needs may still exist, but the Designer should check this out with the supervisor before implementing the program.

What makes a real difference is finding that the same problem no longer exists. If that is the situation, it is profoundly hoped that this information will have come to the attention of the Designer before this point. If not, however, there should still be a delay until the Designer is sure the problem still exists and has not significantly changed. This can avoid having the right program but for the wrong reasons.

On the other hand, the problem may have been exacerbated since the start of the CEM and may be even more important. There might be an urgency now, to improve performance, which did not exist at the outset. In such a case, the need may be the same, but with a stronger vector or force.

Notification of Participants

Although the supervisor may have presented a list of participants, there is no assurance that the participants themselves have received any notification. Unless the procedure is well established, including verification, it can result in participants who receive little or no notice of the training program for which they have been selected. This borders on the ridiculous, but it happens all too often.

There are too many instances of participants arriving for work on a Monday morning and being told not to start but to report to the training site. This happens more often when the training site is located some place in the organization, within the work site, than it does when the participant must travel to some off-site location. The responsibility for the short notice procedure may rest with the supervisor, but the HRD unit must also take some of the blame. The HRD unit should be involved in the notification procedure, so the short notice possibility is reduced, if not eliminated.

Why bother with prior notification? There are many reasons, some physical and some psychological. On the physical side, the absence of one or more people in a work unit is disruptive. It requires shifting assignments, changing work schedules, or even obtaining replacement help. The participant may have made some prior appointments (as with salespeople), or may be part of a carpool which is disrupted by a member being assigned to training.

On the psychological side, particularly with adults, there can be the need to prepare oneself for this experience. If the adult learner has had prior negative learning experiences, some counseling or other pretraining activity can be extremely helpful in reducing the fear of failure during learning.

For a supervisor, manager, or executive, a training program requires a significant shift in behavior. These managerial groups are accustomed to having some control over what they do during working hours. Being part of a learning group, a participant, deprives them of some of their options as to what they will do with their time. Managers are not accustomed to being so constrained and need the opportunity to make the psychological adjustment required by the new constraints. Even the best self-directed learning, with high participant involvement, carries with it some constraints that the manager does not face during the working day. For psychological reasons, prior preparation is important, if not absolutely necessary.

On the physical side, managers have even more need to provide back-ups and alternatives. Managers are generally not as easily replaced as are employees at lower levels in the organization.

Good notification procedures are extremely helpful in assisting the participant to make the necessary arrangements. For some people, mere notification can induce anxiety, and prior notification allows time for some of this to subside. It is a good idea, as part of the notification procedure, to provide the participant with a phone number to call or a person to contact who can respond to questions about arrangements and other items that tend to feed the anxiety fire.

The notification procedure should contain a feedback loop, for it is not enough to merely send a notice to the participant. It is important to receive something back from the participant to show that the notice has been received, understood, and that the participant will attend. Also, it legitimizes the participant contacting the appropriate person in the HRD unit to ask questions or to seek help. The person in the HRD unit who is on the receiving end should be more than a clerk. The need is to do more than just check off that a participant called, for the response to that call is the first step in establishing the learning climate, which we will discuss later.

Some learning programs require precourse reading or work. This is a good instructional strategy that makes effective use of the time available for training. The notification procedure should specify the particular assignment as well as provide the materials required by the precourse assignment. If there are any questions, the participant should be able to call on a designated professional in the HRD unit to seek assistance.

FACILITIES, EQUIPMENT, AND MATERIALS

In the previous event, "Obtain Instructional Resources," the Designer was able to identify the specific facilities, equipment, and materials that would be needed. At this time, a check should be made to assure that what was previously identified is actually available and, for some items, that they are physically on-site.

A liaison person must be clearly identified. Depending upon the nature and location of the program, it could be any one of a number if individuals. The titles vary, but generally include something like: designer, supervisor, program director, aide, or assistant. The last two are interesting positions which provide significant growth opportunities for nonprofessionals or paraprofessionals.

By effective use of these positions, the HRD unit can provide a career ladder for people who are interested in the field, but who lack experience or academic preparation. Caution should be exercised, however, for in some organizations this person can become the "professional," not as the result of a planned developmental program, but as a result of survival. As the professional people move on to other positions or other organizations, the aide remains and eventually, through seniority, moves into a professional position. The result, predictably, downgrades the HRD unit. It is not that aides cannot become professionals in the HRD field, but it should be by more than mere survival or longevity. Still, having responsibility for facilities, equipment, and materials can be a good place to start.

The instructor should know the person assigned as back-up for the particular program. If the instructor is experienced and professional, less back-up is required than when the instructor is a content specialist with little experience in instruction. The HRD Manager must carefully match the back-up (program director, and so on) with the particular program and instructor.

It is helpful to develop a checklist of those items to be reviewed, as related to the training program. Intentionally no checklist is provided in this chapter. It is more important for each HRD unit to develop its own checklist, reflecting the types of programs, the specific organization, and so on. There are books that have checklists, and some of these books appear in the bibliography at the end of this chapter. Using those as guidelines, the HRD unit should develop its own checklist. Even the process of developing the checklist is important, for it can surface differing perceptions among the HRD staff. The checklists should not be permanent, but should be reviewed and modified as experience and a particular program dictate.

OPENING THE PROGRAM

Frequently overlooked elements of planning are the activities related to opening a program. The participants have been notified and are trickling in. The instructor is either in the wings or entering the room, and all is ready to begin — almost.

There is no one way to open a program. It depends on a variety of factors. In some situations, it is appropriate to start immediately with the first lesson. In other situations, there are some activities that should precede the instruction. The preinstruction activities should be clearly identified before the program begins. Some organizations have a standard opening for all programs, while others provide a guideline and leave it up to the individual instructor.

Climate Setting

There have been earlier references to climate setting, and even some activities related to that purpose. Now, at the start of the program, climate setting is crucial.

Climate setting consists of those activities that communicate an attitude conducive to effective learning. It is more than just taking care of logistics, though by no means is that to be ignored. The purpose is to put the participant at ease and to communicate that the program has specific learning and performance objectives and what the nature of the learning activities is. Attention is also paid to the physical needs of the learner, such as indicating when breaks will occur, meal times, and so on. Provision is made for responding to questions and to the concerns of the participants.

There can be a *formal opening*, but it should not be too lengthy as it can slow down the development of a positive climate for learning. Long speeches should be avoided, though some speeches may be necessary and even desirable. Technology can be used. One large organization has a video-taped message from the president of the corporation. It lasts fewer than five minutes and is rerecorded each month, so as to provide for an update. The rerecording eliminates the possibility that a participant will sit and mutter, "Oh, not again! I've heard this speech five times!" By retaping, at least once a month, the tape is always pertinent and communicates the interest of the CEO or other high level official in the training.

There are other kinds of formal openings, and the specific one to be used should be planned beforehand and selected because it is appropriate to the particular learning situation. It is possible, for example, to open a program by having the relevant supervisors present to make statements about their expectations of performance change as a result of the program.

Some programs are best started by an *informal opening*. A method that is frequently used is having a social, the evening before the learning program starts. This is desirable when the participants come from different locations and have to spend time traveling. The social on the evening before the start of the program provides time for relaxation after travel and increases the possibility that the participants will be alert the following morning. Of course, this means that the social should be limited in alcoholic beverages and that the participants should be encouraged to end the social evening at a reasonable hour.

Another type of informal opening starts on the morning of the initial session of the program with some form of "registration." Generally this does not have to be a formal session, but one where the participants get their materials, name tags (if appropriate), and are provided with refreshments to help in climate setting. This is usually coffee and donuts, or some similar morning food. As more and more people are watching their diets, and wellness is a corporate as well as an individual goal, the food service can be juice, yogurt, or other identified health foods. It may seem like a small matter, but it does set the climate. However, if there are people who need coffee for a "wake-me-up," or who have ritualized their morning food (they eat exactly the same kind of food each morning), do not try to break the norm.

Whether or not to have such an informal climate setting experience depends to a good degree on the cultural behavior in the organization. Such an opening may be appropriate for certain levels in the organization and not for others. We can protest that this is not democratic, but violating a cultural norm will not help to produce a successful learning experience. When the presession social, as described earlier, is chosen as the climate setting experience, there should be a sensitivity to the cultural norm as related to liquor. There are organizations where it is forbidden to have liquor on the premises. If that is the case, the Designer may find that the norm persists even when off-premise, as long as it is a company-sponsored activity.

One opening activity that can be either formal or informal is the dinner the night before the opening. Once again, this will be used more for managerial levels, and particularly when the participants are coming from a variety of locations. The dinner can be a banquet where higher level officials of the organization join the participants only for the opening experience. It can also be just a few tables in the coffee shop with participants ordering from the menu.

Whatever the opening, if it is to involve some of the activities just described, it is important that the Designer have provided for this in the budget. It is a legitimate and necessary expense connected with the learning.

When the learning program commences, the participant should be supplied with some essential information. This can be provided by a member of the HRD unit or by the instructor. It should be supplemented by whatever handouts disseminate necessary logistical information. This can relate to parking, emergency telephone numbers, expense reimbursement forms, and similar information.

In terms of climate setting, this presents a choice. By starting with these logistic items, a tone can be set that is rigid and bureaucratic. This is one reason to opt for somebody other than the instructor providing this information. If possible, the information should be given to the participants with other handout materials, but the participant will need time to read these materials. Some participants are not ready to learn until they have some information about expenses, telephone numbers, and so on. Sending the information out with the notification, discussed earlier, is one way of getting it to the participants without interfering with the start of the session. But, if a participant has questions, presession distribution limits the opportunity of obtaining answers.

The design of the learning program influences the opening. Early, if not at the very beginning, participants need to know at least three important items. First, are the *objectives* of the program, or what is the desired end result of the learning. This will be reinforced by the objectives for each lesson, but what are the overall objectives, or the program objectives as identified during "Determine Objectives?" What is the performance change that is expected?

Second, are the *requirements* of the course. The participant should know what is expected in terms of attendance, participation, outside learning assignments, and any other requirements that are either specified or implied by the lesson plans.

Third, and very important, are *mutual expectations*. What does the instructor expect of the learner, and what can the learner expect of the instructor?" This establishes that the learning is a participative activity, with all parties having mutual responsibilities and expectations. The more these can be identified early in the program, the greater the possibility from the outset of positive learning.

OPERATING THE PROGRAM

Once the program actually starts, the instructor should not be left to flounder if any problems should arise. Indeed, problems are always a possibility. The oft repeated Murphy's Law is "If anything can go wrong, it will." To this should be added, "And, it will probably be worse than you thought!" This is not meant to be pessimistic or to cast aspersions on the instructor. Things can go wrong, and the instructor may have little or nothing to do with the causes. It is not important, during the program, to find whom to blame. It is necessary to keep the program going at the optimum level, and then, later, to analyze the situation so breakdowns will not be repeated.

The Instructor

The instructor is only human and there are many things that can happen. At the outset, the instructor may not show up. The reason should be determined, but not while the participants are waiting for the program to begin.

There should always be a back-up position, particularly for the first session of the program. Someone should be present from the HRD staff to be sure the program starts properly. After that, the participants should be notified as to whom to contact if there are any problems, including the no-show of an instructor. Of course, the instructor should also have this information and has the responsibility to notify the HRD unit if he cannot appear. This is not always possible. If the instructor is on the road and has a flat tire, there is very little chance of notifying the HRD unit. There must be a contingency plan for such events.

Other situations can prevent the instructor from continuing the program. The first obligation of the HRD unit is to see that a satisfactory substitute is available. The second is to determine if the reason for the absence reflects on the instructor to the point where that instructor should not be used again.

An infrequent, but possible occurrence, is when an instructor becomes ill during the program. As long as human instructors are used, this is always a possibility. The instructor should know whom to notify, but the HRD unit should have alternatives available.

For some programs, the illness or absence of the instructor can be handled by rescheduling or using an alternative learning unit. In most cases, the lack of an instructor requires canceling the class. If the HRD unit knows this early enough, it might be possible to notify the participants.

Essentially, canceling class should be the last alternative. Once this is done, it will influence the attendance of the participants for the remainder of the program. If the instructor can be absent, why not the participants? Note that it does not work in reverse.

Materials and Equipment

Despite all the plans, something can always go wrong in the area of materials and equipment. Some of the common problems are:

■ Wrong materials

The material arrives in packages and is not opened until the program begins. Then, it is found that the package label does not agree with the contents and they are not what is required for the lesson.

This should have been checked out prior to the start of the program, but may not have been done. The instructor should be advised to check before the start of the session and to notify the HRD unit immediately if the materials are not what is needed.

■ Insufficient copies

It is a general rule to provide extras of materials. If there are 25 participants, it is customary to have 30 copies of materials. This allows for any damaged, incorrectly assembled, or otherwise unusable materials. Despite this planning, the instructor may find that there are not enough copies.

Years ago this was classed as a tragedy or panic situation. Today, with copying facilities so readily available, it is not in quite the same category. The instructor should be able to call for support from the HRD unit for more copies, and to get them quickly. As a follow-up, the HRD staff should determine the reason for the shortage, so as to minimize the possibility of a recurrence.

■   Equipment not functioning

We have all heard of the necessity for spare bulbs for projectors, but despite the constant warning, it is not uncommon to find equipment without a spare. Some of the newer overhead projectors have been designed with a spare bulb built into the machine, which is activated by a mere flick of a switch.

In other equipment, replacement is more difficult, and may require the services of a skilled, or at least an experienced individual. All equipment should be checked beforehand by the HRD staff and it is helpful to provide instructors with at least some minimal training in bulb replacement.

Other equipment problems can be more serious, and the instructor should be advised when to call the HRD unit rather than to attempt on-the-spot repair work. The damage done to equipment at that point may render it totally useless, as well as consuming valuable session time. The instructor, generally, is not expected to be able to repair equipment.

The Program Director

As indicated earlier, each learning program should have one person from the HRD unit who is responsible for that program. Though the Designer may still be involved, the action shifts to the Program Director. The instructor and the participants should be informed who that individual is, where to call or to find that individual, and what his responsibilities are.

The Program Director should make periodic visits to the learning site, not to supervise, but to determine personally that things are progressing as planned. It provides the instructor with a direct and constant link, and indicates to the participants the continuing interest of the HRD staff.

In some situations, the Program Director and the Designer are the same person. Generally this is ineffective utilization of the competencies required of the Designer. However, when they are not the same person, the Program Director should be in contact with the Designer. Rather than merely complain or be critical of what appear to be inadequacies in program design, the Program Director should be communicating problems to the Designer. If this is not done, there should be no surprise when some of the same problems persist in future programs.

A Program Director usually is responsible for many programs and should have a method for keeping a record of programs visited and of suggestions for improvement. These suggestions will generally be about the physical side, as the learning aspect will be reviewed through evaluation and other mechanisms.

When an external facility is being used, the Program Director is probably the person who has negotiated and made the arrangements. It would, therefore, be the responsibility of the Program Director to see that the facility has performed as agreed.

The Participant

Everything possible should be done, by the Program Director, to assure that participants are not diverted from the learning. If a participant has concerns about factors related to the job, family conditions, and so on, it is more difficult to learn. It is not anticipated that the Program Director will assume all the problems of the participant. It is expected that the Program Director will avoid having the learning program add additional problems.

One of the problems is related to *messages*. This may seem like an unimportant factor, until you have been in a training session and could not be reached. During that time, it is not unrealistic to expect that you would wonder if anybody is trying to reach you. Time spent worrying about that is time taken from the learning situation.

There are many ways to handle messages and the least desirable is to put a participant in a position of being "incommunicado." This places training in the realm of punishment and deprivation of rights. Almost all executives and managers expect to be constantly accessible by phone, no matter how loudly they complain about intrusion. The proliferation of portable pagers is apt testimony to the need and desire to be constantly available. Pagers or helpers should be discouraged at a training session. They can easily be replaced by a well-positioned message board that each participant can see when leaving the room for a break or meals. Dire emergencies still require a more immediate response, but most of us do not experience too many such emergencies in the course of our daily lives.

As with instructors, participants can become *ill*. They should not be made to suffer or feel inadequate. If the training is away from the work site, the participant should be informed of the provisions for dealing with illness. With more artificial devices in general use (from contact lenses to pacemakers), Program Directors had best provide for this kind of health care.

EVALUATING THE PROGRAM

During "Build Curriculum," it was noted that the Designer constructs the necessary evaluation instruments to be used during the conduct of the program. Evaluation exercises should be conducted at several points in the program and this type of *formative* evaluation allows the instructor to determine if the appropriate learning is taking place.

At the end of the program is the *summative* evaluation. The results cannot be used to alter the program already conducted, but are very useful for future programs. Particularly, if the present program is to be repeated with other participants, the data collected by the summative and formative evaluation are crucial.

Pretests and posttests may also be used. The pretest may have been conducted even before the participant arrived at the program as part of the precourse work. The more common practice is to administer the pretest at the opening of the program. This must be handled carefully, as it can conflict with the climate setting and produce a negative effect. During the program there are tests, but the most crucial is the posttest. This is akin to the final examination.

The posttest can provide evaluation only of the learning. A good posttest should be as close to the expected job performance as possible, but it is still possible to evaluate only learning. Job performance cannot be evaluated until the participant returns to the job and is asked to perform. At that time, the evaluation is in the hands of the supervisor, though it is hoped that the supervisor will share this evaluation with HRD staff.

There are ethical considerations involved in evaluating the programs we have been discussing in this book, as different from school programs. The participants, in our situation, are usually not voluntary and they are sent to a learning program to achieve a specific goal related to their work in the organization.

Even if voluntary, and this does exist in some company-sponsored training programs, what they are learning relates directly to their present job (training) or to a future job for which they are preparing (education) within a company. As the company is paying the bill, isn't the company entitled to know what they received for their money?

Of course, the "company" is not a disembodied ethereal being. The company is made up of flesh and blood people with whom the participant is working. Generally by "company" we mean the supervisor who is directly concerned with training, or the manager who has concerns about education. Naturally they want to be able to justify the use of the physical and financial resources they have made available to the participant through the HRD activity.

There is nothing wrong with reporting test scores or other evaluation to the supervisor and/or manager. If this is to be done, however, the participant should know this before the program begins. The instructor also needs to know of this requirement and it should be clearly stated when he takes the assignment. If the instructor has any ethical reservations, feels it violates confidentiality, or will get in the way of the learning, all that should be specifically noted before the instructor accepts the assignment.

Of course, the Designer should have determined this at some earlier event. The type of evaluation, the form of the tests, and the manner of feedback will all be influenced by the need to report these data to the supervisors and managers.

The evaluation data, in whatever way it is gathered, is an essential part of the E&FB process.

CLOSING THE PROGRAM

Just as the opening was important, particularly for climate setting, the closing is equally important. The program should not be allowed to wind down slowly and end with confusion. This is often done when an evaluation instrument is administered, with the instruction to "leave when you are finished." The result is that people go out one at a time, whispering to the instructor or other participants, and trying to leave with the least amount of noise. The result is depressing, and leaves a negative last image with the participants.

The closing should be well planned and involve more than the instructor and the participants. It is not always necessary to have a banquet or elaborate ceremony, but there should be an identifiable activity that denotes that this learning experience has now come to an end. The impression should be conveyed that the next step is the anticipated change in performance.

Recognition for Participants

Most people seek recognition. There is nothing wrong with that, and it should be part of a learning program, handled with taste and foresight. There is no one form of recognition that is appropriate for all programs and participants. Rather, the form of recognition that is preferable is one that is congruent with the organization, and observable to all who need to know.

One of the more common practices is to award *certificates*. If you have graduated from a university, particularly with an advanced degree, you may scoff at certificates. You already have more of them than you can possibly put up on your walls, if you wanted to. Such is not the case for everybody.

For some people, a certificate is important. A study done many years ago found that participants framed the certificates and hung them on the walls. At that time, training was not as common as it is today. It would be interesting to determine today how many of your participants have retained certificates (when you awarded them) and what they have done with them.

You can never be wrong in giving a certificate, even if the participant chooses to do no more than file it away. Even if the participant throws it away, after leaving the training site, you have still fulfilled your responsibility in seeing that the participant was "awarded" the certificate.

If a formal certificate is inappropriate, some other *written document* may still be used. It could be a letter from a high-level company offical, or other written notice that the participant has successfully completed the program. It is necessary that "successfully" be defined so that certificates and other documents are not given to participants who did not meet at least some specified minimum requirements. Attendance is one of the common criteria for successful completion.

The certificate should not merely be distributed at the last session of the program, which is the general tendency. Some appropriate *ceremony* should accompany the distribution. It need not be elaborate, for to make it a big affair can be ludicrous. The ceremony should be appropriate to the organization, the nature of the program, and the level of the participants.

Supervisors and managers should be involved. This serves several purposes, the major one being the reinforcement that the goal of the training program is change in job performance. Therefore those who will be looking for that change should be involved in the closing ceremony. Such attendance encourages the participant to take the learning back to the job and to produce the desired change in performance.

Recognition for Instructors

Too often, the instructor is ignored in the recognition activity. If the instructor is *external*, perhaps the major form of recognition is payment. It is doubtful if people become instructors only for the financial aspect. Being a good instructor requires more time, effort, and creative energy than can usually be reflected in payment. Instructors have ego needs, or perhaps they would not have chosen to be instructors.

Recognition for the external instructor is usually best given outside the regular closing ceremony, as this can detract from the recognition for the participants. A letter of appreciation from the HRD Manager is certainly appropriate. If there is an evaluation instrument (and there should be), the results of this should be shared with the external instructor.

When the instructor is *internal*, but not part of the HRD unit, specific recognition is extremely crucial. Such instructors generally do not receive any additional compensation. They may even have to make some sacrifices in their regular assignments in order to successfully instruct in the program. Recognition for them should include a report, sent to their supervisors, particularly if the final evaluation by the participants included laudatory comments.

Some companies find it useful to recognize the internal instructors through an annual ceremony, usually coupled with a luncheon or banquet. At that time, high-level company officials are present and the opportunity to mix with that level is one of the "payments" to those instructors.

For both internal and external instructors, certificates are sometimes awarded. These are not the same as those given to the participants but are specially prepared for instructors. These certificates are less meaningful to the external instructor than to the internal person. The internal instructor is generally not a professional instructor, so the certificate is recognition for some additional competency as well as another contribution to the success of the organization.

Accountability for Equipment and Supplies

There is no ceremony, no certificate for being accountable for equipment and supplies. You might even question why we include such an activity in the closing of the program. In the pressure that builds up as a program reaches the climax and the closing, it is only too easy to ignore some of the physical details.

It is generally the Program Director, or someone delegated by the HRD Manager, who must take charge before the participants and the instructor depart. This could be the same person who has the responsibility for the closing ceremonies and the preparation of the appropriate certificates. There must be at least one person with specific responsibility for the accounting at the close of the program.

This person checks all the equipment to see that it is returned to the proper place or rental facility. The unused materials may be retrieved, particularly if they represent a significant expense item. The facility is checked to be sure that the participants have not left anything behind. All this may seem mundane, but if these details are not covered, it can result in much wasted effort at a later time and even panic about equipment and materials that have disappeared.

This activity should be well organized so as not to interfere with the climate set during the closing, and should be handled as a normal occurrence without any fuss. Effective preparation for this activity at the beginning of the program will enable the Program Director to terminate the program on a positive and successful note.

EVALUATION AND FEEDBACK

The objective of this final event was:

■   To conduct the training program previously designed.

We are now at the culmination of the design process. The program has been conducted, but there is still the need for E&FB. In this phase of the event, the Designer moves back into an active role.

Analysis

The analysis of this event must be carefully planned, as it survives as the written record of the conducted program. Therefore, some Designers opt to have the analysis contain a brief historical record of what happened in the design process and some of the decisions that were made during the different events. There is no doubt that this is useful, but it may be of no interest to those who are concerned only with the end result of learning and job performance.

If the historical data are important, the Designer is advised to present this either as an appendix to the analysis, or as a separate document, available to those who have an interest or a need to know.

The most important part of the analysis is: What have the learners learned?

This can be reported in a variety of ways and usually involves some statistical manipulations. The Designer should avoid using the analysis report as a way of indicating competency in statistics. What is most important is that those who are expected to read the analysis should clearly understand what happened. If statistical manipulations are necessary, and they may be, they should be presented in clear terms, with accompanying definitions as required. The end result of the learning could be stated clearly so that the reader does not have to wonder about the meaning of a particular number or table.

The evaluation can only be limited to learning, yet the basic objective is job performance change. Perhaps, at a later time, the HRD unit will be invited, or at least, allowed to follow up on the job. At that time, a supplemental report can be issued. At the completion of the learning program, the HRD unit can only report on how the level of learning achieved is likely to affect job performance.

The analysis should also contain any recommendations for improving the program, if it is to be offered again. These recommendations are not limited to only the lesson plans, but reflect each event in the CEM. For example, perhaps the objectives should be changed or the content varied. Such recommendations should be made at this time so they can be reviewed and be available for future offerings of this program.

It is also helpful to use this opportunity to review the use of the CEM. The Designer may include recommendations for designing future programs. The Designer may recommend, for example, the types or levels of personnel who should be involved in E&FB in future design efforts. Or, the Designer may recommend how "Identify Learning Needs" could be improved. The analysis report provides the Designer with a mechanism for having the organization look at the design process, as reflected in the CEM, as well as at a specific program.

Feedback

The report should be shared as widely as company policy and individual privacy permit. If the evaluation proves to be negative, if insufficient learning took place, it would be detrimental to provide for an extensive distribution. It is not that the Designer is ashamed, but that it could prove embarrassing to participants, supervisor, and others, and be considered a violation of an implied trust.

Even for a successful program, one where the learning objectives have been met completely as indicated by the evaluation, there could be some hesitancy about a wide distribution. The supervisors involved may not wish others to know of their problems. The participants, particularly those who did less well, may consider such information a violation of their privacy. If there are negative feelings about the feedback of the analysis report, the Designer will experience less cooperation in future design efforts.

Decisions

Although there are few actual decisions to be made at this point, some questions need to be asked.

    1.   Does it appear that the results of the program have solved the initial problem?

At this time, those who requested the learning program can only conjecture. The final answer will not be known until the participants have returned to the job and have performed. It is possible, however, to get some reactions from the supervisors and others as to their perceptions of the validity of the program as compared to the purpose for which it was designed.

    2.   Is there a need to repeat this program?

The repetition should not be for the same group of participants, but there could be other participants who would benefit from this program. Presumably it would be repeated because there are more employees involved in the problem than could be accommodated by a single offering of the program. It is also possible that other supervisors, with the same problem, would now be interested in having their subordinates participate.

    3.   If the program is repeated, are modifications required?

The same program, for another group of participants, may require some modifications. The problem may be similar, but not identical, and with only some minor design modifications, the program could be appropriate for others. It is always possible, after a program has been conducted, to then identify factors that were not obvious during the design process. These modifications could be in any aspect of the CEM. It is possible that some major changes are required if the program is to be offered again. Even successful programs can be improved with modifications.

CONCLUSION

We have now come to the end—at least of this use of the CEM. I realize that some of what has been presented may have sounded simple, because we have been dealing with designing one program at a time. It is obvious that in most cases the Designer is involved in many programs at the same time.

    In such situations, the Designer will find it helpful to use the CEM diagaram as a flowchart or condition board. Each separate program can be traced on a different CEM chart, and the Designer, as well as others, will always know the status of each program being designed.

As you, the Designer, become more competent using the CEM you will evolve your own patterns of behavior for the various events. That is not unusual, and is expected, when one uses an open model. You may even make variations in nomenclature, decision questions, and other elements of the CEM. You should not feel guilty, and I will not feel rejected.

As each of us grows professionally, we change. Using models enables us to see how we are changing, and developing additional competencies. I, and many others, have found the CEM a useful tool. It is anticipated that you will have a similar experience.

11

Support Systems
for Training

With the preceding chapter, we have completed the CEM. A learning experience has been designed and delivered, and that experience must be seen as part of the organization. Therefore it is helpful to identify those activities that should be usual organizational behavior in order to support a training program.

Once again, note the emphasis on training—as different from education. The model described and discussed in this chapter is entirely appropriate for training, but if education is the objective of the learning, a different model must be used. At present, I have found few models related to training and none that focus on education.

Allow me to personalize a bit by indicating how I became interested in this topic. During the 1950s and 1960s, many of us became concerned about the lack of success of some of our programs. We were designing and providing good learning programs, but somehow they seemed to have little effect on the work situation. Gradually this concern was translated into an activity called "organization development" or OD. In its early days, it was based on the concept of "critical mass." That is, it was assumed that if sufficient numbers of people were exposed to the training program, it was more possible for performance to change. Since that time, OD has moved in many directions, but there are still elements of it in training programs that involve the total organization.

The critical mass approach can be useful, but is also extremely costly. It encourages having employees complete training programs that are not related to individual learning needs. It attempts to create a climate of change through mass numbers rather than specific actions.

During the 1960s, the federal government mounted several programs related to helping the disadvantaged enter the world of work [1]. Towards the end of that decade, the *Harvard Business Review* asked me to do a study to see if we could identify which company practices contributed to the success of these programs. (See references in Chapter 4.) Although most of the programs I studied were education, not training, a pattern began to emerge that I then pursued further. This led to the concept and model that I labeled "Support Systems." I do not claim that I was the first nor the only person to identify this aspect of organizational behavior. Unfortunately, however, too little has been written about the specific actions that should be evident if an organization is really supporting its training programs.

In 1980, Mary Broad researched this aspect of organizational behavior and training and reported it in her dissertation [2]. Some of the material in this chapter is from her study, with her permission. There are some alterations, in words not in concepts, and I will take responsibility for that. Her study produced an instrument which is the basis for this chapter and can readily be used by those who wish to identify the support practices in their own organization.

The model is presented in Figure 11-1. For those who have read my earlier work, you will see one significant change. It is an important difference, one that Broad contributed to the evolution of the Support Systems model and will be discussed under "Upper Management Involvement." In this chapter, I will be using some of the statements from the Broad model.

Underlying the Support Systems model is the difference between *commitment* and *involvement*. Unfortunately, we tend to use these terms interchangeably and thereby lose an important distinction.

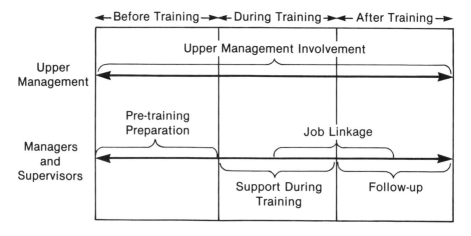

Source: Broad, Mary. "Identification of Management Actions to Support Utilization of Training on the Job." Unpublished Ed.D. dissertation. School of Education and Human Development, The George Washington University, 1980. Reprinted with permission.

Figure 11.1

Commitment is a promise. It is generally a statement, a speech, or some other verbal activity. It is heard when somebody in upper management talks about training. During the 1960s and 1970s, it was heard when company officials attended functions sponsored by the National Alliance of Businessmen and pledged to employ certain numbers of the disadvantaged. Commitment is important, but it is not action.

Involvement is action. It is observable behavior related to a particular topic or goal. It makes commitment a reality; it goes for beyond promise and becomes behavior.

There is a dramatic comparison that sharpens the distinction. When guerrillas and similar underground groups recruit members, there is a ceremony in which the newcomers commit themselves to the cause. History has proven to such groups that commitment is not sufficient. Therefore the initiation ceremony includes some overt action that is observable to all, and therefore signifies involvement. It can be a raid on a bank, building, or office of the "establishment." It could be marching in a parade, where others can see the initiates out in the open. Whatever the act, it is one that binds the recruit through observable involvement.

Within organizations, we have all been exposed to the speeches, policy statements, and other forms of commitment to projects or ideas. It does not take us long, if we are to survive, to distinguish between the intent and the action. Good intentions are desirable, but positive action is essential.

The actions discussed in this chapter focus on observable behavior that should take place to support a training program. In the Broad study, we have the first such listing of which I am aware. It is hoped that other studies will refine and expand the list, so that management, at all levels, will know what is expected behavior when supporting a training program.

The model contains five major action areas. Under each are specific actions.

UPPER MANAGEMENT INVOLVEMENT

It is always difficult to be specific about levels of management. In a hierarchical organization, it is possible to draw a line someplace on the organization chart and be specific. When an organization is designated as a "flat organization" (having few levels of management) or a "matrix organization" (drawing from various parts of the organization for tasks), upper management is more difficult to identify. As used here, it starts with the CEO and stops someplace around what is generally termed middle management. You would have to draw that distinction for your own organization.

In my original model, the term "Management Involvement" was used and was the first element. Broad has changed this, and improved it, by focusing on upper management. She has also identified that these are actions that may not relate to a single program but are continuous in any organization that has training programs, as shown in Figure 11-1.

Names appropriate personnel to the training design committee

In some organizations, the Designer works alone though the CEM has continually emphasized the need for the Designer to work in conjunction with others. In some instances, it is possible for a small group to work with the Designer during the entire CEM, and they are designated as a Design Committee.

The personnel assigned to this Committee should be carefully selected but, when appointed, upper management should make a public announcement. There should be no doubt about who is on the Committee. This also means that it is clear that these Committee members will be provided with the time and resources to participate actively.

Participates in preview of training programs

Although upper managers are not directly involved in most training programs, they should make time available to participate in previewing some programs. It is not expected that upper management will preview all the training programs, as this would prove too costly. The higher level managers, however, should show their involvement by attending previews, usually called briefing sessions, on the major elements of the training programs being designed and offered.

As will be seen later in the model, there is a pretraining phase when managers and supervisors are given an indication of the training program to be offered. Upper management should also be involved in some of these previews. This produces congruence at all levels of management concerning the previewed training programs.

Issues statements on new performance levels expected following training

As training is concerned with performance, it is expected that there will be changes in performance as a result of that training. The Designer, and others, will have identified the desirable performance changes during the CEM. The contention here is that there will be greater change in the organization if those performance levels come from upper management. These statements will merely confirm what has already been determined, but the source of the message can do much to assure that performance change does take place.

Requires attendance at training for certain categories of employees

Too few organizations have policy statements regarding training, and HRD in general. The intent here is to have upper management continually reinforce the idea that training opportunities should be made available to all employees in the organization, and that once selected, attendance is required.

Authorizes released time or changed work hours to allow participation in training

I have previously defined Human Resource Development as having three components and one is "a definite period of time" [3]. This action statement underscores the need for time to be allocated to training. Even JIT requires time, which is under the control of the supervisor.

For most training programs that take place off the job site, there is the need for a specific policy, backed up by the necessary resources. Employees must be released from their regular duties, if they are to engage in a learning experience. When shifts are involved, or alternative work scheduling (for example, flex-time), upper management should make provision for changed work hours.

Provides appropriate physical facilities for training programs

It is the responsibility of upper management to see that the financial resources are made available to obtain the necessary physical facilities for training. "Appropriate" is a nonspecific word, and upper management relies on the HRD Manager to make specific recommendations. If upper management does not make the necessary provision, this can communicate nonverbally a lack of interest in training to the entire organization, as physical facilities do more than support the learning. They are indicative of upper management support of the training program.

Provides for written notification of selection for training

Although the selection of an individual for training will generally be within the area of the supervisor, it should be reinforced by written notification from upper management. This communicates several things to the employee selected.

It shows that upper management is aware of the decision to train. It also indicates an interest by upper management in the employee, as well as in the training. The tone and content of the written communication should indicate that perspective. It reinforces the decision of the supervisor, and also indicates upper management's awareness of the involvement of the supervisor in training programs.

Approves use of confidential organizational data as resources for training

This action is not designed to open the corporate files indiscriminately, but to avoid having the Designer and the training program stymied by bureaucracy. Do you recall the incident, reported in an earlier chapter, where the organization had an extensive and well-developed performance appraisal system, but the data could not be shared with the Designer? The current action addresses that problem.

The Designer need not be given access to the entire performance appraisal of an individual, but should certainly be able to see that part which relates to training needs. Upper management should approve the release of such data so that the Designer is not forced to fight the system.

Another example is when upper management has some plans that will impact upon expected performance, as relevant to a specific training program. Some parts of the confidential data could be made available early enough in the CEM so that the Designer and others will not produce an inappropriate training program.

Participates in one or more training sessions

The involvement of upper management is certainly evidenced by physical presence. Everybody knows how busy people in upper management are, and attendance at a specific training session is an effective communication of their involvement. This requires more than just a five-minute observation from the back of the room.

The Designer, in exploration with upper management, can identify those programs where upper management participation is not only desirable but essential. Then, a specific role for upper management can be identified, and those who will attend can be given adequate briefing on the participation expected.

Not all programs require the direct participation of upper management, but people from that level should be involved in the climate setting or in other activities to indicate support through participation.

Meets with HRD people to discuss ways to apply new performance

Just as upper management should participate in selected sessions, they should also participate in selected activities during the design process. By meeting with the designer, and with other people from the HRD unit, upper management can gain a better grasp of some of the training programs, while indicating their own thoughts about the expected performance. It is also helpful to have the supervisors in such a meeting, and serves to indicate to them that upper management is supporting training.

Provides for salary increase on return to job or after successful on-the-job experience

Apparently, this action is controversial. On the face of it, it would appear that this is an important factor related to training. However, in the Broad study, fewer than 50% of the respondents (presidents of ASTD chapters) listed this action as being important.

If training relates to immediate job performance and to that area referred to as productivity, increased performance should be reflected by a salary increase. Of course, where performance is not tied to salary, one would not expect such a direct relationship.

Authorizes production differentials for trainees for short period back on the job

This action addresses an interesting and often overlooked performance factor. When a learner has achieved an acceptable level of performance, at the end of the training, the general assumption is that this can immediately be transferred to the work site. It could be just the opposite. The protected environment of the learning situation has allowed the learner to explore new behaviors and to perform in ways different from those expected on the job. When he returns to the job, the employee strives to integrate the new learning into the regular job performance. There can be a brief period when performance is lower than anticipated while the integration is taking place. This possibility should be recognized by upper management and specific limits be established as to how long the lower performance level is acceptable.

PRETRAINING PREPARATION (MANAGERS AND SUPERVISORS)

These actions are generally associated with a particular training program. They would be repeated for each new program, and sometimes for an existing program. These are actions to be taken by managers and supervisors rather than by upper management, as was the case in the previous section.

Actively participates in the design of the training program

This action has been emphasized repeatedly in the CEM. In every event, there has been provision for active involvement and certainly in the E&FB.

Rather than repeat, the reader is urged to return to each event of the CEM and note those actions that would be pertinent in your organization. This would start with "Identify the Needs of the Organization" and terminate with "Conduct Training." Under those general headings, you should be able to make a specific list of those actions that are desirable and allowable in your organization.

You can also create a list, from the CEM, of those actions that are desirable, but not allowable at this time. It will provide directions for change that the HRD unit should work on to more actively involve managers and supervisors in the design of training programs.

Actively participates in the selection of in-house instructors

Although this is also reflected in the CEM, it is highlighted here because it is not a common practice. *In-house instructors* are defined as those people who are not from the HRD unit, but who are called upon to instruct. They might instruct for only one session, or handle a complete training program. Their basic job in the organization is *not* that of instructor, so careful attention must be paid to this special assignment.

At the outset, there should be a process for identifying and selecting these instructors. It should not be done by the HRD unit but by the manager or supervisor concerned. The responsibility of the HRD unit is to establish the criteria so that others can make informed and intelligent choices.

Care should be exercised so that this assignment is not seen as a way of employing an unemployable. Assignment as an instructor should be seen as recognition and reward for high performers in the subject area of the training program. Being selected as an instructor should be clothed in all the positive factors that are customary in the organization. Various qualified people should be vying with each other for such assignments. It is not a way of getting out of work, but of working harder in an area where one is a subject matter specialist.

This places special emphasis on the "training of trainer" aspect. (Remember, it is really instructing of instructors.) As needed, managers and supervisors should make adequate provision for the potential instructors to be released from other duties. It should also be made evident that there are benefits. The employee instructor will return to his manager or supervisor with additional skills that can be helpful in OJT and other instructional work outside of the training program.

Actively participates in selecting employees for training

When training is problem focused, as in the CEM, this action is obvious. Some training programs may lack that focus, and may be offered for reasons other than problem solving. It still requires careful selection of employees, with a clear understanding of the objectives of the program and the reason for selection.

For any training program, there should be criteria for selecting those to attend. Managers and supervisors should participate in specifying the criteria against which they will select.

Individual Development Plans (IDP) are still not common, though their use is becoming more prevalent. The IDP may be part of an overall career development program or an aspect of performance appraisal. Where an IDP has been developed, the manager and supervisor should be able to relate the training program to the IDP, and that will clarify mutual expectations.

Before assigning a subordinate to a training program, that subordinate should have a discussion with the supervisor, and even with the manager, to surface mutual expectations. The subordinate should know the reason for the program and the performance expected when returning from the program. Though this is contained in the objectives, there should be a review during the selection process.

During the CEM, reference has been made to including the learner in the design process. For similar reasons, managers and supervisor should include potential learners in the selection process.

Discusses training plans with union officials representing potential trainees

Within the CEM, little reference has been made to the role of unions. Generally, up to this time, unions have not indicated much interest in training, as long as it was not used as a tactic for weakening the union. There is the possibility of some change in previous attitudes. Unions are becoming more interested, not in specific training programs, but in those activities that directly involve their members.

It can even be helpful to involve union leadership, both in-plant and outside, for training seldom has a negative impact upon the union. The distrust that still exists is partly historical and partly due to a lack of communication. Discussing a training program provides an opportunity for a nonconfronting meeting with union leadership. The absence of such a meeting, or at least the opportunity to have one, can contribute to some of the misunderstandings prevalent in management-union relationships.

Notifies employees of selection for training

The general approach to this was discussed in the previous section, related to upper management. Actions by management and supervisor must be very specific, as they are the people closest to the selected trainees. There must be clear verbal and nonverbal communication about the positive aspects of being selected for training. Training is provided to solve problems and improve performance, and should not be communicated as being punishment. The provision of training is a positive action by managers and supervisors for the benefit of the subordinate, as well as the organization.

The selected subordinate should have sufficient lead time to prepare both emotionally and physically. On the physical side, consideration must be given to the reality that the subordinate will be expected to be away from the plant or site, and this applies to upper level managers as well as to those at lower levels of the organization. Arrangements will have to be made for work coverage—at the very least. Travel arrangements may be required. For some employees, a travel advance may be necessary, to avoid financial difficulty. Even with on-site training, work coverage is a factor. Some employees may have to make plans not only to cover their current work but also the anticipated tasks that may arise while they are away at training.

When training is not at the home city, there can also be family considerations. A manager or supervisor may think that the training shows concern for the employee, but it may be a penalty in the eyes of the subordinate. The family should be considered and concern exhibited through early discussions with the employee being selected. The trainee should be allowed sufficient time for the physical and emotional preparation necessary. Some people require more time than others, and this should be explored with the potential trainee, sufficiently in advance of the program, so that work and family needs related to the training program can be identified and dealt with.

Arranges for trainee to attend all sessions

When a training program has more than one session, and this is the general practice, managers and supervisors should make all the necessary arrangements so that there is uninterrupted attendance by the trainee.

Primary, of course, is making sure that the work is covered. It is important that the trainee should not have to wonder about what is backing up on the desk or work site that will have to be dealt with upon his return. If this is a concern, it will detract from the experience and cause the trainee to waste energy planning on catch-up, rather than on learning.

As indicated earlier under upper management, there should be a policy that provides for the training on company time. This is the general rule among U.S. companies, though some still insist that the trainee should go on his own time. A distinction must be made between training programs offered by the employing organization and those offered by others. When the employing organization offers the training program, there is no reason why it cannot be on company time. If, for reasons of scheduling, this is not possible, adequate provision should be made through compensatory time or some other arrangement so as not to punish the employee who is sent for training.

When an employee is sent to an external program, the mutual expectations should be made clear. In a tuition reimbursement program, the employee attends a college or university and the employer pays. In such a situation, it is common for the employee not to expect any compensatory time or other arrangement, although there is nothing to prevent an employer from providing time during work hours for such attendance. Managers and supervisors should be aware of the policy in their organization and provide accordingly.

If all of these logistic elements are attended to, there is no reason why a trainee should not attend all sessions, as attendance at the session should be considered the same as a work assignment. Of course, for reasons of health, an employee may miss work and similarly may miss a training session. Whenever a trainee is absent from a session, no matter what the reason, the appropriate manager or supervisor should be informed immediately. Working with the HRD unit they should explore appropriate action. In some instances, it may be necessary for a trainee to drop out when certain sessions are missed.

Care should also be exercised to determine the cause of absence. Perhaps the trainee does not need the training and is signaling this by missing a session. There could be many reasons, and the managers and supervisors should be encouraged to explore and share with the HRD unit.

Evaluation

There is never a time when we will give sufficient attention to evaluation. It is crucial to any learning experience and for the benefit of all concerned. If managers and supervisors are to receive useful evaluation data, they must involve the HRD unit. When performance is to be evaluated at the end of the program, it is necessary to make pretraining data available for comparison.

The data may take many forms depending upon the nature of the job, the practice in the organization, and the need of managers and supervisors. In some situations, the baseline (pretraining) data may be gathered from co-workers or subordinates, depending upon the objectives of the training program.

DURING TRAINING (MANAGERS AND SUPERVISORS)

When a person goes to training, it is important that managers and supervisors should not drop out of the picture. While in training, that employee is still responsible to the manager or supervisor, but merely on a temporary assignment to another function.

During the previous section, "Pretraining," managers and supervisors will have made provisions or arrangements, as described in that section. At this time they will carry out what they have previously planned. It is important that managers and supervisors follow-up to make sure that the arrangements they made are actually being implemented.

Checks up on work coverage arrangements

First and foremost is making sure that the trainee is actually released from normal duties. It is not uncommon, unfortunately, to find that the trainee is expected to report into the regular work situation sometime during the training day. It may be by phone or actual physical presence. This is more common among supervisor and management personnel than among employees who do not have such responsibilities. Many an instructor complains about trainees rushing for the phone during a break, in order to call the office, not recognizing that the break is an integral part of the learning situation.

When a trainee goes for an extended period of time, there may be the need for a replacement. Managers and supervisors should not only provide for this, but check up to be sure that the replacement actually reports. There is the expectation that this will happen but, if for any reason, the replacement does not show up there can be chaos and recriminations. It is best to determine this as early as possible and certainly before the trainee is scheduled to return.

Some training programs use the spaced learning approach discussed in an earlier chapter. The trainee rotates between the learning situation and the job situation. This can make for good learning but difficult scheduling. When a training program uses the spaced learning design, managers and supervisors should be fully aware of this, and recognize the unusual demands this makes on work scheduling, meetings, and so on.

Avoids work-related interruptions of trainees

It is easy for a trainee to be interrupted during the training program and thereby experience difficulty in reaching the objectives. It is as simple as the manager or supervisor forgetting that a particular employee is not available due to training. A manager can ask to communicate with an employee, others may hesitate to remind the manager of the training assignment, and so the trainee is needlessly interrupted.

Emergencies do arise, and there are times when interruptions are unavoidable. Too frequently, the interruptions are not necessary. The trainee should be advised not to call the office, or do anything else that indicates a less than full commitment to the learning situation. This is not meant to block all communication with the job situation, for it is desirable that there be continuous communication in some learning situations. There is a difference, however, between keeping the lines of communication open and interruptions.

Participates in one or more training sessions

To reinforce the value of the learning situation, managers and supervisors should physically take part in the training. This should not be limited to merely observing or making an unannounced visit. The participation should be carefully planned and directly related to the training objectives and future performance.

Managers and supervisors are excellent resource people, but they may need some help in actually making a presentation when the lesson plan calls for an interview, dialogue, panel, or similiar instructional strategy. The particular session should be carefully chosen, and the manager or supervisor provided with an adequate briefing or similar preparation.

Managers and supervisors can participate in other ways. A supervisor might arrange to meet a trainee for lunch, when it will not interfere with the learning situation. Observation of a training session is desirable, as long as there is adequate preparation. It would be disruptive to the learning situation to have visitors coming in whenever they wished. It is important to plan the visit to the benefit of all so that participation in the training session becomes a positive experience for all concerned.

Awards certificates on successful completion of training

It is fairly common to acknowledge the successful completion of a training program, even one that is only one or two days in length. One of the most common practices used is to award a certificate. For many of us, this may seem almost juvenile, but that is usually because we have so many certificates, they have lost their meaning. However, I have visited offices and seen training completion certificates framed and carefully mounted on walls—sometimes in offices where I least expect them.

If the award is not meaningful, perhaps it is best to dispense with it. When the award (for example, certificate) is important, why not have it presented by a manager or supervisor? Certainly those people have more prestige in the eyes of the trainee than the instructor, or anybody else in the HRD unit. This is not meant to deprecate the HRD unit, but to acknowledge that the trainee has prime responsibility to the supervisor or manager concerned.

JOB LINKAGE (MANAGERS AND SUPERVISORS)

This is a crucial part of the support system, and an aspect that is frequently overlooked. There should not be a gap between the training and the job. If the newly learned performance is to have an impact on the job, there should be a carefully planned flow from the learning situation back to the job situation. Job linkage bridges the training and the job.

Reentry, returning to the job with new learnings, has always been a difficult problem. One of the driving forces that contributed to the growth of Organization Development was the need to enable learners to bring their new performance back to the old job site. Too often, the learner found that those who did not attend the learning were not sympathetic or helpful when the learner tried to use the training experience.

Managers and supervisors can take specific actions that will facilitate the movement back to the job and will increase the possibility that the learning will be applied.

Plans for evaluation when the trainee returns to the job

Evaluation should not come as a surprise to the learner. During the training program, evaluation is built into the learning process. Likewise, there is evaluation on the job and this too should be clearly identified.

Even while in training, the learner should know exactly what will be expected when he returns to the job. This requires that managers and supervisors, working with the HRD unit, plan for that evaluation. This also assures that the evaluation relates to the training program.

Helps trainees set realistic goals

While in training, an employee can be swept up by the momentum of the challenge presented by the learning experience. This is good, but can prove counterproductive when the trainee returns to the work situation, because, obviously, on the job there is less opportunity to experiment with new performance and a high penalty for failure. The work situation, rightly or wrongly, demands results.

Managers and supervisors should be involved, as part of job linkage, to help the trainees establish realistic goals for performance when they return to the job. It is also possible that the managers and supervisors will see new resources and opportunities through the eyes of the motivated and excited subordinate.

Prepares for the return of the trainee

A part of the reentry phenomena is the kind of greeting or reception the trainee receives when he returns. It can be anticipated that there will be a certain amount of teasing, particularly if the trainee was at a pleasant site with the country club effect. The greeting might be, "So you had a good time at the country club while the rest of us sweated here!" This may be intended as light teasing, but can easily become bitter. Managers and supervisors cannot, and should not, try to stop this kind of greeting. It will happen—but it should not be the only greeting the returned trainee receives.

Managers and supervisors should prepare the work group for the return. Reentry will always have some kind of rituals and if managers and supervisors do not make specific preparations, the rituals can become cruel and counterproductive. Which employee would be interested in attending training when the return is marked by criticism and ridicule from others in the work group?

Reinforces the use of new job performance by trainees

We know that new learning, if not reinforced, tends to fade and disappear. Knowing this, we should be doing something about it. Managers and supervisors should not be expected to be completely familiar with this aspect of learning theory, but when reminded they could probably cite many instances when it has occurred.

Sometimes the new performance, learned during training, cannot be used immediately. Managers and supervisors should be assisted by people from the HRD unit in finding ways to reinforce the new performance until it can actually be used on the job. Then, the new performance will be constantly reinforced by direct usage on the job.

It may seem that this discussion is focusing on employees at the lower end of the scale. This is certainly not true. Take the case of a manager who goes to a training course to improve skills in conducting staff meetings. Upon his return, the manager may find that it is not possible to use these skills immediately in the next staff meeting. There could be many reasons for this, such as crisis, changes in personnel, or other factors outside his control. The tendency is for that manager to lose what had been learned concerning conducting staff meetings and slowly revert to previous performance. By the time the immediate crisis or need has been met, the manager is less likely to apply those new skills.

Provides for some work assignment related to the training

Another aspect of the previous action is for managers and supervisors to specifically plan situations where the trainee can immediately use the material from the training program. This may require temporarily assigning the trainee to a different unit or another part of the original unit. Care should be taken that the trainee is not permanently transferred, as that is not the objective of training. (It could be an objective for education.) If a supervisor finds that after training the subordinate is transferred out, the inclination will be to send people to training whom the supervisor would like to lose.

In many production situations, output is measured. Upon reentry, the trainee may be producing at a lower level, rather than higher. Too often this is used as criticism of the training. Quite the contrary. It takes time to integrate new performance into the existing situation. The trainee has an adjustment to make. If, upon returning to the work site, the trainee is subjected to criticism for lower production, we can expect the trainee to forget what has been learned and revert to earlier and less productive performance. During the period of integration, managers and supervisors should provide for a dip in output which will be more than compensated for later when integration is completed.

Provides for trainee to share the learning with others

Though the trainee is not expected to become a peer instructor, managers and supervisors find that a returned trainee can contribute to the general improvement of performance by sharing. If this is to be done, the trainee should be helped to prepare for this while still in the learning situation.

For example, an employee (trainee) is sent to a conference, which is work related, and is expected to come back with new ideas. The conference is, in effect, a learning situation. The trainee returns, and apparently nobody is interested. All the questions relate to the social aspects of the conference, not to the learning. This encourages the trainee to keep the learning to himself and tell grand stories about drinking and socializing. The conference becomes a fringe benefit rather than a learning situation.

This can be reversed. Provision can be made for the trainee to share the experience with others. Questions should be: what was learned, how can we apply that learning here, what else needs to be learned?

For a formal training experience, as different from a conference, the same questions should be asked. The trainee should expect to have to answer these questions on returning, and should be prepared to do so. This is beneficial to the trainee, and to those who did not go to the training but might learn something vicariously.

Provides for conferences among trainee, instructors, HRD unit, managers and supervisors

This action emphasizes that, while in training, the trainee is still the employee of a manager or supervisor who is not part of the HRD unit. Too often, while in training, the trainee becomes a nonperson to the manager or supervisor who originally sent him. The more positive approach is to retain some direct connection.

The HRD unit can facilitate the conferences (brief meetings) which should take place during the training program. Particularly it is essential that there be at least a brief meeting prior to the end of the training and before return to the job. It should be acknowledged that this is very seldom done. We do not have the research to indicate why there is this gap, but the gap does exist. The HRD unit cannot expect the manager or supervisor to initiate these meetings, and therefore, somebody in the HRD unit must take the initiative and the responsibility for working with managers and supervisors to achieve this action.

FOLLOW-UP (MANAGERS AND SUPERVISORS)

This is the last part of the Support System Model. Follow-up should not be confused with evaluation. Follow-up is concerned with what happens after—much later. For convenience, reference will still be made to the "trainee," though by now that employee should not be seen as still in training.

Initiates conferences with trainee after a period back on the job

Good managers and supervisors have frequent conferences with employees on a variety of topics, and some of these conferences should be a discussion of the training program. After a reasonable period of time, the trainee should be asked to respond to questions regarding the training and its relevancy to performance. The information gathered during such a conference should be shared with the HRD unit.

Such conferences can be valuable in helping the trainee understand something of the opportunities and problems. The opportunities may be obvious in that the trainee may now be able to perform in ways that were unknown or unachievable before the training. The problems may occur when the trainee has new performance capabilities, but is unable to use them. If such problems are not explored and resolved, there can be a negative effect the next time the trainee goes for training. The attitude engendered may be, "Why bother to learn something new if they won't let me use it back on the job?"

Approves regular meetings of groups of trainees

When several different groups of trainees have been through the same training program, but over a period of time, their getting together for a meeting should be facilitated by managers and supervisors. In this way, they can reinforce the learned performance, whether it has been used on the job or not.

A possible resultant problem is that such employees could become a subgroup or a clique within a unit. To minimize this possibility, managers and supervisors should also arrange for the sharing which has been described under another action.

Informs trainee of changes in job performance attributable to training

When a trainee returns, and his performance has improved, what feedback is provided by managers and supervisors? Improvement is taken for granted, for if the training was successful, everybody expects performance to improve. Has this ever been directly communicated to the trainee? Such feedback is important not only for the present, but also for the future.

If the trainee receives positive feedback, attributable to training, there will be a positive attitude when training is needed, again, that reduces the possibility that training is seen as either punishment or as a fringe benefit. Instead, training is related directly to the job (as it should be) and the manager or supervisor is providing direct recognition of that.

Provides continuing reinforcement

Reinforcement of learning is still not used as effectively as it could be. It is probably the single most essential element that is missing, as the trainee leaves the learning situation and returns to the job. Reinforcement should be positive, even when criticism is involved. Reinforcement can come from another direction—from the trainee himself. If the manager or supervisor asks the trainee to report on how the training is being used on the job, the expectation of reporting will encourage him to use the learning.

When there is insufficient opportunity to use the training, the manager or supervisor should seek or make opportunities to reinforce seldom used skills. The closer the manager or supervisor was involved in the design and implementation of the training program, the less need there will be for this kind of reinforcement.

Identifies new learning needs

Learning is a continuous process. As a result of a good training experience, the learner may discover that there is much he does not know about other areas. As part of follow-up, the manager or supervisor should encourage the employee to identify other learning needs. Learning can open many doors, and some of them will relate directly to the job.

Some adults hesitate to become involved in a learning experience because of past failures. After a good training experience, it is not unusual to find the employee confident in his ability to learn and eager to learn more. Such learning can go beyond the present job and, therefore, indicates a need for education.

CONCLUSION

A Support System, if one does not already exist, is not easily constructed. It must be introduced into the organization slowly and must be congruent with other behavior in the organization. It will take time, and there may be many attempts to encourage managers and supervisors to take action before one can really feel that a Support System is in place.

With a good Support System in place, the value of a training program is greatly increased. The results are certainly worth the effort. A good Support System will complement the work done by a Designer and other HRD people who use the Critical Events Model to design training programs.

REFERENCES

1.   If you missed what was happening during that period you might want to read "Has Federal Legislation Affected Your Training?" by Leonard Nadler, *Training in Business and Industry*, August 1967. This was later reprinted in the *Congressional Record, American Institute of Management Newsletter*, and *Management Review*. Another source is *Federal Training and Work Programs in the Sixties* by Sar A. Levitan and Garth L. Mangum. (Institute of Industrial and Labor Relations, University of Michigan, 1969.)

2.   The dissertation by Mary Broad is *Identification of Management Actions to Support Utilization of Training on the Job*. Unpublished dissertation in the School of Education and Human Development, the George Washington University, 1980. This university offers graduate programs in Human Resource Development.

3.   The definition of HRD appears in references cited earlier, but to refresh the reader at this time it is: organized learning experiences, during a definite period of time, to produce the possibility of performance change.

Appendix

·

RESEARCH IS NOT EVALUATION

To explore this activity, we must first distinguish between research and evaluation. *They are not the same!* Confusion has led some people to use the label "evaluative research" or just to combine "research and evaluation." Not only does this avoid making the important and necessary distinction, it also blurs both areas and gets the least out of each.

Every learning experience should be evaluated. However, not every learning experience needs to be researched. Figure 1 provides a comparison, obviously a bit simplified, as it is not the purpose of this article to discuss the two areas. The comparison is necessary if we are to focus on research activities of human resource developers.

Evaluation has the purpose of finding out if learning took place . . . what happened as part of the learning program. Essentially, did the learner learn, and if

	EVALUATION	RESEARCH
Purpose	**What?**	**Why?**
Focus	Learning Objectives	Hypotheses
Approach	Actual Situation	Experimental
Strategies	Data-gathering	Data-gathering
Utilization	To Improve Program	Varied
	Immediate	Long Range

Figure 1

(This is extracted from "Research" An HRD Activity Area, *Training and Development Journal*, May 1979.

so, what? Research endeavors to explore why learning took place, or why certain behavior occurred.

Evaluation is measured against the learning objectives determined and stated before the learning program began. Research can have many hypotheses, or predictions, as to what will or will not happen. Research can go far beyond the learning situation to explore factors *outside* of the learning situation, which may have impacted upon the learner and the situation. Research can also be done, as will be shown later, outside of the learning situation and perhaps having nothing to do with a particular learning situation.

Evaluation uses the actual learning situation as the approach to determine what happened. Research can set up experimental or comparative approaches which must be carefully controlled. Research may focus minutely on one part of the total situation or probe it in depth.

Strategies of evaluation and research appear similar and this has contributed to the confusion. Both use some form of data-gathering though research must be more rigidly controlled. Both tend to use statistics to gather and report data.

Evaluation is designed to improve the program which has been evaluated. One must be careful not to use the evaluation of one program to predict results in other situations. Research can be more varied, but with specific controls it can lead to important generalizations for our field. Evaluation should be used immediately, while research can produce the basis for long-range actions. Some research (longitudinal) may take place over a long period of time and have to account for factors other than those which could be evaluated as part of the learning program.

Given the distinction, we can now proceed to examine research as an activity area of human resource developers.

Index